JACK LINDSAY

The

TROUBADOURS
&
THEIR WORLD

*of the
twelfth and
thirteenth
centuries*

FREDERICK MULLER LIMITED
LONDON

First published in Great Britain 1976
by Frederick Muller Limited,
London NW2 6LE

ISBN 0 584 10316 6

Printed in Great Britain by The Anchor Press Ltd
and bound by Wm Brendon & Son Ltd
both of Tiptree, Essex

TO WALTER LOWENFELS

Man in his dire divided state
broke down the atom : what he met
was his own void, the end of all,
the murder in the universe.
He saw his own reflected fate,
his fragmentation and his fall
into the vortex, money's curse,
his blind reduction to a thing.

But there's another way we know
of integration and you sing
that way of love and Lillian,
brushing the stars and still as near
the hidden heart of entangled Man.

These poets here
faced a quite different challenge, yet
they sang uncowering at death's threat.
Out of the past their words resound,
they echo from the future clear
as well, the truth of brotherhood,
of naked lovers : that deep truth
where all things are redeemed and good.

Contents

List of Illustrations

Foreword

I first began working on the Troubadours in the late 1930s, attempting to make versions which would carry over the exact rhyme-schemes of the complex originals, and I have returned to the subject on and off since then. A programme of my versions, with originals sung by Martin Best, at the Mermaid Theatre in 1973 strongly renewed my interest, and the result is this book. In the poems here completely translated I have preserved the stanzaic and rhyme-systems of the originals, though I have added to them some short passages and in some cases prose versions, where I was mainly concerned with the content – thus helping also to ease the pressure on the reader of too many pages of verse. At the same time I have tried to give enough background information about the period and about the poets themselves to make the poems fully intelligible to the reader with no special knowledge. To escape any effect of an anthology of verse translations I have alternated chapters which deal with the general issues with those presenting the poets. I trust that the result is to produce a book which can be read as narrative and not merely as literary discussion. Indeed the story has its clear structure and its dramatic climax, with the breakdown of the independent culture of Languedoc through the crusades and the Inquisition.

Many tributes have been paid to the Troubadours as the inaugurators of European vernacular literature, and there have been many excellent studies. H. Davenson remarks that the Troubadours set out "a new conception of love which has profoundly moulded the structure of the western psyche." And C. S. Lewis declares minor changes in convention "must not blind us to the fact that the most momentous and the most revolutionary elements" of Courtly Love as expressed by the poets "have made the background of European literature for eight hundred years. French poets, in the eleventh century, discovered or invented, or were the first to express, that romantic species of passion which English poets were still writing about in the nineteenth century. They effected a change which has left no corner of our ethics, our

xi

imagination, or our daily life untouched, and they erected impassable barriers between us and the classical past or the Oriental present. Compared with this revolution the Renaissance is a mere ripple on the surface of literature." Such comments could be multiplied. In 1949 E. R. Curtius considered that "the passion and sorrow of love were an emotional discovery of the French Troubadours and their successors." In 1960 R. Bezzola in *Les origines et la formation de la littérature courtoise en occident*, asked:

Why is it that this new poetry, which expresses a new conception of man, which gives an absolutely new image of woman, which presents the relations between human beings in an absolutely new manner, rises up just at this moment, in the eleventh and twelfth centuries? . . . What remains to be almost wholly explained is the new conception of love.

I believe these statements to hold a great truth, but they are expressed too vaguely and generally. So a scholar like Peter Dronke can reply:

I should like to suggest that the feelings and conceptions of *amour courtois* are universally possible, possible in any time or place and on any level of society. They occur in popular as well as in learned or aristocratic love-poetry. Like Dante in the fourth book of *Convivio*, I hold that there is a *gentilezza* which is not confined to any court or privileged class, but springs from an inherent virtù; that the feelings of courtoisie are elemental, not the product of a particular chivalric nature. In the poets' terms, they allow even the most *vilain* to be *gentil*.

But this statement is even more general and ends by dissolving entirely the specific contribution of the Troubadours. There is indeed in that contribution, as this book attempts to show, a great new vision and concentration of human experience, from which all later European literature derives in the sense that the Troubadours set the stage, create a new dimension of experience, and posit certain crucial problems together with a method for tackling them. In short we cannot reduce the contribution to an exposition of Courtly Love, but must estimate it by grasping fully, in a single focus, both *the form and the content* of their work. My book is an attempt to explain this point and show what is indeed the great and revolutionary achievement of the Troubadours.

The line-drawings are not for the most part meant as direct illustrations of the text, but rather as an independent commentary on medieval daily life, with emphasis on the forms of entertainment.

Jack Lindsay

Guilhem of Poitou

IN the late eleventh and early twelfth centuries there appeared a new kind of poet, the Troubadours. Before their advent vernacular poetry did not exist in any clearly defined form. In the Germanic and Norse areas the kind of poems developed in tribal days were still carrying on; and in the later eleventh century a new matter was coming in from Celtic lands, Brittany and Wales, through musicians playing *leis* with words. Everywhere of course there were songs of the folk, and songs were sung, though not written down, at the tables of the lords and in the market-places. There were songs of work and dance, of play and festival, songs telling tales heroic or humorous, love-songs. A large number of minstrels, jongleurs and entertainers moved about the country, bringing in new songs and tales, but the written literature was almost wholly in Latin; and there was nothing in the vernacular to express the great new developments that had been going on in social and cultural life.

In France there were indeed the *chansons de geste*, relatively primitive in form, which in their material looked back to earlier feudal days, especially those of Charlemagne. They were composed in strings of assonantal lines, irregular in number, called *laisses*. The greatest of them, the *Chanson de Roland*, was composed in the late eleventh century, though drawing on earlier material. Its theme is feudal loyalty seen in terms of the Christian empire defending itself against the infidel Moors; to separate oneself from the system is to become a vile traitor like Ganelon. Nothing could be less like the poetry of the Troubadours with its strong individualism and its quest for new ways of life. The *chansons* were sung by jongleurs such as Taillefer who was killed at Hastings, or Berdic who, serving William I, held three villas in Gloucestershire. Similar in character must have been the songs that many warriors sang; thus the warrior Bertolai, *preux et sage*, in *Raoul de Cambrai* promises to sing of the battle in which he takes part. These songs were sung mainly to the *vielle* (violin) which had recently come in from the east. A canon of Rouen composed a *Life of St Alexis* in a hundred and twenty-five *laisses* about the middle of the eleventh century; it told how he refused to consummate his marriage and later lived unrecognised in the family-house as recluse under the staircase. In southern France there were *laisses* on St Rides.[1]

We find however indications that stanzaic rhymed poems in the vernacular were attempted at least from the mid-ninth century. We have a German hymn to the Logos, dated 863–71, by an Alsatian monk Otfrid of Weissenburg; here a hundred lines are articulated into stanzas of rhymed couplets; the five central stanzas have a four-lined refrain. There seems a link with the church-sequences elaborated in this century. In north-eastern France, in a manuscript made at the monastery of St Armand about 882, there is a song of St Eulalia in French couplets: *Buona pulcella fut Eulalia.* "An excellent young girl was Eulalia." We are told of her martyrdom. "Quickly they tossed her to burn in the flame. No flaw was in her: to no hurt she came." Shortly before 1065 Ezzo, priest of Bamberg, composed a chorale in German stanzas for pilgrims going to the Holy Sepulchre that year. In a manuscript of music from Saint-Martial in Limoges, about 1096–9, there was written down a vernacular song which shared its tune with a familiar Latin Christmas hymn. The jongleur begins by calling the audience to hear a new song and to learn it for themselves.

> Friends, trusty listeners, turn
> and your trifling *gazel* spurn;
> for a new tune you must learn
> de virgine Maria.

> I'll not lose my virginity,
> I'll keep forever my chastity,
> as stated in the prophecy
> pois(er) virgo Maria.

> The angel Gabriel am I,
> a loyal salutation I cry,
> God is descending from the sky,
> in te, virgo Maria.

(What the word *gazel* means we shall discuss later.) The song may have been acted out. Mary finally says: "Since it's you that tell me, I'll believe. I yield, myself to him I give, *ego virgo Maria.*"

These examples are scanty, but they do show that a certain amount of experimentation was going on in vernacular verse, linked with the developments of Latin religious song. Without a doubt there was much more of which we have no record; and there are various hints and fragments of folksong, with which we shall deal as our story goes on. But, however we analyse the evidence, there is nothing at all like Troubadour poetry.[2]

That poetry was characterised by precision of form and complex rhyme-schemes, and by a particular set of themes which embodied a new world-view capable of expressing the deepest aspirations and inner conflicts of the age. The poets had a conscious system in which techniques, methods and themes were carefully considered and continually revalued. There was nothing like them before in the medieval world, or as far as that goes, in the ancient world's literary schools and systems, unless we go far back to the age of the Greek Lyric Poets in the seventh century B.C., to which Alkaios and Sappho belonged. There too we see a sudden and rapidly extended growth of precise lyrical forms (linked with music). The Lesbian school had the outlook of an aristocratic group, its background a richly developing culture based on the stable growth of mercantile towns; they were intent on enjoying life in the new world, opening up and expressing the new kind of individual assertion that had been made possible. But apart from these general points we cannot compare the Greek lyric poets and the Troubadours – though we might add that the Greeks heralded the great expansion of classical culture, just as the Troubadours did much to unloose the forces that lead into the European literature of the following centuries, with influences and effects that are still with us. Clearly, then, the latter need more attention than they have yet had, despite many devoted studies. In part they have suffered from the fact that the language in which they wrote, the Langue d'Oc, suffered a sharp arrest at the end of the thirteenth century as a result of the Albigensian Crusades, and thus does not directly underlie any of the great modern literatures of Europe.[3]

Before we explore the situation further, it would be best to deal at some length with the first known Troubadour, Guilhem IX Count of Poitou and VII Duke of Aquitaine. After we have considered his work and got some idea of the base on which the new movement was built, we can examine the cultural situation of Western Europe in the twelfth century and the particular forms it took in southern France. Thus we shall be able to understand how the Troubadours expressed the needs of their world, and we can go on to ask in more detail how their aesthetic and ethic arose. After that we can deal with other Troubadours, with the development of their poetry and its ideas, and describe the tragic events that led to the wrecking of the culture of the Midi.

Guilhem, handsome, bold, brave, gay, and witty, was born in 1071 and at the age of sixteen inherited a third of France, a vast domain larger than that ruled by the French king. But he seems too complex a character to succeed as a feudal ruler; he entered light-heartedly on enterprises without proper consideration. In 1098 when his brother-in-law Raimon of Saint-Gilles, count of Toulouse, was away crusading, he tried to wrest Toulouse from him; and in 1114, during the minority of the new count, he made another unsuccessful attempt to gain the city. In 1101 he took the Cross and led a huge host, said to number 300,000 men, to the East; but the expedition broke down on the way and those who carried on were destroyed by the Saracens in the plains of Asia Minor. We are told that he composed and sang a poem "before the princes, the barons, and the assembled Christians, on the miseries of his captivity among the Saracens, with joyous modulations" (Ordericus). In fact he was never captured but spent a year amid the pleasures of Antioch as the host of Tancred; he may then have learned something of the Arabic songs in Syria. He seems to have been well read; we hear of his father collecting a large library of manuscripts.

He had many links with Spain. In 1064 his father had carried out an expedition with the king of Aragon, taking the rich Moorish alcazar of Barbastro, with much booty and many captives; an Arab author mentions in this connection the wonderful Moorish women-singers. The commander of the force, William of Montreuil, got some 1,500 girls, some of whom were sent to Byzantium. As the result of a vow, Count Guilhem VIII was buried in Spain, at the shrine of St James of Compostella. When in 1094 the Aragonese king was killed before Huesca, Guilhem IX married his young wife Philippa and may have spent the summer and autumn of that year in Spain; he does not seem to have been in Poitou. The wedding occurred some time before the end of the year. Philippa, aged 20–22, was daughter of Guilhem IV of Toulouse and the heiress of the county; her uncle Raimon would not tolerate her presence at Toulouse and it was through her that Guilhem IX claimed Toulouse in 1098. She would have had many jongleurs in her train, including Aragonese, so that her husband would have had many chances to hear Moorish songs.[4]

There were other links with Spanish royalty. One of Guilhem's sisters had married Pedro of Aragon; another, Alfonso VI of Castile, the conqueror of Toledo. Guilhem would have been too young to join in the Toledo expedition, but Limousin lords such as his friend Hugues of Lusignan took part. In 1098 and in 1114 he was in Spain; in 1115 he took part in the raid of Alfonso of Aragon into Andalusia, going as far as Granada and the environs of Cordova, and bringing back into Aragon many thousands of Mozarabs. He was again in Spain in 1119 as ally of the Aragonese king. In 1127 he died.

Contemporary judgments stress his reckless character. "He was daring, gallant, and full of mirth, outdoing even the strolling players in the gaiety of his entertainments" (Ordericus). It seemed "as though he believed all things were moved by chance, and not ruled by providence." He was "the enemy of all decency and holiness," wrote Geoffroi le Gros about 1031. Several times he was excommunicated for his scandalous life, his disregard for the church's teachings and property; but he was not in the least concerned. When the bald bishop of Angoulême called on him to dismiss a mistress, he replied, "I'll do it the moment this comb curls the hair on your head." William of Malmesbury says that he was a great jester, evoking gusts of laughter. His biography as a poet tells us that "he was one of the most courtly men in the world and the cleverest at deceiving women." He loved hospitality, festivity, shows and songs. Jaufré de Vigeois, annalist of Limousin, tells us:

Eblo, viscount of Ventadour, had made himself very agreeable to Guilhem, count of Poitou, through his skill in turning a song. One day he arrived at Poitou, at his suzerain's court, at the dinner-hour. He was served a sumptuous meal, but the preparations had needed some time. At the meal's end Eblo said to the count, "It wasn't necessary, truly, to put yourself at such an expense to receive a small viscount like me." Sometime later, when Eblo had returned home, Guilhem arrived close behind him, exactly at the hour when Eblo dined, and he entered the castle-court in a rush with more than a hundred horsemen.

Eblo, realising the count wanted to play one of his tricks, had water poured out at once to wash hands. During that time livestock was quickly requisitioned from all the peasants around and taken to the kitchen, which became a remarkable heap of hens, ducks, birds of all kinds. Soon there was served up such a banquet that the partakers seemed to be at a royal wedding. And in the evening, without Eblo knowing of it, a peasant came leading a bull-drawn cart, who called out: "Approach, Knights of the Count of Poitou, and see how wax is delivered at the court of my master the viscount." Then he got up on the cart, armed with a big carpenter's axe, and set himself to smash in the casks. Out fell quantities of tapers, all made of the finest wax. Then the peasant, as if he had been dealing with poor cheap wares, got back on his cart and went home quietly to Maumont. Guilhem couldn't stop praising the valour and courtesy of his vassal. Later, the latter recompensed the peasant by giving him and his descendants the fief of Maumont.

In this world prodigality was liable to become an end in itself. Jaufré tells how the great barons of the Midi, in the festival given at Tarascon in 1174 to Alfonso of Aragon, vied with almost ridiculous display.[5]

This then is the man who may be claimed as the founder of European poetry. His poems, of which we have eleven, are divided into those with themes from popular songs, tales, jests, and those with serious love-themes. First, the lewd light songs. "Wisdom and folly I know well," he himself claims, and again:

> Comrades, I'll make a song – refined, no less.
> The only sense it owns is foolishness.
> Love, Joy and Youth are all mixed in, I must confess.

> Who fails to understand it, a peasant is he:
> who in his heart won't learn it deep. We see,
> if a man finds the thing he wants, he holds it steadfastly,

He is addressing his *Companho*, his male friends, in one of the songs that Ordericus says kept the table in a roar; and he goes on to tell of the troubles caused by two of his mares. "I cannot keep them both: one can't abide the other." The first is wild and restive from the hills; the other was "raised down there by Confolens. You never saw a comelier mare." Then in the ninth triplet he gives the game away; he is really talking about two mistresses. "I can't decide with which to stay: with Lady Agnes or Lady Arsen."

The triplet form is an exact imitation of one of the *conductus*, strophic compositions in Latin which had been developed at the monastery of St Martial, an important musical centre in Guilhem's own dominions. The *conductus* were more elaborate than the older hymnody for one or more voices. A man like Guilhem would delight in taking over a religious form and turning it to bawdy uses.

In a second set of triplets he tells how a lady has complained to him of being shut in, guarded by three men. He warns: "You'll hardly find a keeper who sometimes doesn't sleep." Never yet has he seen a lady who, if her pleas are ignored, "excluded from true valour, won't make her peace with baseness."

> If all good company she's thus denied
> with what's at hand she'll soon herself provide;
> and if she cannot have a horse, she'll buy a hack to ride.

> There's no one who can give me here the lie.
> If, sick, strong wine he's bidden to put by,
> then water he will swallow down before of thirst he'll die.

Marcabru took up the theme some thirty or forty years later. He attacked husbands who were "jailers of their own wives, husbands of wives of others." And he makes the same threat as Guilhem: the jailer won't escape his merited punishment. *Girbauts* (a term for domestic servants) will do the job; "and so you'll end by caressing little *girbauts*, thinking that you embrace your sons." Thus the world goes from bad to worse; the poet, like most men of his time, believed in the heredity of vices and virtues.

In a third set of triplets Guilhem expiates further on the matter of locked-up wives and sets out a creed of free love:

> Comrades, I've had much miserable fare,
> I can't stop singing still with a vexed air,
> though I don't want my little doings talked-of everywhere.

> Listen, and my dislikes I'll here unlatch:
> a guarded cunt; a pond – no fish to catch;
> the brags of worthless men, with which no deeds they match.

> Lord God, King, Ruler of the Universe,
> why not on the first cunt-guard set your curse?
> No servant or protector ever served a lady worse.

> Well, here's the law of cunt and how it goes.
> I speak who suffer through it many woes.
> Other things, taken from, grow less. Not so with cunt. It grows.

> And those who don't believe me or agree,
> come to a park by woodlands. There we'll see:
> for every tree cut down, there grow up two or three.

7

Thicker the cut wood grows. And so, no dues,
no property the owner there can lose.
Why then cry damaged goods and shout abuse?

When goods aren't damaged, do not claim you lose.

Again we can feel how Guilhem would have enjoyed using a *conductus* form, with a vernacular text, with such a cry to God. No doubt he used church-music for his tune.[6]

Next we have a poem that narrates a bawdy love-adventure. Here again the stanza is based on one of the forms of the *conductus* with a rhyme-scheme AAABAB, though in this poem (unlike another in the same form) Guilhem leaves the fifth line unrhymed:

I'll sing, since deep in sleep I'm drowned,
stand in the sun and stroll around,
Wrong-headed are some ladies found –
    I could say who.
They don't feel bound, though a knight loves,
    to yield his due.

She who won't love a loyal knight
sins mortally. If faith she'll plight
with monk or clerk, her wits take flight
    in blind desire.
Her they by right would burn alive
    with brands of fire.

O, in Auvergne, past Lemozi,
alone I wandered, sly and free,
and there the women of Guari
    and of Bernart
greeted me with kind courtesy
    by St Launart.

One in her high-class chatter said:
"Sir Pilgrim, grace be on your head,
you seem to me wellborn and bred,
    indeed you do.
But crazy folk who roam the world
    too oft we view."

Now listen to my apt reply.
No *bat* or *but* said crafty I;

for wood or fire I didn't cry,
    but I began,
"Barbariol, barbariol
    barbarian."

Then Agnes bade Ermessen heed.
"We've struck the very man we need,
by God, let's take him home with speed:
    he's dumb, this man,
and so we're safe, he'll never blab
    our little plan."

A cloak they raised and round me spread,
back to their chamber I was led,
a pleasant room with stove and bed.
    The fire was in.
Glad at the charcoal-warmth I stood
    to warm my skin.

Capons at once were ready there,
not only two, as I declare;
no cook or scullion anywhere,
    only us three.
The bread was white, the wine was fine,
    and pepper free.

"My sister, he's a cheat, I fear.
That he's not dumb will soon appear –
so run along and bring us here
    our ginger cat.
If he can speak, we'll make him tell
    what game he's at."

Then Agnes fetched the beast. With awe
a tom-cat fierce-moustached I saw
come bristling out and nearer draw,
    to my dismay.
My courage and my blithe pretence
    all ebbed away.

I drank and swallowed as they pressed me;
then quickly, roughly they undressed me;
on top they set the cat, to test me;

1. A medieval cat. (J. Jackson, 226)

    then, growing bolder,
they dragged him down me, to my heels,
    right from the shoulder.

They pulled his tail. The villain cat
dug in his claws and tore and spat,
a hundred gashes laid me flat
    immediately.
But for my acting they would soon
    have ended me.

Said Agnes after that, "You hear!
He's dumb: that certainly is clear.
Come now, let's take our bath, my dear,
    and take our pleasure."
Then, in that stew, eight days and more,
    I lay at leisure.

I fucked them, I precisely state,
a hundred times, plus eighty-eight.

I thought I'd split my loins, the rate
became excessive.
To tell the after-pains I find
no words expressive.

To tell the after-pains I find
no words expressive.[6]

ı he adds another line to the stanza. Here he uses the meta-
phor of dicing for the chances of life and love, and sets over against
it his skill in love and gaming, his ability to judge men and unite the
tested one with him. He asks the hearers to tell if there's good *color*
in the song he has brought along out of his workshop, *obrador*: "for
I'm here that in this craft obtains the flower; and that's a fact." *Color*,
which can mean "manner, kind, quality, brilliance, deception," here
refers to his images and the nuances or levels of meaning that he gives
them. "Folly and wisdom I know well; Honour and shame I've learned
to tell; courage and fear," and if he has a game-of-love set before him,
he's not such a fool but he can tell the best chances there from the
worst.

I know who speaks with courtesy,
yes, and who seeks to injure me,
the one who smiles beguilingly;
if brave men like my company.
I know it's true:

Trusted by them I needs must be,
and solaced too.

The *juec d'amor* is a debate on love, but here it has the double-meaning
of copulation. The "best chance" is success in seduction, and looks on
also to the question of choosing the true man from the hidden or open
enemy; it further suggests "the better side to choose in a debate". The
uncertainty of the game becomes the uncertainty of life, in which the
most prepared and talented person may be broken by an unforeseeable
twist of events. "The poet chooses the image of the dice throw to represent the master's skill in action; and in this, if we distinguish between the poet and the boastful man he impersonates, we can see a
deliberate moral intelligence at work; for when dice are thrown, all
distinctions are obliterated, all men are truly equal. The world of the
master may seem to be full of fun, a festival world where no one has
to have any identity, so that everyone can enjoy the fun of irresponsi-

II

bility; but it takes no chilly moralist to see that this fun is the accident of a vast uncertainty, and that this world is utterly without continuity, a world of unique instances. This song, with its initial pride in rules and techniques and its final concession to the sovereign power of chance, imitates in its very form a game of chance" (Goldin). After Guilhem has boasted how good he is at the game, he goes on:

> Friends, you won't hear me brag and say
> I wasn't shaken the other day
> at a gross game, absorbed in play:
> at first it made me vastly gay –
> then down I sat.
> One look, my wits went all astray
> and left me flat.
>
> But then I heard her loud complain:
> "To small your dice, my lord, it's plain,
> I challenge you to start again ..."

In this poem, then, there is a far wider range of meanings than in the previous ones, a serious note as well as a lewd one. Folly and wisdom are entwined.[7] In *Farai un vers* the diversity of meanings grows very much more complex. Here Guilhem sets out in paradoxical form a series of opposed states of mind or being: presence and absence, love and loss, indifference and devotion, nothing and everything. The mind is entirely split, yet a deep sense of purpose drives the poet on. In a sense it is an enigma, but with a scope of meaning that breaks all relation to the usual medieval Latin riddle or conundrum. The jongleurs of the north would later call such a poem a *fatrasie*.

> Nothing's the theme on which I write,
> not mine or anybody's plight,
> not Love and Youth and their delight,
> nothing so trite;
> and riding fast asleep one night
> I got it right.
>
> My hour of birth I can't attest,
> I'm neither happy nor distresst,
> not friend or stranger, damned or blest,
> and, I protest,
> my Faery on a mountain-crest
> decreed the rest.

Awake, asleep : I do not know,
if no one tells me how I go.
Broken of heart I almost grow
　　at the sad blow.
Not worth a mouse is the whole show,
　　I swear it's so.

I'm scared of death, my body ails,
and I must trust to people's tales;
I seek a leech down endless trails
　　on hills and dales.
I'll cheer him if his stuff avails,
　　not if it fails.

I love, but do not know her name.
We've never met; it's all the same.
I've nothing then to praise or blame,
　　and that's my aim.
No Frenchman or Norman ever came
　　to explain the game.

It's mad on such a love to stray;
she's never made me sad or gay;
for, missing her, I smile and say :
　　Here's holiday !
I find a fairer one who'll play
　　a better way.

Her dwelling-place I cannot show,
whether on hill or down below,
I can't explain my wrongs, and so
　　none else can know.
Now weary of this spot I grow :
　　therefore I go.

There's nothing. Nothing left to do
but send my song by someone true
to someone else, there in Poitou,
　　and ask anew
if further he can yet pursue
　　the riddle's clue.

The poem of a man so dazed with sexual indulgence that he doesn't
know any longer what woman he has embraced; the poem of a man

2. Entertainment in a Norman House. (Bayeux Tapestry)

who has worn himself down by an unreturned devotion. This remarkable poem is like nothing before it; and if any single work can be said
to originate mature European literature, here it is. The working-out
of its contradictions, its inner conflicts, reach on to Dostoevsky and
beyond. The forces of love and revolt rise up in protest against the
rigorously mapped-out world of authority where everything is severely
rational and has to be answered-for. The enigma, the riddle, is the new
life and its incredible possibilities. The beloved is unknown, yet determines the quest. The dogmatic certainties are mocked out of existence
and from the merry chaos a new cosmos is possible. In Nietzsche's
words: you need a chaos inside if you are to bring to birth a dancing
star. Guilhem has found the creative chaos.[8]

Now we turn to his direct love-poetry. In *Farai chansoneta nueva*
he claims to be making a new song, just as the *conductus* was called a
novum canticum in contrast to the set structure of the liturgy. As
shown by the poem in which he asked the hearers to note the special
color of his method, he was well aware of being an innovator.

> I'll make a song in a new strain
> before the frost comes, wind or rain.
> My lady tests me out again
> to find if she can make me stray.
> Let her provoke with might and main:
> her bond I'll never cast away.
>
> To be all hers is still my aim.
> Me in her charters she could name.
> Don't think me mad or lost to shame
> if her I love in every way.

Without her, my whole life is lame,
and only for her love I pray.

More white you gleam than ivory.
I adore you, lady, utterly.
I'll die if aid's not given me.
Come then and stay with loving play,
in a closed room, beneath a tree,
Saint Gregory! some kissing-day.

What, lovely lady, will you gain
if still my love you thus disdain?
You want to be a nun, it's plain,
I fear that I will waste away.
For wrongs of which I here complain,
make reparation quick, I say.

If I turn monk, what will it mend?
Lost to your service then I'll end.
Yet we've all joy as yet to spend,
lady, if love with love we pay.
Daurostre, sing this song, my friend,
but in no blustering tone, I pray.

I shake and tremble at the threat,
so deep my love and my dismay.
From Adam's line no woman yet
has had such beauties to display.

Each stanza rhymes AAABAB; but the B lines are not here shortened, and Guilhem gives them the same rhyme in all the stanzas (as here shown) so that they bind the whole poem together in a new sort of unity. At the end is a *tornada* or envoy. Certain elements of what came to be called Courtly Love are present. The lady is the most beautiful in the world and the lover is submissive to her power; his readiness to be written down "in her charter" shows a feudal relation. But there is no pretence of a worshipping aloofness. He wants her consummating embrace; the completion of love is contrasted with the renunciations of nun and monk. Love merits love in all its fullness.[9]

In *Pus vezem* he returns to the earlier kind of six-line stanza, but continues to give lines 4 and 6 the same rhyme throughout. (Here I have not carried over this effect.)

Flowering fields again we see,
the meadows rich with greenery,
the springs all rippling lucidly,
    the wind, the breeze.
With every man that joy should be,
    which brings him ease.

Only good things of love I say,
Why does so little come my way?
More may not suit me of love's play,
    Who keeps it well
within its bounds will surely stay
    safe in Joy's spell.

But from my fate I cannot flee.
In what I love no Joy's for me.
So has it been, so will it be,
    though hard I try,
knowing my heart most certainly
    "In vain" will cry.

Of pleasure less I get my fill.
What I can't have I seek for still.
The proverb's true for good or ill
    and should be noted :
There's yet a way where there's a will –
    for the devoted.

Obedience he must not spurn,
bowing to many. In his turn
he must do pleasant deeds to earn
    the love he has sought.
Yes, like a serf he now must learn
    silence in court.

If understood in all it says,
the song's more worth and wins more praise;
and one clear style this song displays
    in every line.
The melody, which myself I praise,
    is good and fine.

Friend Stephen, though on distant ways
    absent I be,

here is the song. About its praise
you'll vouch for me.

Again a feudal touch; he is to behave like a serf. The stress is on
absolute obedience to the lady, whatever pain it brings. The rising of
love is linked with the spring. Whatever the privations and pangs, the
last word is with Joy. Guilhem is also raising the problem as to whether
a song should be clear and understood, or complex and obscure, which
was to stay one way or another with the Troubadours.[10]

In *Mout jauzens* again the keynote is Joy, with the woman as supreme power. In eight stanzas with the scheme ABBAAB the same
rhymes are kept throughout:

> Joyous in love, I make my aim
> forever deeper in Joy to be.
> The perfect Joy's the goal for me:
> so the most perfect lady I claim.
> I've caught her eyes. All must exclaim:
> the loveliest heard or seen is she.
>
> You know I'd never base my fame
> on brags. If ever we're to see
> a flowering Joy, this Joy, burst free,
> should bear such fruit no man can name,
> lifting among the others a flame
> that brightens in obscurity.

He claims that no man can imagine or dream such Joy as his. It has no
like in the world and to sing it worthily could take a year. All other
Joys must yield to it; every other power must abase itself before his
lady, "her charming ways, her welcoming grace." A man who had
won her favours would be sure of a hundred years of life. The Joy of
her love cures the sick, and with one angry word she can kill the most
healthy. She can make the wisest man a fool and snatch from the most
handsome his fine looks. She can turn "the noble to a peasant, the
basest peasant to a noble." He wants to keep her close to refresh his
heart's depths, rejuvenate his body, and preserve him from old age. If
she grants her love, he knows how to take it and show his gratitude.
He'll keep the secret of his happiness, say nothing and do nothing but
for her delight; he'll know how to value her truly and make her praises
resound. But for fear of angering her, he does not dare to send her a
message. Afraid of committing a fault, he does not dare to go in person

and show the full extent of his love. "It's for her to give me her allegiance, knowing well that she alone can heal me."

Here the surrender to love is accentuated. He hopes for his lady's response, but does not demand it; he dares not send a messenger or himself approach her. It is as though only a total abnegation of self can bring the fulfilment of self; only silence can speak. The feudal relation is transferred into a spiritual one: "It is for her to give me her allegiance." At the same time the whole relationship is permeated with Joy and Joy itself takes on a new *color*. It is not an incidental pleasure but a pervasive condition, a central goal in life, an exaltation that comes from the new form of self-dedication. The power of Joy has qualities that are not feudal; it subtly and magically enhances the life-process, which it can transform. The fixed world of feudal hierarchy disappears inside a new redeeming and unifying force. Insofar as this force, attributed to the lady, is a reflection of the power of God or of the Virgin Mary, it indeed remains within the feudal categories; but insofar as it is felt as something inherent in human love realised in its fullness, it is taken away from deity and humanised, with ultimately revolutionary effects.

In *Ab la dolcher* we again meet the six-line stanza, but with the same rhymes repeated throughout the five stanzas.

> Thanks to the sweetness of the spring
> the woods grow leafy, birds all sing.
> Each in his proper tongue and measure
> sings a new song and never tires,
> while everyone seeks for that pleasure
> which man most ardently desires.

Hence his joy. No messenger or sealed letter comes. His heart does not slumber or laugh. He cannot take a step forward till he knows if his lady is such as he would have her.

> Our love, I find, is surely now
> the same thing as the hawthorn bough.
> All night it trembles on the tree,
> defenceless in the frost and rain.
> Then with the sun we brightly see
> the green leaves on the branch again.

> That morning I remember – how
> our conflict ended with a vow.

> A wonderful gift she gave to me:
> her love, her ring. God, end the strain.
> Beneath her cloak my hands will be,
> if yet enough of time I gain.

He has no care of whispering strangers who would separate him from his Good Neighbour. Others can boast of their love; he and she will enjoy theirs.

The motif of the scandal-mongering enemy appears. The image of spring is more subtly entwined with that of love than in *Pus vezem*. There is a deep sense of living at the secret heart of the whole life-process; and this sense of dwelling in a hidden depth of emotion is merged with the feeling of the actual secrecy attending the love-affair which must be protected from the destructive effects of the whisperers. Distance and union are one, doubt and certainty.

Thus the lewd witty poems merge, via the poem on gaming and that evoking the enigma, into the poems of the Joy of Love. But there is one more poem by Guilhem that must be noted. Here the world of lewdness and love is renounced, or rather is said farewell to, under the pressure of time, age, death. The counter-world, which is ruled by the Church, intrudes and takes over. The poem is composed in simple quatrains and seems written in his last years, when he feels a strong sense of failure and fears for his dynasty.

> Since I desire to sing, I vow,
> I'll sing of that which makes me sore.
> In Limousin and Poitou now
> Love's servant I shall be no more.
>
> Going in exile, sadly I grieve,
> in depths of danger, in great fear
> my son at war I'll have to leave,
> while neighbours press him hard, it's clear.

Foulques of Angers has the son (his cousin) and all the land in ward-ship. If he and the French king, "of whom I hold my domains," bring no aid, the son will have many enemies to fear, "Gascon and Angevin traitors,"

> Unless he's brave and wise indeed,
> when I have gone away to you,
> they'll cast him down and pay no heed
> when they his youth and weakness view.

3. Seals of Welf VI (Marquis of Tuscany, 1152) and Raimon Berengar (Marquis of Provence, 1150). (*Archives Héraldiques suisses*, 1916, 57; Blancart, *Iconographie de sceaux . . . Bouches-du-Rhône*, 1860, pl. 2 : Poole, *Med. England* i 342f)

He begs his companion to forgive him if he ever did him wrong, and may he pray to enthroned Jesus "in romance-tongue and what Latin he knows."

> Prowess and Joy have been my love.
> Farewell to them. All that must cease.
> I turn at last to him above
> in whom all sinners find their peace.
>
> Jovial and gay, I felt no care
> but now the Lord won't have it so.
> This heavy burden I cannot bear.
> Therefore towards my end I go.
>
> All that I used to love I quit,
> all chivalry and noble pride.
> Such is God's will. I bow to it,
> and pray he'll keep me by his side.
>
> All friends I beg, when there I die,
> to come and give me honour's due.
> Great joy I've known, both far and nigh;
> also in my bounds, it's true.

Now joy and dalliance I put by,
the vair, the gris, rich sables too.

We are reminded of the passage in the romance where Aucassin ends his decision to choose hell rather than heaven : "And there go the fair and courteous ladies, who have friends, two or three, together with their wedded lords, And there pass the gold and the silver, the ermine, and all rich furs, harpers and minstrels, and the happy of the world."

With the intrusion of the power-politics of feudalism a different Guilhem appears, though he still clings to the memory of his past devotion to Joy. Death ends the courtly game and imposes another set of rules. God takes over from the Lady. But Guilhem does not stress the opposition and draw any moral from it. The change has merely happened.

We see then that the great contribution made by Guilhem was the consistent development of a system of verse-technique and of a set of ideas about Love as the source of self-fulfilment through an ethic of devotion and joy. Elements of the technique or the ideas could be found elsewhere, but the definite and coherent way in which a new poetic system was evolved had no parallel. Music played an important part in this new creation. We saw how both the triplet-form and the basic stanzaic system of six lines rhyming AAABAB can be traced to musical developments of the eleventh century, to the *conductus* which was vigorously worked-out at the monastery of St Martial. (Guilhem in one poem swears by this saint.) Many other elements, poetic, musical, emotional, intellectual went to bring about the new poetry, which we shall come upon as our inquiry continues; but the *conductus* certainly had an important role. Of great importance in the new technical system was the device that Guilhem uses of repeating rhymes throughout a poem so as to produce a textural unity. We have indeed a remarkable anticipation of this effect in a Latin poem by Gottschalk in the ninth century, with stanza after stanza rhyming on the same sound (–e); but this tour-de-force of impetuous emotion, wrung out by the poet's experience of exile, seems to have had practically no effect on the development of the Latin lyric.[11]

Love-poetry has such a long history (and prehistory) that it would be hard to cite any motif appearing at a particular moment as quite original. Most of the elements making up the system of Courtly Love which we find defined in Guilhem's verses can be paralleled in earlier poems; but the peculiar way that they now come together cannot be paralleled. A poem like Ovid's *Art of Love* might be said to set out flirtation, wooing, seduction as a way of life; but the Troubadour system of Courtly Love, first formulated by Guilhem, is a way of life in a quite different sense. It calls on all the energies of man in a single-hearted devotion; it expresses a quest for the innermost meaning of life – a meaning that cannot be defined in any simple way, since it involves all the faculties of the lover, emotional, moral, intellectual, sensuous. *Joy* is the term used to express the total heightening of life that is brought about. (We might say that this term is taken over from Christian hymnology, but with a deep and subtle change of reference.) The shifting balances in the relationship of the loving pair, with their complex fusion of pride and humility, domination and submission, are used to express the movement of the life-process, stable and unstable, struggling precariously and powerfully from one level to another. Life is seen as a union of opposites, which can only be defined in terms of paradox: an enigma which is solved only by the act of living itself, which brings together possession and loss, fullness and dearth, union and separation, closeness and distance.

Such a matured system of complex technique and idea could not have arrived overnight. A lord like Guilhem had many companions who would vie with him, many jongleurs bringing their techniques to bear on the kind of song that was emerging. Guilhem would have built up his own style in jesting rivalry with others. There must have been something of a school around him at his court, though by that term we need not imply any sort of thorough or continuous organisation. Perhaps he refers to it in speaking of his Workshop. Many other developments, such as the musical ideas of St Martial, must have converged at Poitou, and there was an immemorial background of folk song. But at the same time it seems certain that something profoundly new was generated, probably in a fairly short period of time, say in the years 1086–1110. The form of *Mout jauzens*, we may note, is not traceable to any church-song; it provided the basis on which the most characteristic stanza of courtly-love poetry was to develop all over Europe. In *Puy vezem* Guilhem draws attention to the fact he has used throughout stanzas of similar structure and rhyme-scheme. He would hardly have done this if such poems were common. From one of his envoys we learn that he had admirers at Narbonne. Though we cannot be sure of the matter, we can best understand his poetry as representing the rapid maturing of tendencies which had been coming together in the later eleventh century. Out of the large amount of songs that must have been sung at his court his own finally emerged as those which most strongly and richly expressed the new tendencies and suited the spirit of the times.[12]

One further point. Guilhem was a friend of the free-thinking and blasphemous William Rufus of England, and Rufus may have influenced some of his attitudes. The two men must have met and talked much together at the time when Guilhem came to Rufus' aid during the latter's campaigns in France. Guilhem finally pledged his duchy to Rufus. The first known story-teller of Arthurian themes on the continent seems to have frequented Guilhem's court. The second continuator of the *Conte del Graal*, telling of the adventures of Gawain and a dwarf-knight, cites as his authority Bleheris, "who was born and bred in Wales," and who told the story "to the Count of Poitiers, who loved it and held it more than any other firmly in memory." Other details confirm this account. The first continuator also cites Bleheris. Thomas in *Tristan* in the later twelfth century refers to Breri as one "who knew the acts and tales of all the kings, of all the counts who have been in Britain." Maistre Blihis (apparently a corruption through the omission of the overstroke signifying *er*) is invoked as an authority declaring that the secrets of the Graal must not be revealed. The same poem has the knight Blihos Bliheris who "knew such excellent tales that no one could tire of listening to his words." The association of the name seems to have been the reason for making the knight such a tale-teller. Girald of Wales in his *Descriptio* (1194) attacks the attribution of the jest about fishing coracles to *famosus ille fabulator Bledhericus*, while his own tale about pygmies and a truant schoolboy shows the authenticity of the tale that Bleheris is said to have told Guilhem. Similar finely-formed truth-loving dwarfs are found in the *Conte del Graal* and *Huon de Bordeaux*.[13]

The Count mentioned must be our Guilhem and not his son, who is not known to have composed any songs or to have been particularly interested in Troubadours. It may well be significant that the earliest known references to Tristan occur in Cercamon and Bernart de Ventadour, who had connections with the court of Poitou. It seems likely then that Guilhem IX knew the stories of Tristan and Iseult and of the Holy Graal. Tristan and Iseult were fatal lovers and the theme of Courtly Love is not present in their story; but the tragic aspect of lovers devoted to death may have influenced men like Guilhem and

Bernart. Bleheris seems specially linked with the theme of the Graal, and Guilhem and other early Troubadours may have been affected by the notion of an all-engrossing quest for the symbols of redemption – though the only Troubadour referring to his beloved as the Graal is the late Rigaut de Barbezieux. We know very little of how the graal-story developed in France before Chrétien de Troyes wrote the *Conte del Graal* about 1180; but it must have been known in various forms long before that. There is little that is Christian in the *Conte*. Perceval spends several nights of love with Blancheflor, then goes straight to the Graal Castle. The graal is a platter carried by a beautiful girl. Though later Chrétien speaks of the graal holding the Host, that is clearly an after-thought by him or his source.

For some sixty years the Court of Poitou was one of the most brilliant in Europe. Guilhem X had some connections with Marcabru and Cercamon, and his daughter Eleanor, much given to pleasure, attracted Bernart de Ventadour, perhaps in 1155. Andreas attributes to her six Judgments on Love, so she must have excelled in the groups of ladies who made such pronouncements. Also she seems to have carried on her grandfather's interest in Celtic material; she bade Wace trans-late Geoffrey of Monmouth's *Historia* and she must have been con-cerned with the romance of *Troie* in which she is praised.[14]

The Twelfth Century

IN the twelfth century the societies of western Europe made a
decisive leap forward. They were built indeed on bases established
several centuries before; but the whole situation was now lifted on to a
new level. The Troubadours represented one particular aspect of this
development, but to understand them we must see them within the
wider framework of the century. The feudal system had achieved its
first stable basis in the tenth century; it then expanded till it reached its
climax in the twelfth and thirteenth centuries. A relatively unified
civilisation was created in place of the broken-up regional systems of
the earlier period. What had above all made this change possible was the
great agrarian advance, with many technical innovations such as
watermills, the iron plough, the stiff harness, the three-crop system,
and the marling of the soil. There was still however much inequality
of feudal development inside the society of the twelfth century. Parts
of France and Italy had undergone seigneurialisation long before
Germany and England; in southwest Gaul and the Saxon Plain the process was never completed. There large estates of several thousand acres
existed side by side with smaller holdings which were not feudalised
and owned no authority but that of the State. These independent holdings, allods, were especially numerous in Aquitaine, in the areas where
the Troubadours originated and carried on.[1]

In the feudalised areas there was much tightening of manorial
controls, with labour rents and all sorts of exacted services and fines.
Still, there too the peasants struggled to develop their own plots, with
much reclamation and conversion of waste and forest, swamp and
heath, especially in the years 1110–1250. In the later twelfth and the
thirteenth centuries demesne land and the labour-services on them
contracted; seasonal workers, paid in wages but performing customary
duties, were common on seigneurial estates; manorial reserves were
leased out and peasant tenancies increased. In some areas such as
northern France, communities and villages bought enfranchisement
from lords avid for cash. But at the same time there was a counter-

movement that sought to extend serfdom, so that previously free groups were oppressed and the legal definition of their status hardened and worsened. The fief system, whereby land was held in lieu of military service, was extended. In feudal theory every man should have a lord and free tenancy was anomalous.

There were big population increases. It seems that in the period 950–1348 the population of western Europe doubled. The new towns appeared, seeking as much freedom as was possible in a world of feudal exactions and controls. But only in Flemish and Italian towns did there arise a considerable body of urban workers under the artisanate, with its own interests. Generally production was regulated by gilds, which mostly emerged in the later twelfth century. Where manufacturing forces were dominant, artisan gilds at last tended to get a share in civic power: at Florence, Basle, Strasbourg, Ghent. Where mercantile activity was the main thing, the city-authorities generally remained of the merchant class: at Venice, Vienne, Nuremberg, Lübeck.

Trade in the West, we may say, had fluctuated from the early fourth century until the end of the ninth. In the Mediterranean basin it weakened in the fourth and early fifth centuries, revived in the sixth and early seventh, was reduced again at the end of the seventh and in the early eighth, and was probably at a low level throughout the ninth. The West had seen much anarchy from about 850, with the Viking attacks along the seaboard and the Magyar inroads by land; in 878 Sicily was lost to the Moslems and after 843 the Carolingian empire broke up. With the early tenth century Italian seaports began to build up their eastern trade, displacing Byzantines and Syrians as middlemen in the East–West trade; by the twelfth and early thirteenth centuries they were dominant in the eastern Mediterranean.[2]

The twelfth century saw the birth of communes. "A new and detestable name," noted Guibert de Nogent in the early century, while another prelate, Jacques de Vitry, called them "violent and pestilential." They clustered in Italy, Flanders, and, a century later, the Rhineland. The Flemish cities used disputes over the succession to the county to emancipate themselves; the breakdown of imperial suzerainty over Lombardy helped the Italian towns to assert themselves. Communes were also important for a century or so in vassal regions outside the royal demesne in north France where their influence helped to bring about tolerant treatment of the bonnes villes of the Centre and South.

As a result of the population increase, the trade expansion, the

4. Man coining Money. (Capital, St Georges de Bocherville, Normandy)

growth of luxury-demands, and the needs of lords and knights for loot and new land to exploit, there came the thrust of the Crusades. Various groups of western lords were enabled to take over much of the Levant, and western traders strengthened their grip. There were three lines of movement, into Moslem Spain, into the Balkans, and into the Levant. As part of their aggressive momentum, the Catholic crusaders in 1204 sacked Byzantium, which had been the great bulwark against the infidels of the East. Textiles from Flanders and north Italy began to find distant markets; merchants from Flanders and Artois turned up with pack-animals in Champagne, for the fairs of Provins and Troyes. Bridges were built and roads bettered.

In all considerations of the twelfth century we must then remember how the period saw the culmination of a big advance opening up all sorts of new possibilities. The effects were to be seen in every area of life. The Papacy gained enhanced power and wealth, but had to face up against greater threats and resistances from secular forces. The lords like the churchmen wanted more land and income; there was everywhere a challenge to old ways of thought and life. Hence the papal reform movement, intended to centralise the power of the church and make it effective everywhere, able to tackle the new problems. A decree of 1059 excluded the clergy and people of Rome from their customary rights in the election of the pope, which was now reserved for the college of cardinals that had gradually grown up round the Vatican. The rights of the emperor were reduced to a vague reference. (The papacy was taking advantage of the fact that the emperor Henry IV was a child.) Hence the Quarrel of the Investitures.

The struggle was complicated by the fact that, since Otto I, the emperors had needed officials. Unable to rely on dukes and counts, they had drawn on their ecclesiastical vassals, using them for administration and gaining through them most of their armed forces. So they needed a body of loyal bishops and abbots. Under Pope Gregory VII (1073–85) the climax came. A compromise had to be accepted, in the Concordat at Worms, with separation of the temporal and spiritual functions of bishops and abbots. The emperor's claim to universal supremacy was damaged and the rise of a strong French kingdom was facilitated. After Worms came some thirty years of strife and unrest. (France we must understand as a loose group of large fiefs, some more or less independent, for example, the Counts of Flanders and the Plantagenets of Maine and Anjou.)[8]

The political and social crisis we have sketched could not but have strong effects on the monastic system. We must never forget that in the dark ages and the early medieval period the monks were "the Religious." The parish priest was still a very minor figure, more or less in the hands of the local lord, while the bishop was mainly an administrator linked with the state-system. The monks alone were the men who tried to live a Christian life, which everyone felt could only be found by withdrawing from a sin-dominated world. Their attempt in varying degrees to live an apostolic life saved a degenerate world which God was at any moment liable to destroy. Their prayers and intercessions, carefully organised, came between ordinary men and a wrathful deity; and kings, aware of their sins, tried to invoke the appeals of the monks for their personal aid and salvation.

Monasticism had been the first great popular schism in the church, provoked by the latter's acceptance of the Roman State, an unthinkable act for the early Christians or anyone who held to the apostolic idea. The movement of the people out into hermitages or communal systems that rejected property might well have wrecked the church, which was however able to contain it by giving it an honoured role inside itself. But this act of acceptance was carried out at the cost of a break between the true Christians, the Religious, who withdrew to live in apostolic obedience, and the lesser herd, who stayed on as part of the sinful world, conscious of their weakness and failure, but unable to do anything about it. "Few men will be saved and most of them will be monks."

Such positions grew stronger after the breakdown of the Roman Empire in the West. Men, if they dared to think, felt sure that the end of the world would come at any moment. The image of Christ was sublime, hieratic, looking down on guilty worshippers who sought to propitiate him; he was essentially king of heaven and lord of hosts; the psalter was composed of the songs of God's warriors. Thus in the awe-inspiring nave of the romanesque basilica men faced an angry God who condemned them and threatened his day of judgement. Even Christ on the Cross was shown as king and only towards the thirteenth century bowed his head. These generalisations can be modified if one examines the positions from the fourth to the twelfth century in detail; the idea of Christ as the sufferer was never wholly submerged, and so on. But the imagery of power for both Father and Son was dominant. The early abbot of Cluny, Odo (927–42), wrote in his long Latin poem, *Occupatio*:

> Muse on these things with relaxed heart until
> this thought may fix the unstable mind at last
> and each man think that Judgment looms upon him.

He warns: "Now is the Time of Antichrist. Soon the whole aspect of the world will fade away and "our Judge will suddenly come in the flesh resplendent."

The contradictions of the situation had all the while entered into the monastic communities themselves, who found it impossible to maintain for long the fervent spirit of ascetic devotion with which they began or which individual recruits from time to time might emulate. And the admiring laymen helped to ruin the thing they admired, by the gifts they made to the abbeys; moved by the monks' glorification of poverty-in-Christ they made the abbeys rich and magnificent. In the confused days leading up to the eleventh century the Benedictine code, variously interpreted and applied, had been sufficient; the Order reached its height under Anselm. Many cathedral chapters had been reformed in the eleventh century; and in non-cathedral churches college-chapters were set up, with incomes drawn from urban land and market-taxes. The cloisters became important sites for the expansion of religious education and study. Old abbeys, once outside city-bounds, found themselves enclosed in the city. Some formed themselves into chapters; others took a share in the new economic life. The outstanding example of the latter trend appeared at St Denis where the humbly-born Suger became abbot in 1122; he at

5. Designing and Building. (Knight iii 201)

least tripled the abbey's income by selling enfranchisements, devising more effective tax-methods, planting new villages. Some of the money was used for charity, but most went into rebuilding the abbey. When Louis VII went crusading in 1147, Suger was made regent of France.[4]

But the house which most strongly revealed the new situation was Cluny, founded in 910 by Count Guilhem of Aquitaine and set in immediate dependence on the papacy. Here there was a centralised system, which helped the wide expansion of Cluniac houses; and the Cluniac code developed step by step out of a gradual clarification of customs to suit the situation. The ideal as set out by Odo involved the overcoming of the world, the return to a state of innocence, the anticipation of the afterlife with the gaining of eternal peace and the foretasting of eternal silence, the participation in an eternal feast, the attainment of an angelic state and of intimacy with Christ. The successful order, however, established a way of life very far from apostolic poverty, with endless concessions and grants of landed property from popes, emperors, princes, lords. The abbots were among the most powerful seigneurs in Europe; the monks, freed from manual labour, gave themselves up to liturgy and prayer; they were in effect the representatives of a new spiritual aristocracy, their position expressed in efforts to turn monastic life into something magniloquent

and splendid, with an elaborate liturgy of praise and with rich buildings echoing God's glory. They thus reflected the general social and
economic expansion of the tenth and eleventh centuries with a
diminution of the apostolic aspects of cenobitic life. The monastic
growth was helped by the considerable increase of pilgrimages linked
with a boom in relics; tenth-century abbots were very active in getting
hold of relics that would attract pilgrims, shrines were built and made
as rich-looking as possible; expositions, venerations, feastdays drew the
people along and there was a multiplication of saints' lives and
miracle stories about the tombs.

Earnest men in the church, including some abbots, deplored and
attacked the secular absorption of the monks. Early in the eleventh
century Bishop Adalbero of Laon accused the monks to the French
king of living like knights and lords, travelling to Rome to defend the
interests of their sovran abbot, since "King Odilo of Cluny is my Lord."
A poem, probably by Serlo, canon of Bayeux, described itself as:
"Invective against a Soldier, who, because he was poor, left the world
and became a wealthy Monk." St Peter Damian in Italy attacked the
mania for building; Richard of St Vanne, he said, though venerated
as a saint by the monasteries of Verdun, would have to spend eternity
climbing up scaffoldings. Abbot Joannelinus, Leo of Ravenna, and
others echoed such complaints, but without effect. Others, yet more
revolted, took practical steps. Many hermits, singly or in groups,
moved away from the settled areas. Bruno of Cologne left his chair
of theology in the cathedral chapter at Rheims and founded La Grande
Chârtreuse near Grenoble; he himself ended as a hermit in Calabria in
1101. That year Robert of Arbrissel, from the district of Rennes, a
preacher who deeply moved young women, founded a convent at
Fontevrault. Earlier, around 1075, Robert, a gentleman of Champagne,
who had become abbot of St Michel at Tonnerre, left his abbey and
led a hermit group near Auxerre, finally founding the abbey of
Cîteaux among wooded marshes, where the Benedictive Rule was once
more purified and the monks were expected to live strictly in poverty,
penitence, prayer, labour. In 1112 a young Burgundian noble, who became St Bernard, entered the abbey and gave a strong impetus to the
life there. Soon there were too many monks for the house to hold and
Bernard set up an affiliated abbey at Clairvaux, for which he drew up a
Charter of Charity.[5]

Thus, as usual, the problem of reviving apostolic poverty in houses
or orders which had grown wealthy was found too great; the only

6. Henry I's Dream of Insurgent Peasants. (John of Worcester MS)

effective reform was to found new houses which began once more to attempt to live like Christ the Poor Man. The Cistercians with their return to labour came soon to play an important role in extending land-clearances and in developing efficiency in agriculture. They were interested in conduits and drains and water-wheels; they pioneered in plumbing, and in England they re-established furnaces for smelting iron ore and exploited the main ironstone of the north fairly systematically. At Fountains they worked iron and lead, and at Furness used the haemitite ores of the west coast, famous from 1235 for the high quality of their iron. Most Cistercian abbeys had some mineral rights. So, with their managerial work in agriculture and industry, they too ended by being closely entangled with the world, though in a different way from the Cluniacs who had expressed and helped to heighten the period of expanding feudalism.

Through the eleventh and twelfth centuries; then, monachism was undergoing an increasing crisis of worldly involvement, which could not but deeply shake a society in which monks were supposed to be the true Religious following the way of apostolic poverty. One important result was the growth of heretical groups who tried to follow that way in the world itself, not in withdrawal; and in the thirteenth century the church tried to meet their challenge with the mendicant friars. How soon even the Cistercians had lost respect can be seen by the comment on monks made by John of Salisbury, who had been secretary of two archbishops of Canterbury, in the mid-twelfth century:

They are proud of their pale faces, and sighing is with them a fine art. At any moment they're ready to shed a flood of tears. They walk about with downcast heads and halfclosed eyes. They move at a snail's pace, muttering prayers all the time. They cultivate a ragged and dirty appearance, humbling themselves so that they may be exalted.

From 1175 a series of general chapters tried to forbid the acquiring of wills, altars, and other sources of revenue. The 1182 chapter stated: "It is evident to all that when possessions increase, scandals arise both inside and outside the monastery."[6]

Meanwhile the urban schools had been slowly coming into existence and seeking to free themselves from church controls, thus providing the first basis for thorough-going discussion and dissident ideas. They were strongest in the main areas of urban growth, in Italy, especially Tuscany, and in the Lowlands. At Ghent, for instance, the burning-down of a church and its school in mid-century gave the townsfolk the chance to open their own schools, while the clergy attacked them for "insolence of the laity." The monasteries on the whole stood outside this new development, interested only in training persons to become monks; among the exceptions were Cluny and houses in Lorraine and Normandy. The intellectual life of the age tended to be concentrated in the cathedral schools and city chapters, and till the end of the century there was a shortage of teachers for the eager students. "In 1100 the school followed the teacher, by 1200 the teacher followed the school" (Haskins). Chartres and Paris were the outstanding centres; but with Abelard Paris gained the lead. Early in the century there was the episcopal school on the Île de la Cité; then teachers moved off and set up on the Montagne Sainte-Geneviève (the Latin Quarter) in 1108; on the same hill the college chapter of St Victor was founded. It was directed by Hugh, a young man from Laon, who wanted to use all branches of learning to clarify the Scriptures. "Learn everything and then you will see that nothing is superfluous." In his quest for knowledge he was ready to hold discussions with Jews. Paris, in the words of John of Salisbury, became the goal of the keen scholar: "roused from the dead or from sleep by the knocking at the gate of an ardent talent." Among organisational problems were the enrolment of students, the conditions under which they lived, the courses of study and the examinations. As a more formal system was worked out, the schools moved towards the universities of the thirteenth century.[7]

The new spirit of inquiry produced many problems for the church jealously guarding its dogmas. From the late tenth century men had begun to feel the need to develop an instrument of logic for ensuring that they reasoned correctly in their scriptural analyses. In men like Gerbert the term dialectic was used to signify a correct reasoning from statements considered in terms of probability. Many of Gerbert's ideas were elementary, but none the less important in their attitude and direction. Inevitably there were tales of him as a necromancer who had sworn fealty to the Devil; he was said to have fled to Moslem Spain to study forbidden sciences and there, seducing the daughter of his Saracen host, he stole with her aid a book that "contained all that is to be known." Adelard of Bath set out the new convictions:

Aristotle with his sophistical wit, would entertain himself by using the arguments of dialectic to maintain a false statement to his hearers while they defended the truth against him. The truth is that once they are assured of the aid of dialectic, all other arts may tread firmly, while without it they stumble and reel about.

Men with this newfound and increasing faith in the powers of human reason were sure to come into conflict with the church. Berengar of Tours, born about 1000, became head of the episcopal school there, dying in 1088. "Why err with everyone if everyone errs?" he asked, and showed readiness to follow where his reasoning led. He applied the dialectic mainly to the question of the eucharist:

No one short of wilful blindness will dispute that reason is inconceivably the best guide in the quest for truth. It is in the nature of a great heart always to have recourse to dialectic; and to have recourse to that is to have recourse to reason, and whoever does not do so denies that which honours him most, since reason is the image of God in him.

He had to defend his positions against Lanfranc. Finally at the Lateran Council of 1079, always proposing "new interpretations of words," he so confused and baffled his opponents that at last they refused to argue any more and demanded, he says, "that I should confirm this also by oath, that I would henceforth interpret the writing which I held in my hand according to their interpretation."[8]

A younger man was Roscelin of Compiègne, who died in 1120. Abelard heard him preach at Loches. Roscelin rejected the Platonic position that objects perceived by the senses were mere reflections of ideas, the true and higher reality: the position called Realism. He held that by the term Man we imply two realities: the individual human being and the word in its physical existence as speech: the position called Nominalism. Analysing the Trinity, he argued that it could not exist outside the Three Persons constituting it; any other assertion confounded the members. Opponents replied that his position led to the conclusion: "If custom allowed, it would be truly said that there are three gods." (He meant that there were three distinct substances with one power, one will.) He was tried for heresy in 1092, but not convicted. The church was still uncertain before the claims of dialectic.

Lanfranc opposed Berengar. Anselm attacked Roscelin, though he shared his faith in reason. Defending the dialectic, he denounced "the heretics of dialectic who consider spiritual substance no more than a breath." For the monks of Bec who wanted everything to be based on rational argument side by side with scriptural authority, he wrote a treatise on God. We see in him also a passionate desire to unify faith and knowledge through love. "God, let me penetrate through love that which I taste through knowledge." He composed a long prayer to the Virgin. There were however many thinkers who felt sure that the elevation of reason would only work out as an aid to heretics. Peter Damian, the monk who was counsellor to several popes, attacked philosophy itself: " 'We shall be as gods, knowing good and evil.' There, brother. Would you learn grammar? Learn to decline God in the plural." St Bernard, who did much to advance the theology of the Virgin, wrote on his own mystical experiences, and advocated strict monastic discipline, accepted the dialectic as long as it took a second place. He wanted the direct experience of God aided by Biblical positions; the apostles "did not teach me to read Plato and unravel the subtleties of Aristotle, but they taught me how to live, and that is no small science." He grew ever more intolerant.

More trouble was coming up in the schools. Peter, later called Abelard, was born in 1079 and round the turn of the century he left his home near Nantes for Paris. "I had a father who had some training in letters before he put on the trappings of war. Therefore later he grew so fond of literature that he was disposed to have all his sons instructed in letters before they were trained in arms. And so it was done." Peter, his firstborn, was educated with the greatest zeal, and surrendered his patrimony and knighthood to a younger brother; we see how concern for letters was invading sections of the knightly class.

I totally abdicated the court of Mars to be received into Minerva's bosom. And since I preferred the panoply of the arguments of the dialectic to all the documents of philosophy, I exchanged other arms for these and esteemed the conflicts of disputation more than the trophies of war. So, traversing various provinces, disputing wherever I heard that the pursuit of this art was flourishing I became an emulator of the Peripatetics. Finally I came to Paris.

He made a powerful advance in the application of the dialectic and in setting up of standards of intellectual rationality and integrity. In his arguments with William of Champeau over Universals we see under the abstract terms his intense feeling for individual existence. He also had a deep sense of personal relationship with Christ, making of him a human example and companion. He stressed will and aspiration : God loves rather than judges. His teaching was reinforced in a subtle way by his own life and sufferings : his affair with Heloise and the castration with which he was punished, as if he too had to die in his love in order to be reborn – with the love of a woman taking the place of the love of Christ in a complex play of self-denying devotions. Thus Peter the Venerable broke the news of his death to Heloise :

So Master Peter brought his days to their end; and he who for his supreme mastery of learning was known wellnigh over the whole world and in all places famous, continuing in the discipleship of him who said, "Learn of me, for I am meek and lowly in heart," so to him passed over, as I must believe. Him therefore, O sister most dear, him to whom you once clung in the union of the flesh and now in that stronger finer bond of the divine affection, with whom and under whom you have long served the Lord, him, I say, in your place or as another you, has Christ taken to his breast to comfort him, and there shall keep him, till at the coming of the Lord, the voice of the archangel and the trump of God descending, he shall restore him to your heart again.

Here Christ and Heloise almost become interchangeable. She represents the earthly love which is subsumed in the higher love, but then again, at a yet higher level, after the change of the Last Judgment, she resumes her place as the other half of the complete union in which is found self-fulfilment. We see here clearly revealed something of the secularising process of religious ideas that is important for the Troubadours.[9]

Abelard had been found guilty of heresy in 1121 for his book on the Unity and Trinity of God. He infuriated the monks of St Denis by proving that their founder was not the author of the famous treatise attributed to Dionysios the Areopagite (identified in turn with the Athenian whom St Paul converted). Driven out, he set up a hermitage near Nogent-Sur-Seine, where disciples gathered round him. Afraid of new charges of heresy, he accepted the abbacy of St Gilas on the Bay of Morbihan. Meeting Heloise again, he wrote *The Story of my*

Troubles. In 1140 he was condemned at the Council of Sens, where his views were pronounced "pernicious, manifestly damnable, opposed to the Faith, contrary to Truth, openly heretical." But at last, after a peace had been arranged with St Bernard, he died unmolested.

He had declared in *Sic et Non* that "In truth, constant and frequent questioning is the first key to wisdom." He added, "Through debating we come to inquiry and through inquiry we perceive the truth." In his list of questions to be debated the first is: "That faith is based upon reason, *et contra*." Other questions are: "(32) That to God all things are possible, *et contra*; (38) that God knows all things, *et contra*; (84) that man's first sin did not come into being through the persuasion of the devil, *et contra*; (79) that Christ was a deceiver, *et non*; (85) that the hour of the Lord's resurrection is uncertain, *et contra*; (122) that everyone should be allowed to marry, *et contra*." We can imagine the horror felt by large bodies of the clergy at the very idea of debating such matters.[10]

William of Conches, called the Grammarian, in the first half of the century, scornfully rejected the account of Eve's creation from the rib of Adam. He counter-attacked:

These glib smatterers, if they perceive any man to be making search, at once cry out that he is an heretic, presuming more on their gown than trusting in their wisdom. Because they do not know the forces of nature, so that they may have all men comrades in their ignorance, they don't allow others to search out anything and would have us believe like rustics, asking no reason.

William, abbot of St Thierry, who had written the letter to St Bernard that brought Abelard down, threatened William with persecution. William left the schools, withdrew his book, and put himself under the shelter of a powerful noble. Gilbert Porée, an authority on logic, wrote the *Book of the Six Principles*; he loved Greek philosophy and in effect got rid of God by remarking that if he were substance he must have accidents. When he became bishop of Poitiers, two archdeacons and the clergy of the diocese appealed to the pope; and in 1147 a synod was held in Paris with the pope present. Gilbert baffled his accusers with refutations they could not understand, and the synod was adjourned for a year. His enemies held a private meeting at Rheims to rehearse their tactics, with the archbishops of Canterbury and York and Thomas Becket taking part. They were ready to secede from the church if Gilbert escaped punishment. At the second synod, at Rheims

7. A Nobleman's Carriage. (Louterell Psalter)

in 1148, after much argument, the pope acquitted Gilbert in the some-
what mystifying terms: "The essence of God should be predicated,
not in the sense of the ablative case only, but also in the nominative."
What had helped Gilbert was the fact that news of the secret meeting
had got round and weakened the position of St Bernard, who had in
effect challenged the Roman Curia as less in authority than himself.
By 1175 Bernard had reached the height of his power, keenly casting
round for heretics and served by many informers. St Norbert was rushing round the country announcing the advent of Antichrist.

The campaign against the new learning went on. Even Peter
Lombard, staunchly orthodox, was attacked after his death for daring
to "apply scholastic levity to the ineffable mysteries." In 1163 the
Council of Tours had forbidden monks to study law or science; the
synod of 1164 at Sens, presided over by the pope, anathematised anyone treating theology "in artful words or undisciplined questions." In
1210 a Council at Paris even forbade anyone to read or lecture on
Aristotle's works on natural science. How deeply and widely the
passion for dialectic had spread in the twelfth century can be seen from
the account of the schools of the three main churches in London given
by William Fitz-Stephen (1170–80):

On feast-days the masters call their scholars together at the churches. The
scholars hold disputations, some in demonstrative argument, some in
dialectic. These churn out enthymemes, those more perfect syllogisms.
Some dispute just to show themselves off, as they do at collections [examina-
tions]; while others dispute to establish the truth, which is the grace of
perfection. The would-be sophists are judged happy because of the amount
and flood of their words; others play upon words.

The orators with rhetorical speeches speak to the points so as to persuade
you, taking care to observe the precepts of their art and to omit nothing

38

that is relevant. The boys of different schools compete with each other in verse; or they contend about the principles of Grammar, or the rules of the perfect tenses and supines. Others in epigrams, rhymes and metres employ the common sayings of old, lashing their schoolfellows with Fescennine licentiousness . . .[11]

We have noted how the emphasis of the romanesque world had been on the righteous and wrathful power of God and Christ alike. Even as a child Jesus sat on his Mother's lap in the same watchful and monitory way that he sat on his Father's lap for the Judgment. The dominant view of the Fall and of Sin had been that man voluntarily withdrew from the service of God and entered that of the Devil, as if he were acting in terms of feudal *diffidatio*. By that a man withdrew from one overlord and gave himself up to another. By the feudal rules God, though at war with Satan, could not deprive him of his just rights. How could the situation be changed? Only if man of his own free will turned back to God – which he was incapable of doing – or the Devil forfeited his rights by some abuse of power, by breaking the rules of the feudal game. God tricked the Devil by becoming Man. The Devil failed to grasp the situation. By claiming the incarnated Christ and subjecting him to death he went beyond his valid rights. He had claimed a man who had not come over to him; so now he could be attacked and defeated, and the world could be saved. A popular way of expressing the cheating of the Devil was to say that God baited a mousetrap with the flesh of Christ (Peter the Lombard) or to show Christ catching Leviathan with a fishing-line baited with his fleshly ancestry (the patriarchs depicted in medallions) – Leviathan gobbled down the body of Christ but missed his spirit above.

Anselm flatly rejected this scheme. Man had sinned, man must do the redemption. That meant a new creation, or an angel becoming man, or God becoming man. Anselm tried to show that only the third course was logically inevitable, necessary. Now God and man were face to face. Thus Anselm's position opened the way to that of Abelard. (Not that the old feudal idea died out easily; we find it still, for instance, in the Townsley, Chester, and Hegge mystery-plays, which drew on the Gospel of Nicodemus.)[12]

We perhaps see the transition at Autun, in the church of St Lazarus, begun in the 1120s. Here the romanesque was strongly affected by classical influences, a Roman arch still standing in the town. Gilbert (Gislebertus) carved the richly expressive capitals with sharp contrasts of light and shade reminding us of late Roman work. On the tympanum over the west door was powerfully depicted the Last Judgement; men entered the church under that menacing image. But a new sense of life appears in the rounded figures of Gilbert's carvings, and his naked Eve has a strange sensuous charm. In the Weingarten crucifixion of the mid-eleventh century we see a wholly human Jesus on the cross. With the twelfth century we meet a stress on the Last Judgment as a symbolic event rather than as an historical world-end. Thus Richard of St Victor (d. 1173) defined it as an instantaneous process of judgment within the conscience caused by the "light of divine wisdom." Peter Lombard summarised the various points of view, but did not decide between them.[13]

In the change from the world-image of the angry God of Judgment to that of a loving Jesus who can be felt as a companion in suffering, we see the change from a system in which only the monks tried to live an apostolic or truly Christian life to a system in which the monks are more and more displaced from their central role. It is felt that somehow or other the ideal must be one that all men can attempt to imitate or incarnate. The church ceases to be primarily a place where one gathers in pleading prayer under the eye of God or Christ Pantokrator. As romanesque developed, we can see many links with the feudal castle. Consider the third building (early twelfth century) at Cluny with its two naves, its great central chancel tower, and its outer range of towers. We are reminded of the typical castle-structure with its central tower and keep or donjon, and its outer circle of smaller defensive towers. The church is God's stronghold in the Devil's world. But now, with the new sense of man having a more secure and even harmonious place in the universe, we come on Gothic. Cistercian architecture aimed at austere simplicity; but the sense of a new great flowering of life found its noblest expression in Gothic with its soaring spires. Much advance in engineering and building skills had been needed to devise the rib-vault, the pointed arch, the flying buttress. Great height was needed to express the new upward flight of the spirit, its new cosmic dimension – with the coloured glasses giving the effect of a paradisiac transformation. Chartres was meant to have eight spires; Rouen six. At Laon five towers were completed. The vehement verticalism of the exteriors was "the supreme expression of the heavenward urge" (Pevsner). By the 1250s and 1260s the great cathedral drive had exhausted itself.

The German monk who wrote under the name Theophilus gives us the feelings of the men who made and enjoyed the Gothic cathedral:

. . . you have adorned it with so much beauty; you have embellished the ceilings or walls with varied work in different colours and have, in some measure, shown to beholders the Paradise of God, glowing with varied flowers, verdant with herbs and foliage, and cherishing with crowns of varying merit the souls of the saints. You have given them cause to praise the Creator in the creature and proclaim him wonderful in his works. For the human eye is not able to consider on what work first to fix its gaze; if it beholds the ceilings they glow like brocades; if it considers the walls they are a kind of paradise; if it regards the profusion of light from the windows, it marvels at the inestimable beauty of the glass and the infinitely rich and varied workmanship. But if, perchance, the faithful soul observes the representation of the Lord's Passion expressed in art, it is stung with compassion. If it sees how many torments the saints endured in their bodies and what rewards of eternal life they have received, it eagerly embraces the observance of a better life. If it beholds how great are the joys of heaven and how great the torments in the infernal flames, it is animated by the hope of its good deeds and is shaken with fear by reflection on its sins.

But though hell and judgment cannot be altogether left out, the stress is now on enjoyment, on heaven in all its radiance; and as a result the earth too is irradiated with new values, new elements of joy and hope.[14]

Jesus on his mother's knee comes alive, plays, smiles. He is fed from her breast and she too comes to life, taking up an old tradition that had died out in the West though surviving in Byzantium. Tales of her loving kindness multiply, spread, are collected. Until the twelfth century she had played only a minor role in the miraculous interventions recounted by pious writers. The lack of relics of her person helped to keep her cult in abeyance. Now she was shown as ready to succour even the sinful if they loved her. Thus, a thief who worships her is held up by her for two days after he is hanged; when the hangmen try to tighten the noose she prevents them with her hands on his throat; at last he is let go. A sacristan has a mistress, but he always says an *Ave Maria* on passing her altar; drowned on his way to a love-tryst, his soul is restored to his body at her intercession. St Bernard in his *Memorare* prayer declares: "Never was it known that any who fled to thy protection, asked for thy help, or sought thy intercession, was left unaided." With the feudal right of asylum in a church, the church becomes her sheltering body, another form of paradise.[15]

As part of the general intellectual advance and the stronger critical sense that was developing, there was much codifying work in law, both secular and ecclesiastical. The church had got itself into a state of much confusion, incorporating in its statutes many customs from the barbarian areas; various collections tried to deal with different spheres such as General Councils, Roman Synods, Papal Letters, and so on from the sixth century. To collate the material and make sense of it was difficult. Systematic case-books were begun, for example by Bishop Burchard of Worms (first half of the eleventh century), who complained that the confusion brought ecclesiastical law into disrepute. The compilations in general were incomplete, with interpolations, canons attributed to imaginary Councils, falsifications. With the quarrel over Investitures the papacy needed more secure ground under its feet. There were continual pamphlets and treatises justifying each side and making statements that were hard to verify. The Justinianic Digest was rediscovered and led to a rebirth of studies of Roman law, at Rome, Pavia, Ravenna, Bologna. Ivo of Chartres in the later eleventh century attempted a set of rules; in the prologue to his collection of canon law he stated: "Do not at once break out into reproaches if the authorities I have quoted seem to contradict one another. . . . It is necessary to take into account the circumstances in which they wrote, the time and place and those for whom they were writing." He used the distinction in Roman law between justice and equity in an effort to find a compromise for the dispute between emperor and pope. The arguments roused by Roscelin and Berengar increased the need for clarity. The idea of systematisation derived from legal work (for instance, that of Gratian on canon law at Bologna) was taken over by theologians. Peter the Lombard at Paris in his *Sentences* tried to make conflicting authorities concur and his work was the basis of theological studies till the seventeenth century.[16]

The economic advance had led to increased division of labour and the need for more efficient administrators and officials by the governments, the great lords, and the church. Cities too needed scribes, and tradesmen more and more needed a certain amount of education. The number of physicians grew, and for the first time there was a widening spread of culture outside the church. All the while the available Latin classics were read and studied. Ovid was copied even at Cluny. There was considerable advance in letter-writing, sermons, treatises. At monastic centres there were libraries from which books could be borrowed.

The quotation from Ivo showed how an historical sense was appearing. Both that sense and the new sense of the individual appears in such works as the biography of Anselm by Eadmer (who had known Anselm well) and his *History of Recent Events*; Suger's *Life of Louis VI the Fat*; William of Malmesbury's historical writings with their clear critical sense and their desire to make a coherent story with cause and effect; or Salisbury's *Historia Pontificalis*, which dealt with recent events. John evaded the obligation to write a universal chronicle by pretending that his work was the continuation of a well-known chronicle – the only connection being that the latter ended with the year 1148 when John's close link with the papal court began. A new critical perspective informs the autobiographies of Abelard and Guibert of Nogent; and the Crusades stimulated direct accounts. With Geoffrey of Monmouth we meet the incorporation of legend in an attempt to build a sense of national purpose and continuity.[17]

At times a sceptical attitude is stirred. Guibert, son of a lesser nobleman turned monk, wrote *On the Relics of Saints* and was often jesting in his treatment. When two heads of John the Baptist were claimed, he remarked that the saint had two heads or one of them was a fake. He asks how five churches have Christ's foreskin; and if the abbey of St Medard has indeed a tooth of his, can he be said to have risen fully from the dead? William Rufus was a mocker of holy things. Girald of Wales commented, "Many hide secretly their unbelief among us today." A priest, criticised for an indecorous celebration of mass, told another: "Can you out of this bread make flesh? out of this wine make blood? can you imagine that God the Creator of All took flesh of a woman and wished to suffer? Do you think a virgin can conceive and remain a virgin? do you think our bodies, reduced to dust, will rise?" Such sceptical attitudes had been helped by the too-literal arguments about the real presence in the ingredients of communion.

Journeys were slow. John of Salisbury said that it took seven weeks to go from London to Rome, though a man ready to kill his horses could do it in four. But there was considerable movement, and many of the persons who did the travelling were those most useful in spreading ideas, stories, songs. There were the wandering scholars, often acting as a kind of jongleur; Latin poems of the kind they recited grew richer, more sensuous in treatment of love-themes. Thomas Brown, an Englishman, became a judge in Sicily, then went to Arabia where he got the title of Kaid Brun, and ended as an official under the English Henry II. The hagiographical works about Becket, written in England, were to be read in Icelandic translations within three years of his

8. A Blind Wayfarer. (Wright, 328)

death. A law of 1157 against Rhenish weavers mentioned "men of the lowest class who move frequently from place to place and change their names as they go."

Pilgrimages saw much exchange of culture and stimulated the growth of stories or poems about the martyr and his tomb as well as other themes, as we see from the *Chanson de Roland*. The idea of quest – for God, for the Graal, for the Lady – was also stimulated. Life itself was seen as a Progress into sin or redemption, a movement from one territory or sphere to another. St Bernard, dealing with the Prodigal Son, said that he wandered from the Paradise of Good Conscience into regions of Sin, then with the guides Fear and Hope attained the Castle of Sapience, where he was prepared for reunion with God.

Trade, pilgrimages, crusades all helped to bring about a convergence of cultures. Peter the Lombard drew heavily on the Greek theological encyclopedia of John of Damascus. After the Norman conquest of Sicily there was an increased inflow of Byzantine and Arabian elements; Roger II, who even had his harem, protected Arab-speaking poets and scholars who rubbed shoulders at his court with Latin writers. A sound legal code, the Assizes was developed. The Byzantine emperor sent a copy of Ptolemy's *Almagest* in 1160; a scholar at the medical school of Salerno in south Italy at once travelled to Palermo to see it. The geographer al-Idris, educated at Cordova, worked at the Norman court, and Roger II commissioned a treatise from him as well as a religious history from a Greek monk.[18]

Spain was however the main centre from which Arab learning spread. The story began with the strange figure of Gerbert, the first man of the West to lecture systematically on the whole range of logical treatises inherited from the ancient world. He also made important contributions in arithmetic, geometry, musical theory, astronomy, and brought in the abacus (on an Indian system) as a calculating device; his pupils had astrolabes. In 967 when aged about twenty-five he had set out for Catalonia. There were already a few translations from Arabic science, e.g. a work on astronomy done by Llobet of Barcelona. At Ripoll the monastery had Mozarabic monks; through them and through merchants going from Barcelona to Cordova many Arabic works became known and were translated. After his period in Spain Gerbert went to Rheims for nearly ten years and absorbed what was taught of logic there; finally he became Pope Sylvester II. A humanist scholar, he loved the ancient poets, orators, philosophers, and searched for manuscripts; he bewildered people by saying that he sought consolation in philosophy rather than in prayer.

In 1106 the baptised Jew Moses Sefardi, who took the name of his patron Alfonso I of Aragon, calling himself Pedro Alfonso, travelled in various Christian lands. About 1110 he was in England as physician to Henry I. His main work was in astronomy, though only fragments of it survive. He stressed the need for observation and for the dissemination of scientific knowledge; he also made a lively collection of tales, *Disciplina clericalis*, which had a very wide circulation. He influenced Adelard of Bath, who seems to have studied at Tours and taught at Laon, then travelled in Italy and Sicily, Cilicia, Syria and Palestine; at some time he was in Spain or took over material from Pedro Alfonso, since his version of the astronomical tables of al-Kwatizmi show corrections made at Cordova. In 1126 he was back at Bath. Among his works were versions of Euclid's *Elements* from the Arabic and his own *Natural Questions*. He was curious about everything. Why aren't fingers all the same length? Why don't babies walk at birth? He noted down his impressions of an earthquake in Syria, believed in the continuity of the universe and the indestructibility of matter, and had a fair idea of gravity. (He said that if we could drill a hole through the earth, an object thrown in would come to rest midway.) He felt the need to develop precision instruments. His tradition went on to Robert Grosseteste and Roger Bacon.[19]

A convert like Pedro Alfonso could hand on direct a good deal of Arabian science, but in general there was a need of translators. In the second quarter of the twelfth century there were many in the Ebro region. At Tarazona, some sixty miles west of Saragossa, the bishop installed after the reconquest commissioned Hugh of Santalla to do a dozen scientific works, with astrology bulking large in the list. A great problem was the method of translating, which for some time was rudimentary, with each word taken separately and little concern for context. Versions tended to be more garbled according to the number of languages the work had gone through, e.g. Syriac or Arabian into Greek and then into Latin.

Among the translators were Jews and Mozarabs, Spanish clerics who had learned Arabic, and foreign scholars drawn in by the lure of knowledge, like Hermann of Carinthia, perhaps a Slav who had studied at Chartres, and Robert of Chester. These two planned to work together on astronomy and meteorology, but after a while went in different directions. Hermann, after a period at Laon, went to Toulouse in 1143, where he completed a version of Ptolemy's *Planisphere* from the Arabic, which he dedicated to his master Thierry of Chartres, and composed a philosophic work of his own, the first in Europe to be deeply affected by Arabian cosmology. Robert had gone to Pamplona and Segovia, and was in London about 1147; his main work was a translation of al-Khwarismi's *Algebra* and tables of astronomy adapted to the meridian of London.

At Barcelona an Italian of Tivoli, Plato, aided by Jews, worked at translations from Arabic and Hebrew (1134–45). About 1138 he did a minor treatise of Ptolemy, and about 1145 a work on practical geometry, the first in Latin to give a complete solution to a quadratic equation. In 1185 at Toledo, capital of Castile, the king had a "school of translators." The first bishop was blamed by the Moslems for breaking his word in turning the great mosque into a cathedral; but his successor fostered cultural exchanges. Many works were translated, with a rising standard of method. Versions of Galen and Harpokrates and a host of Arabian medical writers superseded the few crude works used at the start of the century. There was also a change of interest from directly scientific works to philosophy and to Aristotle. In 1141 Peter the Venerable, abbot of Cluny, on a visit to Spain, watched the translators of the Ebro region at work. He had the idea of a complete and accurate Latin version of the Koran, so that effective controversies could be held with the Arabs. For a while Hermann and Robert of

9. Doctor and Patient: "Put out your tongue". (Trinity Coll. MS)

Chester worked at the project; finally with the aid of a Moslem and a Mozarab the text was finished. Peter however failed to interest St Bernard. We see the change from the fixed idea that a work like the Koran must be a product of diabolic deceit, and the growth of a belief in the efficacy of intellectual discussion. The German author of the *Willehalm* in the early thirteenth century treats the Saracens as "God's handiwork" as much as Christians, and throughout his work poses the problem of the non-Christians as human beings in their relation to Christians. We are in a totally different world from that of the *Chanson de Roland*.[20]

A decisive change had thus occurred in the attitude of thinkers to the physical universe, which was seen, not as an imperfect copy of a higher reality, but as a system to be studied in all seriousness for its inner workings. The naive desire for secrets that would at once confer great power on the discoverer was giving way to genuine scientific curiosity, from which in turn came the wish to devise philosophic systems that would synthesise the discoveries and give them an adequate setting. There was special interest in the works attributed rightly or wrongly to Aristotle, and to commentaries on them by Arabs like al-Farabi or al-Kindi. In 972 no work by Aristotle on natural science was known in the West; by 1204 there was keen study of works under his name dealing with physics, the heavens, meteorology, the soul and the senses, respiration, and so on. There was also much interest in contemporary systems such as those of Averroes or the Jew Maimonides. All these influences from Spain intensified the effects of the dialectic developed by Anselm, Abelard, and others. A wide range of subjects was opened up, including physics, optics, mechanics, biology. There was much that was confused and rudimentary in these ideas and attitudes, and there was a long fight ahead for those who sought to apply the new positions. But the decisive movement had occurred. The ideas might be checked, driven under, but their effects could not be eliminated.

The pointed arch, essential for Gothic, may well have come from the Moslems. Crusaders would have noted it in parts of Syria and Asia Minor, and it is even possible that Moslem masons were taken westwards. But no doubt there could have been influences, and masons as well, from the nearer area of Spain. The new architecture also needed the increased precision of geometrical studies and the revival of Euclid, which merged with the use of symbolic schemes. Once the system had been started off, the master-masons or architects were capable of developing it; though it is clear that patrons also played a role in determining styles and methods.

The Troubadour area of southern France, so close to Catalonia, shared in the spread of the new science. In 1140 at Marseille, Raimond adapted the astronomical tables of Toledo to the local meridian. At Narbonne, soon after that, Abraham ben Ezra began his series of versions from Arabic into Hebrew for the Jewish communities of Languedoc and Provence. The counts of Barcelona were connected by family with Narbonne.[21]

Even the brief sketch here given of cultural developments in the twelfth century will have brought out the powerful and far-reaching nature of the changes occurring. The economic and social expansion had reached a point where there was a rapid movement on to a new level of artistic and intellectual comprehension and expression. Feudalism, in maturing, created a large number of inner conflicts and contradictions, which appeared particularly in the towns and communes. A new spirit of questioning arose, quickened from the heart of Western society itself, but stimulated by various influences from without, from the Byzantine and the Arab worlds. The advance of society expressed itself in the breakdown, or modification, of ideas that had ruled earlier medieval thought and emotion. The stern God of the Last Judgment began revealing more sympathetic features, and the Virgin Mary asserted herself as an emblem of love no longer tied down to rigid moral systems. There was a large-scale expansion of monasticism, which at the same time increasingly showed up its weaknesses and limitations. The Christian way could no longer remain the preserve and refuge of a chosen few who cut themselves off from normal life and who, to the extent that they took that life into themselves, became corrupted and unworthy. Both the new concepts of natural science and the new Gothic architecture expressed an acceptance of the earth and the cosmos as sources of fulfilment and happiness, despite the prevailing ideas and dogmas of earthly life as hopelessly permeated with sin and degeneration.

Such a situation could not of itself have created the new poetry which we saw coming about in the work of Guilhem of Poitou, but it made it possible.

III

Cercamon, Marcabru, Rudel

JUST as we could not make out, except in a very general way, the other poets or singers who must have surrounded Guilhem, so we cannot see in any detail how the new type of poem was developed in the first decades of the twelfth century. We have, however, poems by three troubadours composing in the period after Guilhem's death in 1127. Cercamon is said in Marcabru's biography to have been his teacher, but it has been argued that the roles should be reversed. However, the two poets are so different that it is impossible to decide such a point, and it is best to see them simply as two divergent lines of development that follow on Guilhem. Cercamon is a rather vague figure who seems to have been active about 1135–45 in the courts of Poitou and Limousin. His Provençal biographer calls him a Gascon jongleur with the name of Court-le-Monde, Runabout-the-World, a phrase that suits a wandering jongleur who did not succeed in finding any settled court-home. He wrote a *planh* or lament for Guilhem X of Poitou in 1137; and an exhortation of his that aid should be given to Edessa in the East must have been made about 1146–7. We have seven of his songs, and an uncertain eighth. One of his poems is a *tenson* or dialogue-song with Guilhalmi, which shows him in what looks like a jongleur-role. Guilhalmi is trying to get out of making gifts to him by saying that he'll do well, with "palfrey or rent," when a certain princely marriage comes off, probably that of Eleanor of Aquitaine and the future Louis VII (which was first arranged for 30 May 1137). Cercamon is unimpressed. "All your fine words at less than a farthing I rate. Better a quail held fast in my bosom here than a whole poultry-house locked up by someone else. Rely on another's gifts and you gape at empty air."[1]

We see from his love-songs that the ideas thrown up with imaginative force by Guilhem have been developed into something like a rhetorical system and yet are being effectively used to penetrate into complex moods in which opposites are merged.

> When bitter the sweet breezes turn
> and from the bough bring down the leaf,
> when a new speech the birds all learn,
> I sing as still I sigh with grief
> of love whose power on me is set
> though power on love from me has fled.

The same rhymes (ABABCD) recur through nine stanzas and two envoys. He declares that he has gained only toil and torment from love. Nothing is so hard to get as the thing that he desires; nothing fills him with such longing as the thing that he can't get. In his lady's presence he is dumb; away from her, he loses his wits altogether.

> The loveliest lady ever beheld
> near her has not a glove's poor worth.
> When darkness holds the whole world spelled,
> where she is, there is light on earth.
> God, let me live to have her yet
> or watch her getting into bed.
> I shiver, tremble all over, burn;
> asleep, awake, in love I shrink,
> afraid of the sure death I'll earn;
> of asking her I dare not think.

Perhaps if he is her suitor for two or three years she'll guess the truth. He doesn't die, live or recover, or feel his sufferings though deeply he suffers. He's happy when she sends him mad and makes him stand gaping, staring still; he's happy when she laughs at him, mocks in his face or behind his back. For the good time will come after the bad, and quickly too, if it's her whim. If she doesn't want him, he wishes that he had died the day she took him as servant. "Lord, with what gentleness she killed me, and locked me in such an enclosure there, I never want to see any other." He is beset with worries yet enjoys them; it all depends on her, if he fears and woos her, whether he'll be false or true, a peasant or a courtly lover, tormented or at ease.

In another poem he tells of his grief in a separation caused by scandal-mongers (the enemy motif). He is sorry for crediting tales about her and for complaining of her infidelity. She is loyal, true, pure; she can still make him happy by granting what will enrich him:

> Messenger, God protect you, go
> and somehow to my lady appeal.
> For long I cannot live, I know,
> and nothing my deep pang can heal

> if I can't hold her in embrace
> and kiss her naked body there
> within a tapestried close-place.

He mentions the dawn-parting of lovers, though not in a dawn-poem or *alba*.

> Holy Saviour, grant me haven there
> where she, the fairest, dwells, and we
> may kiss at last and love may share
> in true accord. She'll give to me
> all she has promised, and then go
> at dawn, possessed and mine, although
> harshly the jealous brute behaves.

And he links Joy with Love: the reward granted to the small number of true lovers. "God grant that I have joy of her."

The conceit about her body shining in a dark world may have come from Spain, where the Jewish poet Ibn Gabirol, born in Malaga 1021–2, wrote: "Who is this that, rising like dawn, looks down and shines with the brightness of the sun? . . . See, the world would be dark now, but for your light." And again on roses: "A light shines from their faces like the day's bright splendour."[2]

With Marcabru we meet a very different character, a poet of powerful originality and damn-all boldness, who has some of the qualities of Guilhem IX but who approaches the world of the twelfth century from below, as a commoner not as a lord. He was born in Gascony, probably about 1110, and may have been the first professional Troubadour, unless Cercamon can claim that title. His Provençal biographer tells us:

Marcabru was dumped at the door of a rich man. It was never known who he was, nor where he came from. And Sire Audric de Vilar had him brought up. He stayed then with a troubadour named Cercamon, and thus it was that he began to sing. At that time he was called Lost Bread, but after it he bore the name of Marcabru. At this time all that was sung was called *vers*, not song. He was very renowned and much listened-to by the world, as well as feared because of his tongue. He was indeed so slanderous that he was at last killed by the castellan of Guyenne, about whom he had said many bad things.

Another text tells us that he was born in Gascony of a poor woman named Marca the Brown. That is what Lost Bread himself declared. He seems not to have known where he was born; he only knew that he had seen the day under a star propitious to satirical instincts.[3]

10. Ladies hunting Deer. (Royal MS 2B vii)

He was active around 1130–48 and frequented camps as well as courts. His first ten years (perhaps 1127–37) may have been spent at Poitou. He took the side of Guilhem X in more than one poem and links his death with the end of Munificence and Valour, the two virtues that Troubadours stressed in their patrons. Then he went visiting the great courts of the Midi and Spain, finding no settled patronage. Peire d'Auvergne, about 1157–8, refers to him in the past tense and suggests that he has fallen into neglect. We have some forty-two poems of his, which show much variety: love-songs, *pastorelas*, *tensons*, crusade-songs, songs of satire and invective. The last-named were his main vehicle, and he often introduced, deliberately, a gross popular note. Throughout we feel his lively personality, his clear and fearless moral tone. At his best he attains in his denunciations to a prophetic power; and his passionate urgency at times makes his work harsh and difficult, thus creating what was called the hermetic style, *trobar clus*. "I go sowing my remonstrances on the rock, where I see no seed or flower take root." "Then sleep who will. Myself I think and muse on grave matters, according to nature and against nature." "Against the plague Marcabru rises in his wrath: alone, without companion." After thanking God and Saint Andrew, he declares:

> There's no man has more sense than I.
> I don't self-flatter
> nor merely chatter.
> It's my opinion. I'll tell you why.
> Sadly is spent
> long argument,
> entangled, with no proper ending.
> Judgment's in vain
> if you can't explain
> the subject-matter you're defending.

My head so teems
With brilliant schemes
it's hard to make of me a fool.
The fool's bread oft
I eat when soft
and warm, and let my own bread cool.

So he cajoles the fool and eats his bread, then goes off with his own. It's right for a fool to act like a fool while the wise man watches out for what he can get away with. A man's doubly stupid who is fooled by a fool.

With Breton stick
or sword I'm quick.
At weapons none has better wits.
I hit my foe,
ward off his blow,
but he can't dodge my masterly hits.

In his woods still
I hunt at will.
My two small dogs I set to barking.
The third, my hound,
off with a bound,
is boldly there the victim marking.

My private place
is hard to trace :
none can enjoy its charms but me.
So barricaded,
it's never invaded :
I've locked it up so capably.

He is full of serpentine tricks, with a hundred *colors* from which to choose the best. He carries fire here, and water there, for putting out the flames.

Beware my part;
for with such art
at living and at dying I play,
that bird am I,
so shrewd and sly,
the starlings feed its chicks each day.

That is, he is the cuckoo, the lord whose bastards fill up the ranks of his order.

There he is both vaunting his own skill and mastery, his insight into the world's betrayals, and pretending to act the part of one of the betrayers, the worst of them all. He cites Scriptures, Ovid, popular sayings or proverbs; and in denouncing the world for having taken the wrong turn into violence, villainy, corruption, he is never far from singing of the failure to sustain love as the core of the whole disaster. In his dialogue with Ugo (Uc) Catrola he starts off by denouncing false love, while Catrola tries to soften his blows.

> "Marcabru, truly I can't approve
> when you say aught but good of love.
> Hence this debate. My point I'll prove:
> Love gave me birth and fostered me."

Marcabru brings up the case of Samson. Catrola replies:

> "Marcabru, if you truly mean
> that love and lying are akin,
> then giving to the poor's a sin:
> treetop and root are levelled, sure."

> "The love you find such virtues in,
> switches dice secretly, to win.
> Watch out when a good throw you spin.
> Heed Solomon's and David's lore."

Catrola says that Love has declined because youth loses valour. "Anger and dread cry in my heart, for vile things you have said of Love." Marcabru replied: "O, Love scorns no one, dark or light; indeed prefers the earth's worst scum." Catrola says that he doesn't believe Love ever loved Marcabru. "For Love scorns nothing more than jongleurs who've gone daft like you. . . .

> "When I feel bad, with weary stress,
> and my sweet friend gives a caress,
> a welcoming kiss, as I undress,
> I leave her feeling good once more."

> "A fool's in love with the wine-press;
> his coins skip off and still grow less –
> show him the road to emptiness
> which other fools have traced before."

Like Guilhem, Marcabru uses effects of church music and prosody for his own purposes, as in a litany of thirteen stanzas with each stanza having for its fourth line: *Listen then!*

O, I will make no more delay
in starting off my song today,
for true are all the things I say.
  Listen then!
Who does no good while yet he may
stands out among unrighteous men.

Youth falls and crumbles fast away;
and all those who admit Love's sway
his tithes must quickly to him pay.
  Listen then!
For quittance none on earth can pray.
All to the end must pay, all men.

"Once Love was just, but he became twisted and flawed in every way. Nowadays he bites you deep. *Listen then!* Or else he licks you with a tongue rougher than tongue of any cat." "Marcabru by Marcabrune was brought forth under such a star that he knows all the ways of life. *Listen then.* He never loved a woman yet, and there's no woman who loved him."

In other poems he describes the world as deranged. Like the winch of a well that rises and falls grinding and whirling, all goes from bad to worse. The world's end is near. Perversity spreads out on a trellis, while Joy grows stunted on a single prop. Perversity is a Tree "wonderfully big with boughs and leaves," which covers with its shadow Spain, Guyenne, Poitou – princes hang from its branches, their throats squeezed by the cord Stinginess. The monster with a thousand aspects is transformed into a mercenary who attacks the castle in which Prowess at bay seeks refuge. "They've taken the armoury. Alone the keep holds out. There Youth and Joy and Prowess are condemned to cruel affliction. . . . She is prisoner, the noble thing, and cannot hope for pause or end unless she turns recluse or nun. And then each man tears her apart, beats her and breaks her teeth. I know no longer any kin of hers, from Portugal to Frisia."

The ethic of Love has become distorted. Now a husband wants to be a gallant and woes his neighbour's wife; the neighbour then pays him off in the same coin. The forsaken women console themselves; betrayed, they take vengeance. It's in vain to shut them up. The culprits are not the women but the barons who have welcomed any innovation; also the Troubadours hiding ugly things under fine shows. "With no more sense than children they prattle to honest folk indeed of great despairs.

11. Eve and the Serpent in the Garden. (*Speculum Humanae Salvationis*, Augsburg, 1470)

In words confused they torture truth and put on the same footing True Love and False Love still." Vile men have gained the confidence of the great. "They govern them in their own way, and the whole house they're starving out." As a result, "the bad grow fat, the good are fed on wind." Today there are "no more rich men whom games and festivals please."

Here we meet the typical complaint of the Troubadour who needed to live on his songs. Marcabru does not shrink from criticising the emperor:

> He's pleased I'm keen to put to flight
> the wicked ones, the recreant knight –
> why does he keep his teeth clencht tight
>   to stop all praises issuing? . . .
> Emperor (help me, God), I cry,
> if your largesse you still deny
> no much-praised pond for fish I'll try,
> I, Marcabru – and that is why
>   I've lost all faith I'll catch a thing.

He sums up the situation in the seven stanzas of *Pus mos coratges*. He sees himself as joyously chosen by Love. Such a man "lives gay, lives wise and courtly too." The rejected one is "committed to total destruction. And he that seeks to blame noble Love becomes so fondly bemused

57

that in delusion he imagines his end is upon him." Such are the false judges, thieves, cheating husbands, perjurers, impostors, flatterers, hired tongues, convent-looters, adulteresses, murderers, traitors, simonists, sorcerers, lechers, usurers, stinking witches, drunkards, cuckolds, false priests and abbots, false recluses of both sexes. Such is the world. Then the poet begs Love for mercy on himself. "Protect me from that torment, so I may not linger there."

> More than the others I here constrain
> myself and probe despite the pain.
> He who accuses, as it's right,
> must view himself in a ruthless light,
> for fear that, tainted deep, he reeks
> with all the evils of which he speaks.
> Only then may he strike again.

He sets out a positive ideal in attacking those who fall away from the true ethic of Courtesy, Courtliness, *Cortezia*. He'll try the courtly manner, he says, "if there's anyone now to listen to it. And since I'm committed to the attempt, I'll do my best to make it fine." *Cortezia* is not to blame for the failures. *Mezura* (Moderation, true Balance) is essentially linked with it. "That love is to be prized which holds itself dear; and if I say anything crude against it, wanting to blame it for some ill, then I agree it's right to make me wait a long time to obtain what it has promised me." He opposes *Amors fina*, *veraia*, to *Amors falsa* or *Amars*. True love is defined by its opposite; it is all that is loyal and steadfast in quest as contrasted with the loose pleasure-seeking world. In one poem he seems to reproach man for not following the animals "the right way," which in turn may be one with living according to Christ's message and example.

In his pastorela, *L'autrier jost'*, he has been taken to affirm the need for feudal degrees of hierarchy, because the shepherdess, accosted by the poet (knight), insists on her lowly birth and observes at the end: "Good sense suffers badly when degrees are not observed by men." But the real point of the poem is that she, the peasant, represents true love and the wooer is false through and through. He tries to convince her that a girl of such charm must have had as father a knight who begot her on some "courtly peasant-girl."

> "Master, my lineage, I avow,
> I trace back only, then as now,
> still to the sickle and the plough,

my lord," replied the peasant-wench.
"And those who rank as knights like you
would better work as our folk do,
six days a week and never blench."

Such a retort can hardly be taken as a defence of hierarchy; rather it implies that the higher orders exist only by exploiting the peasants. This parasitism of theirs is linked with the falsity of the knight in his efforts to seduce the girl. In this way Marcabru's attack on the world for *Amors falsa* becomes an attack on all its falsities, its various pretences and rationalisations that in any way mask inhumanity and oppression. Here then we see what we may call the troubadour ethic breaking through its limitation to matters of love, of the relations of two lovers on their own, and finding a basis on which it applies to the whole of society.

Acquainted with the scholastic tradition, he draws on allegory, symbolism, proverbial wisdom. He seems at times to invent new words or to devise new forms and combinations of old ones. He can be both harsh and graceful in diction or rhythm; at times he twists language in his desire for sonority and rich rhyme-schemes. Certainly his contemporaries seem hardly to have understood him and found him obscure. He clearly found pleasure in vaunting his complexity of aim and method, his finesse with many *colors*. "My private place is hard to trace." He starts off fires but he has to hand the water for quenching them. "Beware my part; for with such art at living and at dying I play." His headlong style can be picturesque as well as powerful, comic as well as savage. As examples of his word-play we may take his terms for the painted and scented parasites grown fat and idle in the castles, the born foes of the bold adventurer (soldier or singer). He calls them cruppers-on-earth, wine-tunners, firebrand-breathers, adze-sharpened beaks, cutting-tongues.

> Who grasps each word of mine is wise,
> I most whole-heartedly declare :
> who sees what each song signifies
> and how the theme's unfolded there.
> I take much trouble and devise
> ways to clear up obscurity.

In the next stanza he speaks of Troubadours with childish minds who torment what Truth has put forth and take much trouble to leave their words entangled, upside-down, *entrebeschatz*. This maltreatment of words he links with False Love, which seeks only bodily pleasure and rejects the complex discipline of True or Courtly Love. *Al departir* shows how his own kind of difficulty arises:

> Now the rough weather's passed away,
> sap rises in each branch to bring
> the broom and heather quickening.
> Frogs in the fishpond sing and play;
> willow and elder budding sway;
> the peachtrees all are blossoming.
> Before the heat dries everything,
> I think I'll make a song today.

In five more stanzas and envoy with identical rhymes he elaborates his idea, "unfolds his theme." The trees are of good stock and make a fine show of leaf and blossom, but the fruit are hollow. At fruiting time, what seem to be apples turn out to be willows and elders. With the head defective, the outer limbs are in a bad way. The good old trees are dead. The surviving ones are all twig and straw, no use for great undertakings, though busy in idle play. They are full of promises, but "in keeping them, mere willows and elders." We then move on to the persons whom the poet censures: the lords Stephen, Constant, and Hugo, who boast a lot by the fire at night, vying with one another, though by day in the elder-shade they do nothing but shout and amuse themselves, "with their bets doubled." Then we return to the tree-symbolism. Only the elders still live; you're lucky to find a laurel or an olive. Even the gardeners go off, putting on fine clothes instead of "simple smock and boots." The *tornada* sums up:

> God keep the brave with merit inbred;
> the wicked great-ones are elder-trees;
> and so the world is weak in the head,
> confused and shattered by disease.

Each sixth line ends with *saucs*, elder-trees, the emblem of weakness and uselessness. "Weak in the head" is perhaps a reference to the papal schism of the 1130s; if so, the poem is early.

A crusading song seems connected with the campaign against the Arabs in Spain, in which the Marquis of Provence and the Knight Templars took part. Here a strange effect is achieved by using a deliberately homely image for something meant to be extremely holy. The baptismal font is called a *lavador*, a washing-place, and seems to refer both to the holy war itself and to the shrine at Santiago, on a pilgrimage to which our Guilhem X (mentioned in the last stanza) had died.

> Pax in Nomine Domini!
> Marcabru made the words and song.
> Hear then my plea.
> The Lord of Heaven of his grace
> has fashioned for us close at hand
> a most remarkable washing-place.
> Not by another such you'd stand
> save in Jehosophat's far land
> and it will comfort your sad case.
>
> Washt, morn and evening, we should be,
> and any other way is wrong.
> Please trust in me.
> Now here's a chance to wash your face
> till hale and whole your life is crowned.
> Go straightway to that washing-place
> where our true source of healing's found.
> We're doomed to lodge on lowly ground
> if through death's door unwasht we pass.
>
> But Meanness yet and Perfidy
> to part Youth from his friend are strong.
> What misery!
> They seek that hole, in scrambling race,
> where hellish profits most abound.
> If we don't reach the washing-place
> ere mouths are closed and eyes are blind,
> for all our pufft-up pride, we'll find
> in death the Enemy face to face. . . .

He ends by calling on Christ to protect Poitou and Niort. In another crusading poem he attacks the rich who don't respond to calls for sacrifice. They prefer to lie on easy couches and think that it's enough to praise the men who do go to fight. "But I tell them that a day will come when from their palaces they'll exit, with head behind and feet in front."

There is a third poem dealing with the crusade led by King Louis VII after Jerusalem fell in 1147; but here love is set against war and against the religion that causes war.

In the orchard where a fountain's seen
and grass on sandy banks is green,
where a tree's shadow slants along,
in pleasant setting of white flowers
and the new season's ancient song,
I found the girl. Alone was she
and did not want my company.

She was the daughter of a castle-lord. Just as he was thinking that the birds and the greenery, "in the sweet new time," must be filling her with joy, and she'd be pleased to hear his little speech, she burst out into her lament. She reproaches Jesus for causing her grief. "All best men of this wide world go off to serve you : that's your pleasure." Her lover has gone too. "Ai, damn then that King Louis, he gave the orders and the sermons." Marcabru remonstrates : "He who makes the woods break into leaf has the power to grant you joy in abundance."

"Lord, I believe it's true," said she,
"that God indeed may pity me
in the next world, in eternity,
with other sinners gone astray.
But here my one true love he has taken.
What matters now? I lie forsaken :
The man I love has gone away."

Marcabru is then the poet who makes the decisive expansion on the bases provided by Guilhem. The new lyric structures sketched out by the latter are stably elaborated; and the theme of courtly love is used to provide an ethic by which the world can be judged. In Guilhem the coarse poems and the poems of love stood in separate compartments, though, especially in his enigma poem, he raised urgently the question of the relation of the lust-daze to the quest of true love. Marcabru merges the popular element and the element of high aspiration, producing a complex body of poetry in which the conflicting elements are unified.

We may note that while he opposes true love to mere lust and promiscuity, there is no suggestion in his work, or in Cercamon's, that the poet does not see true lovers as fully consummating their love. The term Fin'Amors is often translated Pure Love; but the adjective means "fine, quintessential"; "pure" in the sense of admitting no extraneous factors, no imposed morality, no derelictions, not "pure" in the sense of being wholly spiritual, of accepting an imposed morality of restric-

12. Catching birds by clap-net. (Knight iii 197)

tions which forbid consummation. A much more complicated situation in this respect appears with the next poet we consider.[4]

Marcabru ended his poem about *Cortezia* and *Mesura* by saying that he wanted to send it and its melody "to Sir Jaufré Rudel, beyond the sea." It seems then that he knew Rudel or at least felt close to him. Rudel was castellan of Blaye with the title of Prince. He was on good terms with his distant cousin William Taillefer, count of Angoulême. He was in the Holy Land in 1148, and round that time was friendly with the crusaders Hugues VII of Lusignan and Alphonse Jourdain of Toulouse. By 1167 he was dead, as another member of the family held the fief of Blaye. There could hardly be a poet less like Marcabru with his dark angers and his passion for righteousness. Rudel has a limited vocabulary and range, but he uses them with assured charm and succeeds in constructing a warm spontaneous world:

> Enough that round me, I possess
> song's masters and song's mistresses:
> orchards and trees and flowers are here,
> and birds whose plaintive trills come clear . . .
> Shepherds in piping find their ease
> and foolish games will children please:
> as happily do I employ
> the loves that bring me home such joy.

All his six poems are of love. Two seem based in a real situation. He describes the lady as "plump and soft and lovely," with every aspect of her adding to the total charm. "Good and delightful is her love." She seems to live some distance off, and in a spring-setting he tells how he is lost between dream and reality.

This love absorbs me, every bit,
waking and then in dreaming sleep.
I feel such joy, enjoying it,
rejoiced in and rejoicing deep.
No profit from her charms I keep,
for no friend has revealed to me
how pleasure from them I might gain.

So eagerly to her I ride
in haste to bring about our meeting,
still backwards I appear to slide
and she is steadily retreating.
So slow my horse, my heart stops beating.
Unless she halts and waits for me
I'll never reach her, I complain.

Then in the last two stanzas he turns in another direction, saying that
he must go crusading – "follow God to Bethlehem" – and therefore
must restrain his longing, though "his heart still rejoices" in the love
he has known. The account of riding may however be only a symbol
of his divided state of being, in which every attempt to gain the lady
seems to distance him from her. In the second poem he tells how he
was defeated by the lady's guardians. One night, perhaps drawn by a
false message, he was hoping to gain her. At dawn she came, late, and
told him that the enemy have started such a tumult, "we cannot drown
it now and share our pleasures as we would." He was attacked and
jeered at, unable to defend himself. "It would have been better to lie
down clothed than naked under the sheet." The attackers ran off laugh-
ing. "I tremble still and sigh for it." He decides to throw from his
shoulders the "foolish burden," but no matter how deeply he sleeps,
fear wakes him.

And now I see, I know, believe,
that all the torment now I leave
and never back to it I'll go.

"He is mad who is too precipitate." He thanks those whose good advice
he has taken; he has regained the joy of heart that they consider a
source of honour. May they find their reward in his recovery. "Now I
have joy and am rejoiced, now in my worth am I restored, now never
elsewhere shall I go and others seek to overcome." After falling
through the enemies of true love, he has been able to save himself
because true love never deceives or fails those who seek it. True love

(*fraire*, brother) forbids what false love (*seror*, sister) permits and authorises. No man is so wise that he cannot err. He offers this lesson in particular to the Troubadours so that they may spread it abroad. "My song then to be heard I wish. Learn it, you troubadours, I ask."[5]

It is hard to distinguish fancy from fact in these poems. The terms have been understood literally. Thus the sister was ready to be taken, but her brother sent his henchmen to beat Rudel up. Such interpretations seem forced; but we may perhaps surmise that some mishap or shock did deter Rudel from seeking to possess his lady and drove him towards an idealisation of the situation. Certainly separation and the dreams that it stirs are central in his poetic themes. He wants to catch the lady "in suitable places," since "no sigh or tear can avail as much as a single solitary kiss to keep my heart secure and whole." "I've never had joy of her, I know; she never has had joy of me. She won't look on me as her lover or make a treaty about herself." And so, "since daily I've no chance to see her, I'm not surprised I thirst for her."

Two poems deal with a love in a distant land, and another seems to celebrate a woman as shadowy as a phantom. These were the poems that made Rudel famous. In the phantom-poem he writes:

> No wonder if my love should be
> for one who has never seen my face.
> My joy depends upon her grace,
> though I've not seen her. Joy for me
> lies all in her, yet I can't say
> what good in it I'll ever trace.

He develops to their extreme the paradoxes of loss–possession. He is smitten and dies of joy; the sting of love makes him burn; his whole body perishes; never has he felt such a blow followed with such languor. His dreams are grievous. "But when at morning I awake, then all my lovely torment's gone." He'll never be her friend, and she has told him "neither truth nor lie." He ends: "My art is sure, my song is done; everything's in its proper place." It will be sung at the courts of Cahors and Toulouse. Whoever is to learn it from him must make sure not to spoil it.

The legend of Rudel as told in the *vidas* or biographies did much to strengthen the effect of the poems.

Jaufré Rudel of Blaye was a very noble man, the Prince of Blaye. And he fell in love with the Countess of Tripoli, whom he had never seen, through the praise that he heard of her from the pilgrims who came from Antioch.

And he made many songs about her, with good melodies and simple words. And through the desire to see her he took the Cross and set out to sea. And on the voyage a grievous illness fell upon him and those in the ship thought him dead, and he was carried as a dead man to an inn in Tripoli. And the news was told to the Countess, and she came to him by his bed and took him in her arms. And he knew that she was the Countess and he recovered his hearing and his sense of smell, and he praised God and thanked him for having let him live to see her. And so he died in her arms. And she had him buried with much honour in the House of the Templars. And then, on the same day, she became a nun because of the grief that she had from his death.

Such a legend fitted in well with the songs of the Distant Lady:

> When clearer every sparkling day
> appear the waters of the spring,
> and we behold the eglantine
> and nightingales upon the bough
> with ceaseless subtlety essay
> to make their songs more sweetly fine,
> shall I not also sing my song?
>
> Love of a country far away
> has filled my flesh with suffering.
> Nothing can save me but a sign
> from her : to say that she'll allow
> embraces warm in alcove-play
> or under the cool orchard-line,
> since for her company I long.
>
> As never luck of love is mine,
> I burn, and none need ask me how.
> God made all other women clay,
> Christian or Jewess withering,
> or Moor. My girl is beauty's shrine.
> For manna he won't need to pray,
> the man to whom her smiles belong.
>
> Still restless for her love I pine,
> for I am wholly hers; and now
> desire has left me to dismay
> if she's a mercenary thing.
> Though grief is sharper than a spine,
> love has a trick to make me gay,
> and therefore pity does me wrong.

To please Sir Hugo I design
without an inch of parchment now
this simple and vernacular lay.
Filhol is taught what he's to sing.
Poitou and Berri both combine;
from Guyenne town to Breton bay
the praises of my lady throng.[6]

The Distant Lady has been taken as the Countess of Tripoli, Jerusalem, and the Virgin Mary, not to mention Helen of Troy and Eleanor of Aquitaine. Tripoli was on the Syrian coast and its countess was Odierna, wife of Count Raimon I. The story ran that Rudel did not go with the French king to Palestine but went by sea with the count of Toulouse to Tripoli. On landing, he looked at Odierna and at once died. However, as we saw, Marcabru thought he was with the French host. Also, tradition made his beloved Odierna's daughter Melisendis. If that were correct, Rudel must have gone on a second voyage eastward, in 1162. Tripoli had been taken by the crusaders in 1109; a county was formed under its name and given to Bertran of Toulouse, whose descendants held it till 1200, when it became part of the principality of Antioch. Melisendis, born about 1142, was betrothed in 1160 to the emperor Manuel I of Byzantium, but he failed to carry out the engagement. The rejection however increased her fame, and she was reported to be very beautiful and good. But we need not look for any actual woman as the Distant Lady.

When now the days are long in May,
I love to hear the birds far distant,
and when the song has died away,
I dream about a love as distant.
Deep in my longing am I drowned.
The songs, the hawthorn-bloom around,
warm me no more than winter-snow.

But I believe the Lord one day
will let me see this love that's distant.
Ah, for one good, my lot, I pay
with double ills, since it's so distant.
Would as a pilgrim I were gowned,
with cloak and staff to tap the ground,
I'd draw her eyes to note my woe.

What pleasure it would be to pray,
God's love! to own that lair so distant;
for if he pleased, I'd always stay
beside her, I who wander distant.
What sweet discourses will abound
when near the distant love is found;
what charming words we'll whisper low.

And I'll return both sad and gay
if I behold that love so distant.
When will it come? Ah, who can say,
since our two countries are so distant?
What endless ways between each land:
I'm sure of nothing that I planned.
At God's will let the winds all blow.

Love has no joy that won't betray
except this love that lies so distant.
Such charms no woman can display
in any land that's near or distant.
So lovely, gentle, pure, she's crowned:
to see her close, a captive bound
by Saracens, I'd gladly go.

God makes all things in their array.
He's fashioned too this love that's distant.
God, hear my cry and don't delay
but give me yet this love that's distant.
In that sweet lair if I should stand,
garden and room would warmly expand
till like a palace grand they'd glow.

My accuser cries, as well he may,
I'm broken by a love far distant.
With one desire on earth I stray:
it's to enjoy that love so distant.
But my desire's denied and banned;
loving, unloved, I bear the brand –
to my godfather this lot I owe.

With my desire denied and banned,
loving, unloved, I curse the brand
and him to whom this lot I owe.

13. Reaping and Gleaning. (Knight iii 200)

Rudel's poems thus show an extreme cleavage. In the account of his mishaps as he lay naked in bed awaiting his lady he comes close to what seems an actual affair; in the songs on the Distant Lady the woman seems to dissolve into a strange and remote symbol. Yet both the realism and the dream are vital parts of the Troubadour system. The dream-aspect puts all emphasis on the idea of Quest, of an ultimate fulfilment at the end of a devoted pilgrimage, which suggests something like the legend of the Graal, but which at the same time is to be understood in terms of the system of Courtly Love. The separation-theme, with its sense of a tremendous magnetic pull towards the body and soul of the beloved, is not meant to make her unreal or unattainable. From one angle the Distant Lady is every women truly loved and loving, and the symbol of distance refers to the element of the unknowable in her – in every person including the poet-lover himself. The movement of love is towards knowledge of the other and of oneself. But with each deepening of consciousness there is a simultaneous opposition and union; new dimensions of closeness and distance open up.

It is true enough then to see in the Troubadour positions: "Love that does not want to possess but to play with this state of non-possession, *Minne*-love containing also the sensual desire to 'touch' the woman truly 'woman' as well as the chaste distancing, Christian love transposed on the secular plane, which wants to 'have *and* not have'" (Spitzer). But it is not enough to note that this paradoxical game is played; we have to understand why it attracts the singer and what it means in terms of poetic and human realisation. From one aspect the conflict and union of opposites appears at every nodal point of development; for our purposes the question is why the issue is presented to the Troubadours in the terms we have discussed. The poets are seeking to define love as the ultimate good or aim in life and to discover how the human being orientates himself towards it, then goes through various stages in which he more fully grasps this good and achieves the true end of man. The dominant philosophic ideas and idioms of the period are inevitably drawn in, being profoundly changed in the process. Thus, it may be argued that the love of the distant land, the distant lady, is not a reflection of objective reality but is a concrete expression of *naturalis dilectio* in Augustine's sense. It is a universal principle or innate inclination of nature in the search for a happy life; a metaphysical concept of love as an immanent and vital activity deriving from the intuition of one's *esse* (being) as good and pure, and striving towards the absolute truth and goodness to which one feels somehow to be indissolubly bound. In this interpretation the lady is nothing but a form of one's own *esse*. In a broader way the lady could be said to represent the soul which, in Neoplatonic mysticism (inherited by both Christians and Arabs), was considered to be divine with an innate desire to rise to perfection though its union with a material body prevented the beatitude of reabsorption into the first principle.

Such reductions are far too narrow and one-sided to explain the Troubadour position, but they are useful in pointing to aspects of contemporary philosophy and theology which contributed to that position. If we look at the system of mystical experience set out by St Bernard we come much closer to the Troubadours, for he is trying to use the psychology of love to clarify what he considers the ascent to God. Here God, so to speak, becomes simultaneously a symbol of the self in its fulfilment and a symbol of the beloved, insofar as each penetration into her being brings about a sense of new unknown regions to be explored.

The opulence of the psychological vocabulary used in this analysis is the exact verbal reflection of the opulence of love, in its intuitive certainties. They all emanate from the communion with the loved one, in the nuptials of which the drunkenness brings about a total *fiducia* (impossible to translate this word of Bernard's language). All fear is banished, and this spontaneity, gained in the gift of oneself, is simultaneously the fine fruit and the reason of freedom. "Love requires no other cause and no other fruit than itself. I love because I live, I live in order to love. What a great thing is love, provided that it returns to its principle, returns to its origin, and flowing back towards its course, borrows from it what enables it to flow without arrest" (Chenu).[7]

Thus in mystical ecstasy the *excessus mentis*, the going-forth of the mind, is seen as a loss of oneself, of one's *proprium*, as almost an annihilation, but it is in fact felt, by a conformity of the Other, to express the plenitude of being. (Bernard's *fiducia* or total trust is analogous to the total submission of the Troubadour to his lady.) We may then claim that such mystical psychology as that of St Bernard subtly dissects and unravels the structure of human self-knowledge and then applies the pattern abstractly to what is considered a relationship with deity (pure otherness). The Troubadours set about taking the pattern back to the directly human level. Thus they make men and women more aware of the dialectical movements of their being in the deep knowledge of self and of otherness, which reaches its height in love.

One is not claiming that they do so consciously. Rudel would have repudiated any idea that he was attempting to translate St Bernard's interpretations of the *Song of Songs* into secular verse and to give his love-emotions a new dimension in their light. But the relation is there, deep inside the totality of the spiritual and cultural movements of the age. We may go on to claim that the mystical or theological system represents an alienation of human emotion by cutting its earthly roots and transferring the experience-pattern to deity or abstract being. In the process, however, because of the pressure of abstraction, a sharper awareness of the pattern as a thing-in-itself is generated. The poet brings the clarified pattern back into life with all its complexities. In so far as the return-movement is not fully carried out and realised, a metaphysical element remains, an hypostasised structure not fully integrated in the new consciousness of the nature of experience and of human relationships. With Rudel this partially-undigested element shows itself in the extent to which the lady is indeed inaccessible and considered as an abstract principle of beauty, love, an abstract goal of aspiration. But this abstract or metaphysical element is being steadily subdued and used to illuminate the real forms and forces operating in the human quest for fullness of love, for entry into otherness without loss of self. The concrete movement consists of a ceaseless give-and-take between the self and other people (with the whole life of society and nature ultimately involved.) Thus the self is implicated in ever wider ranges of action and understanding. In the dialectical moment the self is at times dominated by otherness, then is enhanced, enriched, dominating otherness in turn. What St Bernard saw as an onanistic relation between the self and God becomes a sensuous and emotional relation of one lover to the other.

As an amusing example of the way in which theological and sexual imagery could be entangled at this period we may take Juda Levi (born 1070–5), a Jewish–Mozarabic poet, whom Heine in one of his poems singled out for refusing to worship the "false god of love" and to praise a castle-lady or a Laura, but instead adored all his life the lowly figure of Jerusalem in her ruins. Juda Levi was in fact one of the first neo-Hebrew poets who sang of earthly love in the sacred language, and he has recently been revealed as a transmitter of popular sensuous poetry in ways that helped to build the Troubadour system.[8]

IV

The South: Languedoc

NOW let us look at the area where the Troubadours originated and developed. What special characteristics did it have that favoured the rise of the new poetry? Since it never existed as a political entity, as did the French North with its kings, there is no name for it. Perhaps the most convenient term is Languedoc. (The folk spoke the *langue d'Oc* – from *hoc*, being the form there taken by the affirmative, while in the north we meet *oïl, oui*.) Languedoc then was the area over which our romance-tongue was spoken with dialectal variations: most of the regions between the Rhône valley to somewhere west of the Garonne and south of the mountains of central France. The language was much closer to Catalan than to northern French. The term Languedoc came into use only at the end of the thirteenth century when officials of the French king needed to define the area they administered, in fact an area smaller than that covered by the speech. Soon afterwards Dante used it. The name Provence came from the Roman Provincia Narbonnensis, but the region thus called was only one part of Languedoc; and the use of the term Provençal in a wide general way dates from the late sixteenth century. The area ruled by the counts of Toulouse was much more important culturally and politically than Provence; the counts claimed jurisdiction over an area as big as that ruled by their nominal sovereigns the kings of France. The Toulousain area by the late twelfth century represented what could have been the basis for unifying the South. Another term for the Midi is Occitania (from Aquitaine). The southerners considered that they spoke *roman*, the term for the vernacular as opposed to Latin.[1]

The Visigoths who had been the main Germanic groups settling in the area, which they held till the eighth century, were the least barbarian of the invaders. Languedoc showed no trace of the Carolingian revival of letters, and monasteries were few and ineffective, with poor chronicles, though some rich houses emerged by the twelfth century: St Sernin, Lézat, St Gilles, La Grasse, Fontfroide. There were no strong political links with the Capetian kings of France since the mid-tenth century. But the area had developed in its own way, so that by the eleventh century it had a strong character all its own. Generally the system was far less feudal than in the north; the ties of homage and the military obligations entailed on land were far less stringent. Manorial institutions were rare; and there was considerable urban growth in the twelfth century, helped by the nearness of the Mediterranean and its trade. The growth indeed went on at a faster rate than in the north; and the towns with their strong positions were able to gain much independence and spread their influence and control over the surrounding countryside. The economic expansion was much stimulated by the crusades, with merchants following behind the armies. The to-and-fro of trade with the East and with Spain brought about an increased flow of ideas. There was far more tolerance than was usual north of the Alps.

Languedoc was thus surrounded by powers militarily superior, who coveted it but were not in a position to attempt to subdue it. Louis VII did try to seize Toulouse in 1114 in the name of his wife Eleanor of Aquitaine; and in 1159 he stepped in to prevent the intrusion of the English. Pressure from the English indeed went on till Raimon VI of Toulouse (1194–1222) married Joan, sister of Richard I, in 1196, when Richard asked only homage for the Agenais. Yet more powerful pressures came from Catalonia through the twelfth century. The Catalans fought Raimon V over Provence and made more attacks after 1181. When Pedro II (1196–1213) gained the crown of Aragon, the pressures slackened, but the Catalans had by no means dropped their aims of dominating or taking over what is now south France. Pedro II held important lands there; and but for the Albigensian crusade there might well have emerged a state of Aragon stretching from the Ebro to the Alps: an event that would have been more satisfactory from the cultural viewpoint than what did happen – the extension of kingly rule from the north.[2]

There was thus a complicated and at times uneasy situation, with the great lords manoeuvring to avoid domination by France, England, Spain, and yet failing to exercise much control of their own areas. There was no interlocked feudal hierarchy. Under the great houses of the counts and viscounts there was a medley of small nobles or knights with slight resources. And such power as the great houses held was often weakened and shared by bishops, abbots, and town-governments all seeking to extend their controls.

The oath of fidelity found in the south used forms from the Caroling-

14. Corn emptied from sacks into store. (Knight iii 200)

ian oath but seems essentially more linked with the contract of *convenentia*; its roots go back into the Visigothic or Frankish past, and it was closer to the court of justice than to the seigneurial castle. The fief here was not connected with the oath and lacked the stricter formalism of developed feudal systems in the north. It gathered something of the atmosphere of Fidelity, but without any binding oath – just as we find the oath used without clear feudal meaning. Hence the lack of inner force in southern feudalism: "a Fidelity without basis in land-tenures, a feudalism without the support of the oath, an aristocracy without vassals" (Magnou-Mortier). The term *onor*, honour, so characteristic of feudality, could designate a fief or a quit-rent; at the end of the eleventh century we find a vineyard given as a fief with an annual rent of 3 deniers.

In Poitou, at the extreme north-west extension of our area, where Guilhem IX had ruled, things were indeed different. From the tenth century there had been a proliferation of castle-building; but on the whole the comital house kept control of the situation. Things took a more normal feudal course. The old free allodial land-owners hardly asserted themselves; the rural exploiters or lords of villages entered into the vassalage of the main castellans. But by the time of Guilhem VIII, the count held firmly in his hands the Poitevin aristocracy. By the end of the eleventh century a dubbed man was held as a noble and there grew up the essential traits of a caste of birth, military in profession. In the Bordelais feudalisation was held back by the existence of an old landed aristocracy of large and small freeholders; the fusion with the world of castellans and the formation of a military nobility had not truly appeared before the end of the eleventh or the start of the twelfth century. In Comminges, a march between Aquitaine, Toulousain, and Aragon "the larger part of the aristocracy was strongly allodial and seems to have ignored till the twelfth century the vassalic structures" (Higounet).

The contradictions inside these areas were yet more strongly at work in Toulousain and Provence. Much of the arable land, perhaps a half, was held in independent allodial tenures with no feudal relations. It was on the resources of his allodial lands, rather than on feudal services, that Raimon VI of Toulouse depended. Yet he, like the Trencavels (viscounts of Albi, Béziers, Carcassone, Razès), had built up a fairly efficient system in his own courts. Another important custom impeding feudalism was that of free bequest. An estate did not descend to the eldest son, but might be cut up among several heirs, some of them even women. Thus members of a family often shared a lordship consisting of a castle or two and a few villages. At one time there were fifty lords of Lombers, thirty-six of Montréal, thirty-five of Mirepoix. The Monk of Montaudon sang: "I hate too many brothers on a small bit of land, too many heirs for a single castle." Such a group might exercise control through a common court, sharing out the revenues which often were only partly in money. To raise dowries for daughters was often difficult.

The situation was further complicated by marriages. A woman might bring in some small fiefs or bits of fiefs, and inevitably there were many disputes, even if some individual was recognised as the family-head and despite the many rules aimed at protecting one co-seigneur against another. Small lords, not directly exploiting their lands, and living on rents and seigneurial rights, were often poorer than their peasants. By the thirteenth century it was not unusual to see a rustic acquire the rents from lands of neighbours, buy land from nobles, and go over to "idleness." Many of these newly-rich married daughters of squires and were accepted as gentlefolk. In general there was a lessening of the distance between knight and rich peasant, between rural and urban bourgeois. Money was a substitute for noble birth and broke up any tendencies towards an aristocractic cohesion on warrior lines; the smaller nobility often wrecked themselves through small expeditions for which they paid by putting their castles in pawn. In any event not many rural nobles got in much income from tenancies and courts of justice, while the obligation of military service was hedged round with so many reservations that it was of little importance. Knights tended to serve simply for pay; and the fragmentation of holdings meant that liege homage was almost impossible. Men changed from lord to lord almost at will. Charges to which commoners alone were in principle submitted were often put on nobles, and bourgeois and peasant were submitted to military obligations reserved for knights. The result was to "dishonour honour." There was thus little difference in dress. Rich peasants and townsfolk were not yet bold enough to woo ladies, but already like nobles, they bore baldricks. These changes came to a head in the thirteenth century, but the conditions making them possible had been growing through the twelfth. The rich townsfolk when not able to buy a piece of land, bought up the *beneficium* and inserted themselves between tenant and lord. They thus became *domini*, assured of small but sure revenues. By the thirteenth century they thus used wealth gained by traffic to live the same sort of life as the small lords, who, not directly exploiting the land, had for revenue only quit-rent or seigneurial rights. The money-rule showed up in the way that "feudal benefices" began to be negotiable and to circulate like transferable securities. We see that throughout the twelfth century the weakness of feudal relations in the Midi was leading in this direction. There was little trace of the antagonism between lesser nobles and townsfolk that we find in the north. Nobles had seats in the consular college at Toulouse, Castelsarrasin, Moissac, Nîmes, Montauban. Such men had nothing of the military might that enabled counts and viscounts to maintain a feudal apparatus. In the towns nobles often lived in houses with watchtowers; at times a street was reserved for them. They made up a sort of urban chivalry, which the richer townsfolk could aspire to enter. In the late twelfth century the shift from ecclesiastical to lay lordships over villages tended to reduce the independence of the village-folk; yet even so the peasants could bargain over rights with their lords.[3]

As for the church, many bishops and abbots held seigneurial powers and were concerned only for their own interests; they were often embroiled with lay lords in property-disputes. There was nothing like the links of church and state that we find in France; the county of Toulouse made little use of ecclesiastical councillors. The bishop of Narbonne, ruling part of the town, had the viscount as his nominal vassal for the rest; the bishop of Agde held the title of viscount; the bishop of Mende, under a grant from the French king, exercised all the royal rights in his diocese, the bishops of Albi and Béziers were lords of part of the

15. Threshing. (Knight iii 200)

town or the whole of it; at St Gilles the abbot governed the town. Such a situation stimulated anticlericalism and led to events like the conspiracy of the townsfolk of Carcassone in 1304 to offer the viscountcy to the Infanta of Majorca, in the hopes that he would grant what they could not get from the king of France: the suppression of the Dominican Inquisition.

Feudal assembles for a whole county were unknown. The count merely called together the local nobles wherever he happened to be. The nobles felt no common bond, and there was much squabbling and petty fighting. There was no accord of church and state, church and nobility; and this situation worsened, if anything, throughout the twelfth century, till it led to the final clash that brought about the papal crusade against the heretics of Languedoc. Raimon V of Toulouse in his free-thinking jests showed the influence of heretical thought. When some lords had forgotten the time for meeting him, he commented: "We see indeed that it's the Devil who has made this world; nothing happens as it should." Playing chess with his chaplain, he said: "The God of Moses, in whom you believe, will not make you win. As for me, I prefer that he does no favouring." The secularising trends made the lords especially keen on display, on expense for its own sake. Raimon V at Beaucaire in 1174 gave 100,000 sous to be distributed among 10,000 knights. We hear of a rich lord having 120 horses burned before his guests; and, as wax was costly, meat was cooked by candles. The Troubadours and jongleurs profited from the readiness to make rich gifts. Raimon VI gave Raimon de Miraval horses, clothes, anything he needed; the pair called one another by the female name of Audiart. Other Troubadours were treated as generously, and barons in general gave gifts according to their means. It showed bad taste to offer a Troubadour a poor horse or a worn cloak. Ladies too were given many gifts.

In the twelfth century the economy was prospering. Agriculture was doing well, with cereal crops, hemp, vineyards, orchards; in the eastern region oil was pressed from the olive. The river-valleys were rich, though there were uplands where life was hard. The population was increasing. By about 1250 Toulouse had some 20,000 inhabitants; Montpellier, 15,000; Carcassone, 6,000. Apart from Flanders, the Midi had a larger population than any other region in what we may call the French area. Abbots and laymen took advantage of the situation by planning and planting villages, *salvetats*, to which they drew settlers by offering special privileges. We hear of peasants emigrating to Spain or to towns where they occupied the bourgs. In the *salvetats* they could enjoy some judiciary franchises, free from market tolls or *leudes*, and could trade without preliminary authorisation. An urban atmosphere was quickly created and many peasants became artisans. The dangers of wandering mercenaries or bandits, and of war in general, helped to make the settlements attractive. Isolated monasteries or merchant caravans were liable to attack. The growth in markets helped the drift to the towns. Townsfolk cultivated allodial plots inside or outside the walls; burghers invested in land; and there was some growth in villages of industrial production (in leather and textiles).

Towns along the coast or near it had been doing well for some time out of pilgrims and the traffic caused by the crusades. Several towns in Languedoc as well as in Catalonia and north Italy became metropolitan in this situation, active in long-distance as well as in local trade, and drawing in foodstuffs from a wide area. We have the records of three ventures made by two partners of Genoa (one investing, one travelling) between autumn 1156 and August 1158; it seems that two of the journeys were to Provence or Catalonia. Wares came in from Flanders, Italy, the Levant, with most of the sea-borne traffic carried on by Italian shippers. Languedoc's strength lay in its balance of agriculture and trade, with a large amount of regionalism in production and distribution. St Gilles was a thriving market-town with a September fair for traders coming from afar; its merchants had privileges in Tyre and Acre; it had commercial treaties with Genoa and Pisa.

16. Fishing with seine-net. (Knight iii 197)

Montpellier dyed textiles brought in from the north for re-export. In the west of the county of Toulouse regional trade was concentrated, with leather, furs, cloth sold in the fairs of Champagne. Wine was carried down the Garonne to England, though Aquitaine and Bordeaux controlled the outlets to the western seas. Goods were taken across country by mule-trains or by barges. Brokerage-fees at Narbonne in the thirteenth century mention two dozen kinds of textiles, eight kinds of leather, fur, dyes, thread, saddlery, iron and steel products, silver, oil, wine, grain, livestock, armour, ploughshares, hoes, wooden spoons, bottles, slaves.[4]

Toulouse was the outstanding example of the growing town. In the later twelfth century the immigrant peasants provided labour for construction and industries, among the earliest of which was milling, using the waterpower of the Garonne. The first trade-fraternities negotiating with the count for privileges and protections were the butchers and the tanners. Documents show also boatmen, bakers, building workers, artisans and craftsmen making leather wares, metal, cloth. A list of gilds in the late thirteenth century mentions cutlers, makers of kegs, dice, bridles, rope, tiles, candles, pastry, and dealers in lumber, oil, wax, secondhand clothes. Men with money speculated in grain, mills, land, or lent money. The town government found no trouble in raising funds to buy freedoms from the count or to finance military campaigns against neighbouring nobles for the purpose of winning exemption from tolls.

Languedoc treated Jews with far more tolerance than any other area in Europe. While the first crusade stirred much violence against Jews in the north, it had no such effects in the south. Jews not only owned property and did business under the protection of the count of Toulouse, they even worked in his administration. The counts thus defied the church, which forbade lords to take Jews into their service and above all to put them into positions conferring authority over Christians. In 1203 the viscount of Carcassone had the Jew Simon as his bailiff; and Jews held similar posts at Toulouse as well as in Catalonia and Aragon. Money dealings were often largely in their hands since, except at Narbonne, such matters were forbidden to Christians. At Toulouse they had a hospice used as school and synagogue. There was no ghetto; Jews lived scattered in various quarters. In their communities, especially at Narbonne, we find them developing the mystical lines of thought that produced the *Kabbala* as well as showing tendencies to asceticism which had affinities with the ideas and practices of the Cathars; there may well have been exchanges between the two groups. The Catholic crusade of the thirteenth century took on an antisemitic tinge, treating Cathars, Lombards and Jews with the same cruel intolerance, and later the Catholic White Confraternity persecuted Jews, pillaged and destroyed their houses, on the pretext of suppressing usury.

The period 1125–60 saw the main struggle of the towns to gain from the lords various privileges, liberties, customs, and to set up their own system of government under Consuls. Such a government was achieved at Béziers in 1131, at Toulouse 1144–73. Moissac asserted its independence already in 1130. At times there were small revolts, but mostly the gains were made peacefully. The bourgeois oligarchies who took over levied their own taxes, controlled a militia, and in ports like Narbonne signed commercial treaties with the great ports of the Mediterranean. At times inland towns like Toulouse used force to enter villages and castles around, so as to suppress heavy tolls, *leudes*, dues that were harming their trade. Indeed the towns could act as anarchically as did the lords, but they did so with much wider interests in view.

If we look at Toulouse, we see the count in 1100 in complete charge, taxing at will and dispensing justice, demanding services and issuing licences to traders and craftsmen while other lords in the countryside around had the rights of tolls on the river and the roads. The townsfolk found it insufferable that seigneurial officials might hold up their packs as they were being carried round and even open up the same packs three times in the same town to demand *leudes*. First a group of townsmen bought freedom from certain dues. The citizens built up municipal courts and took part in the defence of the town. In 1152 a Common Council of the City and the Bourg (the northern and southern halves) set out legislation limiting the count's rights. Steadily they wore down his prerogatives, using negotiation, purchase, and force. The decade after 1180 saw the townsmen gaining control over all their essential affairs. The consuls, defending the bourgeois against general arbitrary acts, guaranteed to all citizens some important rights in personal security. They encouraged the creation of leagues, *amistansas*, where the aims went beyond purely commercial matters and sought to bring about general justice in social relations. In the thirteenth century at Narbonne such a league was formed, with the members promising to aid one another and swearing to defend the rights of town and bourg "in such a way that justice will be done to each man, as much to the poor as to the rich." Narbonne was the first port to proclaim the principle of the protection of shipwrecked persons. At Toulouse already the citizens could be called on for service in the militia or convened to ratify the list of consuls. With the thirteenth century conflicts broke out inside the citizen ranks, with the rise of a popular party. The power of the old oligarchs rested on land-rents and speculations in real estate; the new men included merchants, money-changers, even some tradesmen. Under their rule the rural lords around had to abolish or cut tolls. Soon however the popular party had to share power with the old oligarchy, or to alternate in running things. Further discords came up with the bishop pressing the issues of heresy and usury. During the siege of 1217–18 all citizens united against Simon de Montfort as the ruthless exponent of the papacy and of the feudal reaction. But this part of our story will come up later.[5]

We may note however that the relative peace of the second half of the twelfth century had helped the increase of wealth, especially under the counts Raimon V (1148–84) and Raimon VI (1194–1222). As a result a large number of Troubadours and jongleurs were attracted to the court. In Toulouse the poor, ill, and aged were looked after as well as in any medieval town. At least eleven hospitals and half a dozen leper-houses lay within the walls and in the suburbs by 1200; they were often maintained by individuals who turned their homes into shelters or who left bequests.

We see then that Languedoc was marked in western Europe of its time by a relative lack of feudal divisions and controls, an intermingling of classes, a tolerant tone both in the castles and the towns. The intellectual resurgence of the twelfth century did not have a strong effect here in a scholastic way, though a medical school grew up at Montpellier, with Spanish influences, and there was also a school that began studying Roman law. Late romanesque architecture flowered magnificently in the area, but there was not the same response to Gothic as in the north because of the comparative weakness of the church.

Here then were conditions likely to foster a tradition of secular poetry linked with the gay life of the courts, a poetry embodying the independent spirit of the age, which in this area took the form of a steady movement away from the church's teachings. The same tolerant and free-thinking attitudes begot the Troubadours and allowed the heretical Cathars to carry on unhindered, though songs and heresies were not directly connected. A simple medieval explanation of the complex situation was given by the chronicler Philippe Mousket when he wrote that Charlemagne, dividing the land among his followers, gave Provence to the singers and musicians; hence the love of song among Provençals and their supremacy in poetry and music.[6]

We saw that Guilhem IX and Marcabru each in his own way protested at the harsh treatment often used on women. The lords indeed had little concern for marriage as a lasting relationship; they got rid of a wife when it suited them and could behave callously to women. Knights too were ready to repudiate wives if the whim took them. Raimon de Miraval got rid of his wife Gaudairenca, who wrote "dances," on the pretext that "one poet in the house was enough." She then called on her lover Guillaume Brémon and Raimon handed her over. Brémon then "took her for his wife." The pair may have been married by a Cathar minister after merely signifying their mutual consent.

After the crusades began in 1198 and many lords or knights had seen Syria, buildings grew more ambitious and villas with palisades failed to satisfy a lord with resources. Still, the castles of the twelfth century were relatively small, cramped, and badly lit. The lady lay with her husband in one of the upper halls of the keep. Close by or in the same room, separated by simple hangings, her damsels slept in twos or threes in a single bed. There was little or no privacy, especially in winter when the keep with its one staircase was chilly and draughty, with men coming and going all day along the narrow passageway and everything lying open. When the lord was away hunting or fighting, or travelling on an expedition, his lady was kept secure only by the constant presence of the women about her. She was perhaps the one beautiful and well-dressed women amid so many warriors, who watched and desired her, and who joked about her among themselves. Bernart de Ventadour, like many other Troubadours, shows how strongly aware were the men in the castle of her physical being.

17. Lovers in a walled garden with Devil overhead. (*Der Seelentrost*, Augsburg, 1478)

Throughout my life I'll never quit
while still good health and strength I find.
After the soul has gone from it,
the flesh long flutters in the wind.
Although she's slow and leisurely,
for that she'll get no blame from me,
if now she makes amends for all.

Belovèd, good, desirable,
body fine-modelled, smooth and slender,
God with his own hands fashioned well
that flesh so fresh, fair-skinned, and tender.
You always I've desired alone,
no joy from others have I known,
upon no other love I call . . .

Lady, who make me happily sing,
strike through my mouth now at my heart
with a warm kiss, a pure true thing,
to draw me from my sorrowing
and lift me up to joy, apart . . .

Yes, to the loveliest one I'd go,
see her fresh skin, her marvellous eyes,
and kiss her mouth in all directions,
so that a month the marks would show.
I'd find her where alone she lies,
sleeping or feigning sleep, I'd steal
a secret kiss – not worthy I
to ask for it. Lady, I sigh.
Little we get from love. I feel,
in God's own name, how time slips by:
the best of it, we lose, and why? . . .

What use on earth is it to me
to live if I may never see
my true love bedded pure below
the casement window, in the glow
her body white as Christmas-snow,
and side by side embraced we grow
united in our equal love . . .

Would that it were the right season
for my reward of secret kisses,
if for it all there's but one reason:
my deep desire, and that alone . . .

O love, what shall I do?
Will I grow well through you?
I fear that death is near.
With longing I feel weak

> unless she takes me in at last
> there where she's lying white and clear
> and I may clasp the thing I seek,
> kiss, fondle, and hold fast
> her body plump and sleek.

At any moment she might fall to a bold steward, a crafty chaplain, an astute Troubadour. All around were beds to fall into. One noblewoman told the Inquisitors how she was ravished by a guest while her husband had gone to look at the stables; she said nothing about it afterwards as she knew her husband considered that wives liked to be raped, and she would have been blamed. Another time a knight crept to the lady's bedroom from his own storey, found the door open, and lay under the bed. When the candle was put out, he climbed abed. "Who is it?" "Be quiet, by God, I adore you!" "How, you boor, can I be quiet?" And she called: "There's a man in my bed." The poet Peire Vidal finds his lady asleep one morning and steals a kiss; she doesn't even wake up, thinking that he is her husband. Raimbaut de Vaqueiras, a *razo* tells us, "was able to see lady Béatrice [de Montferrat] when he wished, without anyone knowing it, as long as she was in her chamber . . . And one day the marquis came back from hunting, put his sword by the bed and went off. And the lady Béatrice stayed in the chamber and undressed." She took up the sword, "girt it on as knights do, then drew it from its sheath and brandished it . . . And Raimbaut saw it all through a vent-hole. That's why he thenceforth called her Beau-Chevalier in his songs."[7]

A kind lady could easily give the Troubadour glimpses of her body. She would invite him to assist at her bedding, where he would help her to undress, perhaps take off her shoes. And there was always a chance that she would go further while her girls listened behind the curtain. A woman did not lose her honour if she gave in to a man of higher status than her husband. The Monk of Montaudon tells us that at the time "when lived the count of Toulouse, one of his knights, Sire Ugonet, was caught with another man's wife at Montpellier. The townsfolk led him before the count. Questioned, he confessed everything. The count then asked, 'How have you dared thus to compromise both my honour and your own?' The knight replied, 'Lord, what I've done, all your knights, all your squires, do.' "

In one song three Troubadours exchange opinions as to whether a lady expresses more favour when she looks lovingly at a suitor, squeezes his hand, or presses his foot. Savaric de Mauléon, a great lord

18. Sword Dance. (Royal MS 14E iii)

of Saintonge and Poitou to whom King John gave lands in England, making him viscount of Southampton, declares the glance to be the best proof of love, Gaucelm Faidit, son of a townsman of Uzerche (Corrèze), who became a jongleur after losing all his fortune and who lamented the death of Richard in 1199, champions the hand-squeeze. Uc de la Bachélerie (near Corrèze) speaks on behalf of the foot-pressure. (Biographers say that the discussed event occurred at a meeting of three suitors, Savaric, Jaufré and Elias Rudel, with Guillelma de Benauges. She looked at Jaufré, touched the hand of Elias, and pressed the foot of Savaric.) Gaucelm says of the love-glance: "This sweetness arises from the heart: an honour greater a hundredfold than the other two acts of kindness. The hand-squeeze shows neither disgrace nor favour, I insist, for ladies use it commonly in welcoming." Uc declares: "When the white gloveless hand of a lady gently squeezes that of her friend, love comes out from the heart and the spirit." Savaric claims that the foot-pressure "is hidden from the slanderers; and since the lady had recourse to the trick of pressing her friend's foot with a smile, it seems to me that her love is quite devoid of deceit." At last the three poets decide to put the question to some ladies. Savaric suggests "my Garda-Cors, who has conquered me, and Lady Maria, in whom is great merit" (Marie de Ventadour). Gaucelm suggests Guillelma "with her courtly and amorous speech." Uc says that he could suggest someone else, but two will be enough.

Loba de Pennautier was one of the most famous ladies of the Carcassone district in the later twelfth century; she was married to Jordan de Cabaret, who separated from her but took her back under pressure from the church. She herself was a Cathar heretic if we may judge from her friends, who included Peire Rogier de Mirepoix, Betran de Saissac, Aimeric de Montréal, and others, all Cathars. She gave herself to them provided they kept to the courtly forms and showed themselves generous. The red-headed count de Foix was said to be her favourite; she bore him a son, Loup de Foix. The Troubadour Raimon de Miraval served her, but gained no favours and decided to go. She called him into her room and wept, "Miraval, if ever I've been celebrated afar and here, if I've had the name of beauty and courtesy, it's to you I owe it, I know. I haven't granted you all that you'd wish. Don't believe that another passion has held me back. I was waiting for more favourable circumstances for the moment of appearing yet dearer to you, so that your pleasure would be made more precious. It's more than two years and five months since I held you with the gift of a kiss. Well, I see now that you don't think of leaving me and that you don't trust a word of the calumnies of which I'm the object through men and women who hate me. Since you defend me so well against them all, I renounce all other love but that for you. I deliver myself up wholly to your discretion. I give you my heart and body to do with as you will. I only ask you: Go on defending me with all your might." That is how the tale was told; and the chronicler says that Miraval possessed the lady, who certainly was a bold and resourceful character. As for Miraval, we have his opinion of women in a comment on Azelais de Boissezon: "Who gives the most can enter first."

At small courts there would have been entertainments only at the Calends of each month, at Christmas, Easter, and in April and May. Much of the time was spent by ladies spinning or looking after children, yet the poets almost wholly ignore the fact that children existed. The ladies were not much given to washing. "Don't grow nails so long that the dirt shows in them," said Amaniende Sescas. They cleaned their teeth and put fard on their faces, red on cheekbones, blue under the eyes, saffron or white on the cheeks. (We shall learn more of cosmetics when we come to the Monk of Montaudon.) When possible, Troubadours praised their ladies for their natural tint. As there was no boudoir, much of the toilet must have gone on in the bedroom where anyone might look in – and where indeed the lord received his friends, his squires. But the ladies made up with fine clothes for deficiencies of washing or toilet. Matfré Ermengau describes them "dragging the long train of their rich surcoats," as never having enough of "capes, garnaches [a sort of cloak], gonnelles [overtunics], fine furred gowns of vair, squirrel, cendal [silkstuff]; never enough of fine chemises or footwear." Jaufré de Vigeois, Limousin chronicler writing 1170–80, looked back to the early years of the century and saw a great change in clothes:

Once the great were glad to wear the meanest clothes, so that bishop Eustorge, the viscounts of Limoges and of Comborn didn't shrink from wearing skins of bucks and foxes. Today the simplest folk would shrink from such clothes. Men have been set to manufacture rich and precious stuffs, with colours to suit the whim of each person. The edges of clothes are cut into little spheres and pointed tongues so that those wearing them look like devils depicted by painters. Capes are slashed and the sleeves made as big as on the gowns of hermits, cenobites . . . Young folk now wear their hair long and their shoes with long beaks. By the length of the clothes trained in their rear women resemble adders.[8]

The Troubadours at times were ready enough to mock at their own code of love, which was both a deeply serious matter and a game made exciting by its complicated rules. They could be rude enough to the ladies if they wanted to raise a laugh from their audience, and as professional singers they might be more interested in getting valuable gifts than kisses. Elias Craicel admitted:

> That I sang of your worth and your wisdom it is true,
> but it wasn't at all that I was in love with you.
> Honour and profit were what I wanted to raise,
> like a jongleur who turns to a noble lady with praise.

Others protested that their ardent declarations were taken too literally.

It is worth noting that in towns like Narbonne and Montpellier, where the bourgeois were strong, there was great support of Troubadours. At Narbonne was the viscountess Ermengarde (1143–92), an energetic and capable woman, able to grasp the political situation or direct a military expedition; her neighbours often chose her as arbiter in disputes, and she maintained her estates against their encroachments. She had two husbands. Peire Rogier was her special Troubadour, but she also gained the praises of Peire d'Auvergne and probably of Bernart de Ventadour. She seems to have used her wit on questions of love, as Andreas the Chaplain attributes three judgments to her. He probably did so correctly, as G. de Borneil asked her advice on a question that could have provided material for a partimen, one of the dialogue-songs. Then there was Eudoxia of Byzantium, who was very fond of Troubadours and who died in a humble monastery, repudiated by William VIII of Montpellier after a dozen years of marriage. She had welcomed G. de Borneil and Folques of Marseille, and the latter took up her defence against her husband, though he soon retracted. William too patronised Troubadours such as G. de Calanson, Arnaut de Mareuil, Aimeric de Sarlat, and probably Perdigon.[9]

The tales about women ready and even zealous to commit adultery are not all fiction or antifeminist convention. The twelfth and even more the thirteenth century saw a widespread revolt of women against the standards imposed on them by the men, against the unequal rule in marriage, against the endless insults from the church. The only way in which they could protest was by adultery. The contrast between the homage paid to them by the love-cult and the orthodox condemnation of their sex as innately evil had become extreme. The inquisitorial records in the period of the Albigensian struggles reveal how often women, after suffering the brutality and indifference of their husbands, decided to go their own way without concern for the moral system that had put them in a degraded position. Béatrice de Planissoles decided to give herself to any man who wanted her. Another young woman, Grazida, was seduced by the village priest at the age of thirteen. He married her off to one Pierre Lizier. "In giving yourself to a priest before being married," asked the inquisitor, "and afterwards, when you were married, did you consider yourself sinning?" "As it pleased me at the time, and as it pleased the priest," she replied, "I didn't think that it was a sin, and don't think so now. But today, as it doesn't please me, if I had sexual relations with him, I'd think it a sin." She added, "Though all bodily union of man and woman displeases God, I still don't think they commit a sin, if it's agreeable to both of them."

How widespread was Grazida's problem we may gauge by looking at Andreas' treatise *On Love*. He defines as Pure Love that in which lovers imagine all sorts of embraces and contacts, indulge in touch and kiss as much as they like, but stay short of copulation; as Mixed Love that in which copulation does occur. A man and a woman discuss the question. The woman points out that love is offensive to God, so that the best thing is to keep clear of it. The man replies:

Your statement that God is offended by love can't keep you from it. It seems to be generally agreed to serve God is very great and an extraordinarily good thing; but those who want to serve him perfectly ought to devote themselves wholly to his service, and according to the opinion of Paul they should engage in no worldly business. Therefore, if you choose to serve God alone, you must give up all worldly things and contemplate only the mysteries of the Heavenly Country, for God has not willed that anyone should keep his right foot on earth and his left foot in heaven, since nobody can properly devote himself to the service of two masters. Now since it is obvious that you have one foot on earth from the fact that you receive with a joyful countenance those who come to you and that you exchange courteous words with them and persuade them to do the works of love, I believe you'd do better to enjoy love thoroughly than to lie to God under the cloak of some pretence. I believe however that God cannot be seriously offended by love, for what is done under the compulsion of nature can be made clean by easy expiation.

We see the dilemma created by making the monk and the complete ascetic the only true religious person. Everything done in the world thus becomes a dereliction in the eyes of God, so that the sinner may as well make as good a job as he can of the situation by enjoying the sweets of love. Andreas argues that it is wrong for lovers to refuse mixed love (copulation) since mixed love is true love and therefore said to be "praiseworthy and the spring of all good things." It doesn't seem at all proper "to class as a sin the thing from which the highest good of this life takes its origin and without which no man in the world could be considered worthy of praise."

To realise the deep cleavage of thought and emotion in this world we need to set against the Troubadour poems and the reasonings of Grazida and Andreas' characters, the monkish view of women, which was that accepted in general by the church. A monk of Cluny thus defined womankind: "The foulest of Jakes, the most deadly of Snakes, fair outside and corruption within." And here is a version of a Latin poem by the Venerable Hildebert which sets out the same position at more length:

> Your heart is quick   with filth and trick.
> With chains you should be loaded.
> Your wicked mind   is shrewd and blind,
> with venom lusts corroded.
>
> A viper bitch,   a newdug ditch,
> a darkly closing gap.
> From nought averse,   a guileful curse,
> for all you bait the trap.

A nightmare-sore,   a public door,
a worn and common track,
like flame you burn,   like asps you turn
to sting us: that's your knack.

The man who's stirred   to trust your word
will weep before he's finished.
O curst in fate,   insatiate,
Your lusts are undiminished.

No longer write   in lewd delight
the songs you scatter round,
the songs so base   of love's embrace,
a sad and dirty sound.

Then I no more   will tell the whore
her merits to her face.
On your affairs   I'll waste no prayers,
I'll leave you your disgrace.

My efforts cease,   I turn to peace,
alone I wish to be.
I've closed my heart.   So do your part
and keep away from me.

Think kisses sweet,   hug all you meet,
yes, him and him and him!
O snuggling, call   them darlings all,
according to your whim.

Your mind is blown   of glass, it's stone,
it's iron, lead, a shame.
To break, beguile,   betray, defile,
to you it's all the same.

He that's Allwise   may smash the skies
and start our world anew
ere I'll endure   to grow impure
by touch or smutch of You.

The church in the world, unlike the monks, might abuse women, but it could not forbid copulation. So thinkers like Hugo of St Victor condemned all fleshly desire as evil but held that the copulative act could be accepted when performed solely to produce offspring. In a state of

19. Marriage of the parents of Thomas Becket. (Royal MS 2B vii)

innocence we would cohabit without any fleshly impulse. Peter Lombard argued that desire was not an evil but a punishment laid on men for the Fall. The act, though not free from evil, could be excused "by the good ends of marriage." He cited from an allegedly Pythagorean source the sentence: *omnis ardentior amator propriae uxoris adulter est* (To love one's own wife passionately is to commit adultery). For Thomas Aquinas the evil thing in the sexual act was the submergence of the rational faculty.

The assertion of the joy of love as a good thing, as the supremely good thing on earth, thus ran counter to all the theological positions. The Troubadour love-ethic was a highly sophisticated expression of the revolt against the branding of love as evil and as morally acceptable only when exclusively concerned with the production of children. Women like Grazida were responding to the same kind of revolt in a simple intuitive way.[10]

But the breakdown of the idea that the service of God involved a total rejection of the world led also to the heretical idea that a man might live a life of rejection while still actively involved in the world's affairs. Since the church, apart from the monks, had become an aspect of the world, entangled at all points with state-power and property, to reject the world in the service of God meant that one had also to reject the church. The heretical positions at root involved the idea that one could and should live the apostolic life in the world. No longer was it felt sufficient for a few men to withdraw into monasteries which soon

93

became as much concerned with power and property as the pope and the bishops; no longer was it felt sufficient that men could live violent and self-centred lives, and then at the last moment atone by belated expressions of repentance and rich gifts to monasteries. Men awakening to a new critical sense of the unchristian world that took the name of Christ in vain could not but feel an overwhelming sense of horror, as if suddenly a dark and deceitful cover had been torn away from the face of things. What was revealed was an almost incredible gap between the professions of men and the reality of their lives.

The heretical response took two main lines. First, to condemn the world and the church altogether, to see nothing anywhere but the rule of an evil principle of power and greed, in which the God of the church was an accomplice. In this view the acclaimed God of the Old and the New Testaments was himself the embodiment of evil; for otherwise how could he have created and sanctified such an evil world? Against the church's elevation of evil as the divine principle must be set a total repudiation of the earth and all its ways, with a creed looking to another God, who was not implicated in the creation of matter. Secondly, to recognise in the church a hopeless set of compromises and falsifications, and to attempt to revive outside it the apostolic way of life, accepting the New Testament as revealing the true creed of brotherhood in poverty, of union in Christ.

Both attitudes were strong in the twelfth century in many areas of the West. The first or dualistic creed, which had its variations of absolute or mitigated dualism, owned connections with similar creeds in the East, especially that of Bogomiles of Bulgaria; there can be no doubt that the latter groups, more organised than those in the West around 1100, played a considerable part in supplying ideas and methods. Trade, pilgrimages, and the crusades provided contacts between East and West. In the first half of the twelfth century groups in Italy, France, the Lowlands, and Germany attacked the veneration of Christ or the saints, burial in consecrated ground, and other such practices. They criticised the priests as contaminated by the world, and felt that it was wrong to eat meat. The groups we hear about were mainly in the north. Thus in 1022 at Orleans, Robert the Pious condemned to death some canons with Manichean (dualistic) ideas. We learn however in 1018 already of people in Aquitaine who acted like devout monks in their ascetic ways, but who rejected the cross and baptism. A Council of 1026 discussed steps to be taken against them, and some persons were burned at Toulouse.

Among the northern heretical leaders were Peter of Bruys and a certain Henry who appeared at Le Mans in 1116. Later Henry came south and carried on in the region round Toulouse. He held that prayers for the dead were useless and that the church existed only in a spiritual form (made up of the true Christians), but he respected Christ. He wanted the church hierarchy to drop all wealth and honours. Only faith vindicated baptism and men should confess their sins to one another. In 1119 Pope Calixtus II at the Council of Toulouse denounced heretics who disowned the sacraments of the Holy Orders, Baptism, Marriage, the Eucharist. By 1145 the churchmen of the Toulouse area were distressed at the extent to which heresies had spread. St Bernard was drawn into a preaching mission and found a denial of the trinity prevalent among common folk, especially the weavers. The noble classes either ignored or fostered the growth of opposition to the church, since they often coveted its lands and revenues.

The years 1140–60 saw a steady expansion of the Cathar heresy, which seems to have started in Cologne and Liège and moved south. Probably by 1150 it had taken strong root in Languedoc. The name Cathars came up in the north around 1160; other names for the same sort of heresy were Publicans (north Italy), Patarines, Bulgars (Bougres), though churchmen often used old terms such as Arians, Manicheans, Marcionites to describe such groups. Soon those in the Midi were known as Albigenses from the town of Albi, though that was not their most important centre. In 1163 at the Council of Tours Pope Alexander III declared, "In the regions of Toulouse this damnable heresy not long ago emerged, which, bit by bit, diffused itself in the neighbouring areas in the way of a cancer, so that already it infects Gascony and many other provinces." In 1177 Raimon V of Toulouse stated that Catharism "had penetrated everywhere. It has thrown discord into all the families, dividing husband and wife, son and father, daughter-in-law and mother-in-law. The priests themselves yield to the contagion. The churches are deserted and fall into ruins." He found himself unable to arrest the spread of the heresy. "The leading men of my land have let themselves be corrupted. The crowd has followed their example and abandoned the faith, with the result that I dare not and cannot repress the evil." His account was exaggerated, but the situation was serious from the church's viewpoint. In 1065 a Cathar group under Oliver were induced to come before an assembly of Catholic clergy and laymen at Lombers near Albi. They admitted their rejection of the Old Testament, denied the use of baptism by priests, and gave suspect answers as to marriage

20. Anchorite burning his hand to drive out Temptation. (*Das Buoch der Reiligen Alträtter*, 1482)

and confession, ending with a denunciation of prelates. They were considered heretical, but no action was taken.

A leading missionary from the East, Papa (priest) Nicheta, was said to have met Catharist leaders from north and south France at the village of St Felix de Caraman, where he had them rebaptised in a strongly dualistic tradition. As well as the group near Albi, three new groups were set up, centred on Toulouse, Carcassone, Agen (or Val d'Aran in Comminges, though this is unlikely). By the end of the century the Cathars were organised in sufficient strength to constitute a rival body to the Catholics.[11]

There were two levels in the Cathar church. First came the leaders or more advanced individuals, the Christians or Good Christians, called by the Catholics the Perfected or Consoled, the Robed Heretics; they also became known as the *Boni Homines*, the Good Men. They had been baptised in the spirit by the laying-on of the hands of other Good Men in the rite called the *consolamentum*, which ensured salvation. Below them were the mass of followers, the Believers, who had not been baptised and who put baptism off till the last possible moment. They supported the Good Men, attended ceremonies, gave services or gifts. The community of Good Men elected their bishop, who had as assistants an Elder and a Younger Son, the titles indicating status not age. The three men travelled, preached, baptised. There were also deacons who supervised the hospices for the Good Men and Women. The Good lived in complete asceticism, rejecting sex, wine, meat (any food resulting from sexual breeding). There was thus in effect the same division as among the Catholics between the Religious or Monks and other Believers; but here it was palliated by the way in which the Good did not live a separate life except in the strictness of their discipline. They fasted three days every week and there was a yearly forty-day period of restricted diet, during one week of which only bread and water were taken. Inevitably the Catholics told tales of all sorts of debauchery among the Cathars. Especially the Good Men were accused of homosexuality on account of their rejection of intercourse with women; hence the French term *Bougre* and our *Bugger*. They accumulated property for their church while rejecting individual ownership. They provided security for aging widows and homes for unmarried daughters. They preached in the vernacular and evoked a sense of participation among the Believers. Their simple rites were devoid of mumbojumbo and affected even those who did not join them. Thus they enjoyed considerable respect from all but ardent Catholics.

There were also the Waldenses. This sect was founded at Lyon in 1173 by a rich merchant, Waldes, who took seriously Christ's injunction to sell what one had and give the proceeds to the poor. (St Francis was soon to follow his example.) The clergy mocked and disapproved; but for a while Waldes gained papal approval for a way of poverty. Called before the zealous Henry, once abbot of Clairvaux and now papal legate, at Lyon in 1180–1 he stated:

Whatever we had, we have given to the poor as the Lord advised, and we have resolved to be poor in such fashion that we shall take no thought for the morrow, nor shall we accept gold or silver or anything of that sort from anyone, beyond food and clothing sufficient for the day. Our resolve is to follow the precepts of the Gospel as commands.

But the Waldenses could not forbear from preaching. They were excommunicated and thrown out of Lyon in 1182. Now calling themselves the Poor in Spirit and often called the Poor of Lyon, they wandered around, and were included in the list of condemned heretics of 1182. Soon they were preaching over most of Languedoc. They kept up contacts with Italian and Burgundian friends, and spread over the Pyrenees before the Cathars. They developed increased disagreements with the church. The only true church, they declared, was the believers themselves wherever they were gathered; they held that confession to God alone was needed and that indulgences were worthless; they banned oaths and condemned the death-penalty for crime. Where they differed from the Cathars was in accepting the Testaments and in not denouncing the God of *Genesis* as the Evil One.

The heretical groups had their links with the general movement of twelfth-century thought, its tendency to independence and its readiness to criticise ideas or institutions for inner inconsistency, for failure to live up to pretensions. They were seeking a way of life that held logically together in all its aspects; and having discovered what they felt to be the truth, they wanted to proclaim it and were ready to die for it. Cathars and Waldenses flourished in the same area as the Troubadours, not because of any direct connections, but because of the relatively high degree of tolerance existing there, the weakness of feudal forms and the lack of a strong secular power allied with the church in a determination to maintain a hierarchical structure. We can, however, find certain points of contact between the heretical world and that of the Troubadours, despite the deep differences. The Cathar notion of body–soul division and the need to ascend through a cycle of purifications to a dimension of non-material light had some affinities with the more idealist side of courtly love. Cathar influences may have helped to strengthen that side. Also the Cathars tended to see fornication and adultery, though bad, as less sins than marriage; for the latter, organised to bring about the production of children and thus to perpetuate the world of matter, was a direct glorification of the evil principle. There is little direct link here with the rejection or belittling of marriage in the Troubadour system; but one effect of the Cathar propaganda may well have been to intensify various moral confusions by its attack on all the church's sacraments. Thus people became more responsive to ideas that involved a new way of life and sought in varying degrees to supplant conventional moral positions.

[V]

Bernart de Ventadour

OF Bernart his biographer tells us:

He was born in Limousin, at the castle of Ventadour. He was a man of humble extraction, son of a servitor who did the office of baker and warmed the oven for baking the castle's bread . . . He was handsome and adroit, he could sing well and make verses, and he was well-informed and courteous. The viscount of Ventadour, his lord, grew fond of him through his verses and his songs, and did him great honour. The viscount had a lovely wife, gracious, young, and graceful, and she too grew fond of Bernart and his songs. She fell in love with him and he with her, so much that he made verses on her and on the love he bore her . . . Their loves lasted a long time before the viscount realised what was happening . . . And when he did find out, he chased Bernart from his presence. As for his wife, he had her shut up and guarded. Then she let Bernart know that she gave him his dismissal, she prayed him to leave her and go off. And he left her and came to the duchess of Normandy who was young and of great merit . . . Bernart's songs pleased her much . . . He stayed a long time at her court and he was smitten with her and the lady was smitten with him, and of it all he made many good songs. But the king of England married her and took her off to England. Bernart stayed there sad and grieving. He left Normandy and went to find the count of Toulouse, at whose court he stayed . . . and after the count's death he abandoned the world, verses, songs, and secular pleasures; he withdrew to the Order of Dalou, and there he died.

Uc de Saint-Cire declared that he had these stories from the son of the countess that Bernart had loved so much. But the legend is doubtless based on guesses from the songs and the use of accepted formulas: love conceived from infancy, suffering of the beloved through a jealous person, exile of the lover through the beloved's insensibility, and so on. Peire d'Auvergne says that the mother "used to warm the oven and gather firewood," the father being a crossbowman.[1]

At Ventadour Bernart was under Eblo II, vassal and friend of the count of Poitou and himself a Troubadour. The next count Eblo III continued the patronage. He married in 1148 Margarida of Torena (Turenne) but in 1150 repudiated her; she soon afterwards married the count of Angoulême. The duchess was Eleanor of Aquitaine who married Henry of Anjou in 1152; she was grand-daughter of Guilhem IX of Poitou. Henry, her second husband, shared her tastes. He "loved pleasure and feasts, and in his castles especially before the disaster of the White Ship, he liked to invite ladies and demoiselles, setting an example of gallantry to his knights and mingling assemblies and games with splendid tourneys." Eleanor's court was an important meeting-place of south and north; a tradition carried on by her three sons, young King Henry, Richard Lionheart, Geoffrey of Brittany, who all became legendary figures. Two collections of Italian tales, later but founded on Provençal sources of the thirteenth century, attribute to them traits of liberality bordering on the maddest extravagance. Bertran de Born wrote a *planh* on young Henry: "Lord for you, I want to renounce all joy. All who have known you are henceforth sad and dumb. I value as an acorn the world and all who are in it." The Monk says that Richard "plucked him out of the morass."

When Henry of Anjou became king of England in 1154, he took Bernart across the Channel with him while Eleanor stayed behind. Bernart in the *tornada* to a song composed in England remarked: "If the English king and Norman duke desires it, I'll see her before the winter's come upon us. I'm English and Norman for the king's sake, and were it not for my Magnet I'd stay on till Christmas." Later he must have stayed a fair while at Toulouse, no doubt visiting near courts at Narbonne and so on. Not until 1194 did he die in the Cistercian abbey. The lady he calls Tristan (a male name) seems the countess of Ventadour; the one he calls Confort (Comfort) and Aziman (Magnet) seems Eleanor.[2]

He left some forty-five poems. Of lowly birth, he was one of the first fully professional Troubadours. All but two of his poems are love-songs. His work represents the first maturity of the Troubadour lyric in all the freshness of its young tradition. His themes are limited, but he gives them a sense of immediacy and works them fully out, providing the model for the Troubadours celebrating love. What remained still a relatively abstract sentiment in Rudel's poems on the Distant Lady is now expressed so that we feel it to be truly a part of everyday experience. Bernart introduces anecdotal or narrative material if he wishes, without losing his lyrical verve; and above all he makes the structure of his poems a vivid expression of opposed and alternating ideas or emotions, which come together in the unity of the dramatic moment. His form is subtle yet simple. He attempts no complications of rare rhymes, but manages to make his patterns define the mood of the moment: pathos, anger, despair, joy. In *Chantars no pot* he sets out his literary manifesto:

> Singing cannot much avail
> unless the song wells from the heart,
> unless it's noble love you feel.
> My singing's then supreme. For, bold
> in the deep joy of love, I hold
> and still direct my mouth, my heart,
> my eyes, my understanding art.

The experience of love and the act of song are inseparable; and so he goes on to say that he must remain true to love whatever sufferings it entails. True love cannot fail. Women who love for wealth are "common whores." The love of two noble lovers lies "in accord and in assent. Nothing can be of value in it if the will towards it is not equally shared." The tension lies between that ideal and the fact of loyal but unrequited love.

The negative aspect is put in *Can vei la lauzeta* (which is the first known poem in which the exaltation of the lark's flight up into light is expressed):

> When I behold the lark arise
> with wings of gold for heaven's height,
> to drop at last from flooded skies,
> lost in its fullness of delight,
> such sweetness spreads upon the day
> I envy those who share the glee.
> My heart's so filled with love's dismay
> I wait its breaking suddenly.
>
> I thought in love's ways I was wise,
> yet little do I know aright.
> I praised a woman as love's prize
> and she gives nothing to requite.
> My heart, my life she took in theft,
> she took the world away from me,
> and now my plundered self is left
> only desire and misery.

Her rule I'm forced to recognise
since all my broken joys took flight.
I looked within her lifted eyes,
that mirror sweet with treacherous might:
O mirror, here I weep and dream
of depths once glimpsed and now denied.
I'm lost in you as in the stream
comely Narcissus looked and died.

Now trust in indignation dies
and womanhood I henceforth slight.
I find that all her worths are lies.
I thought her something made of light.
And no one comes to plead for me
with her who darkens all my days.
Woman I doubt and now I see
that she like all the rest betrays.

Aye, pity women all despise.
Come face the truth and do not fight.
The smallest kindness she denies,
yet who but she should soothe my plight?
So gentle and so fair is she,
it's hard for others to believe.
She, who could save, in cruelty
watches her wasting lover grieve.

My love has failed and powerless lies;
devotion bears for me no right.
She laughs to hear my deepest sighs –
then silently I'll leave her sight.
I cast my love of her away.
She struck and I accept the blow.
She will not speak and I must stray
in exile. Where, I do not know.

Tristan, I've made an end, I say.
I'm going – where, I do not know.
My song is dying, and away
all love and joy I cast, and go.

Addressing great ladies, he has no hope of fruition. The conflict of love
and rejection is worked out in *La dousa votz*:

21. Lovers and Garden. (Whicker 67 : French)

The nightingale's delightful voice
deep in the woodland I heard swell.
Into my heart it leaped with joys
that soothed and softened still my care
and the hard blows that yet
are all from love I get.
As here I linger in despair,
another's joy would serve me well.

Yet only a man of base life will fail to have "his dwelling with joy"
and to direct his heart to love, when everywhere all things give themselves up to joy and ring with song : "meadows and parks and orchards,
heathland and plains and woods." He has been rejected. A traitress has
betrayed him and is herself betrayed, "plucking the switch with which
she beats herself." He served her until she showed her fickle heart, but
he'd be a fool to serve her still. "Service without reward, like the hope
of Bretons, makes a lord a mere squire by custom and by habit." (Note
the feudal idiom). He doesn't want to speak of his lady any more.
"Yet if one speaks to me of her, such talk makes pleasant feelings stir."
A curse then on the tale-tellers who caused all the trouble. "The man's
a fool who quarrels with his mistress. So I forgive her if she in turn
forgives. It's only a pack of liars that makes me speak such folly of her."
He sends the poem to a lady of Narbonne.

A complex interplay of trust and doubt, hope and fear, love and suffering, runs through another poem, to Tristan, which begins again with a description of the nightingale singing. Here he says that what makes himself sing is his "great envy", though of what he is to sing he doesn't know. "For I don't love myself or anyone else. And I'm making strenuous efforts since I can't compose good verse when I am not in love." Whatever the pain, he cannot leave the lady. "From each place where she might stay, I turn and go afar. To save myself from seeing her, I tightly close my eyes and pass her by. For he who avoids love follows it, and love pursues him who runs away. But I've a mind to forsake it still, until to my lady it returns." He is forced to realise that no other love will ever light up his heart. "Tristan, you may not think it's true, but I love you more than I used to love." In other poems he keeps on working out the same rending conflict, aware all the while of the redeeming and transforming power of love. Again and again the contradiction between the inner conviction of joy, of stable union and fulfilled love, and the outer facts of separation, suffering and unstable relationships, are explained from different angles.

> My heart's so filled with deep delight
> it changes all I see.
> The frost appears a blossom of white,
> golden or green, to me.
> When the wind blows up the rain, it's right:
> my fortune sprouts with the tree.
> So thrives my worth with freshening might
> and my song gains loftier glee.
> Such is my love and such the power
> of joy and sweetness in its dower,
> each icicle seems to me a flower
> and the snow is greenery.

So the poet triumphs. Whatever happens to his love, he has realised the enormous potentialities for joy that lie in human beings. His senses are distracted, but in a creative way. The elements run together in new matrices. Plenty is born at the heart of dearth. The lover's steadfastness will in the end bring about the universal rule of joy with the old contradictions overcome; and this promise becomes true in the all-embracing joy of the poet-lover in the immediate moment, the here-and-now.

Andreas gives us a decision of Queen Eleanor. He is arguing that a

22. Henry II and his wife Eleanor. (Tombs at Fontevrault)

woman may be called unfaithful if she has encouraged a lover and has advanced to the second or third stage of love, yet then refuses to grant the love she has promised. (He defines the stages as follows: the giving of hope, kisses, embraces, then of the whole person.) It is shameful of a woman to grant kiss and embrace, then go no further; she sins against the nature of love. Eleanor deals with the case of a lover, who, to test the constancy of his beloved, asks and gets permission from her to obtain the embraces of another woman. He does not however really want those embraces and does not get them; but on returning to his beloved he is refused her love. "We know that it comes from the nature of love that those in love often pretend untruly that they desire new embraces, so as to test better the faith and constancy of their lover. So a woman sins against the nature of love itself if she witholds her embraces from her lover on this account or forbids him her love, unless she has clear evidence of his infidelity to her."[8]

There is a certain ambiguity in the use of the term Noble Love. Love is felt to be the preserve of the noble class, but a member of that class only becomes truly noble if he or she is devoted to love. In the

De Amore of Andreas it is argued that it is excellence of character which provides men with the privilege and title of nobility, since what determines nobility is not birth but character. All the same the poor man is excluded because poverty prevents a man from acting nobly and doing good deeds; it limits his role intolerably. A noblewoman argues that a bourgeois is also excluded, since he engages in business. A man who spends six days of the week in thinking of money and dealing with it is not in the position to be a lover on the seventh day. But the middle-class man who woos the woman replies that there is no disgrace in business, since it agrees with his social position and his nature; his aim is not dishonest gain but the winning of a position that enables him to take on nobility of character by doing noble deeds. Also, business saves him from falling into poverty, which would indeed confine him. The poor man is hemmed in with cares and hardships that rob him of all joy; when poverty intrudes, love begins to fail and the lover acts differently to his lady so that he appears abhorrent to her.

A lover suffering from dire poverty is so tortured by the thought of household affairs and his urgent necessities that he cannot heed the impulses of love or allow it to keep on growing as it should. In consequence everyone seeks to find fault with his character and his life, and he is despised and hated by all, and no one will consider him as a friend, since

> When you are fortunate, many friends you'll mark,
> but you'll be quite alone when skies grow dark.

Through all these things a man's face and figure begin to change, and the repose of sleep abandons him, and he can scarcely avoid growing contemptible in the view of his beloved.

A needy woman may accept a rich lover in preference to a poor one, as long as he's the equal of the latter in birth, life, and morals. "For if both lovers," laid down the countess of Champagne, "are weighed down by poverty, their love, it seems certain, will endure only a short while. Poverty brings down a heavy sense of shame on all men of honour and imposes many anxieties on them and is even a great perturber of the quiet of sleep. And so it commonly drives love away."

Thus questions of social status break in on what is seen as matter of pure nature. The art and necessity of love is nature. "Love is a thing that copies nature." Nature is common to all men, all men are one by nature, and love is common to all. This law makes it right for even clerics to love women, though they are vowed to the service of God.

Nature compels all to love and at the same time lays down certain limits. It excludes the aged or the over-passionate from love, it forbids love of male for male. The over-passionate are like animals, moved by their lower nature; the true lover is moved by his human nature, which involves reason and affection. Peasants fall into the same category as animals. Even if against their nature they fall in love, it would be unwise to instruct them in its art; they would then neglect their farms which "through lack of cultivation would prove useless to us." Andreas defines the element of universal nature in the higher or fully human love as "quasi-natural".

The women in *De Amore* often appeal to nature, but in particular to argue that true nobility is of blood, so that lovers should stay in their own class or should seek love from a higher. The plebeian woman states that if she accepted a lover from a higher class, she would be blamed. The man replies that it is instinctive and natural for men to rise through good works and by character. The nobility of character thus gained is not accidental or artificial, but is "quasi-natural." Again, a plebeian woman declares she would take the love of a man of the nobility only under a strong love-impulse.

No matter how much good a man does in this world, it will not profit him in gaining the rewards of eternal blessedness unless it has been prompted by love. Similarly, no matter how much I strive to serve the King of Love by my deeds and works, unless these proceed from the heart's affections and are born out of the impulse of love, they cannot profit me toward gaining love's reward.

The woman who does not help with her love the lover threatened by adversity is like the hypocritical priest who preaches to others what he does not himself practise.

Let us look further at the case of the bourgeois. He pleads that desire and passion urge him to look above his class; he thus follows the law of love that is unconcerned with rank. He cannot hold himself back; the more he forces silence on himself, the more he suffers. At last Love's mighty power "has forced me to ask for great things and seek a cure for my ceaseless pang." He argues: "Just as love makes men of all classes burn, so love should draw no distinction of rank, but should consider only whether the man asking for love has been wounded by Love." The lady ignores the class-issue and replies merely to the claim that love must be requited with love. She agrees that Love compels everyone without distinction to love; but she considers that it is false then to infer "that a lover ought not to distinguish beyond asking whether he who seeks for love is in love." The results would be disastrous if that position were accepted. Even a farmer might force a queen to love him. Everyone would claim a lover in the sphere above him. Rather, Love, agreeing that all men are drawn to someone of the opposite sex, would insist that it was shameful for a man "to pitch his tent at once over against the other person, so that she who is sought in love must be driven to return love at once." In truth Love leaves to a woman to accept or refuse a lover.

The man argues that it is character which confers nobility; as he has cultivated an excellent character, he can be defined as noble. He then cannot be called presumptuous in seeking a love in the nobility; for character, not birth, determines nobility. True, the woman, wooed by a worthy lover, may say yes or no. If she yields, she gains unutterable reward; if she refuses, unbearable punishment. It follows that she should not deny a worthy man unless already under the obligation of loving someone else. We see then that despite some casuistries that try to keep true love the preserve of the nobility, there is a genuine notion of equality in love, which breaks down the class-barriers, at least in theory. The one class that is almost wholly barred from tasting love's nobility is the peasant. Andreas' phrase reveals the recognition that the feudal world depends on the peasant as producer, and any ideas or actions tending to draw him from this role are felt as disastrous. In the relative acceptance of the bourgeois we may trace the effects of the social forces which in the Midi were linking lesser nobles and rich townsmen.

From one angle the Troubadour ideas reveal the general loosening-up of philosophic and moral views that we saw coming to a head in the twelfth century. Part of this trend was the stress on Reason, returning to the positions of Boethius who had seen Reason as the *summum bonum* of human nature and the key to all blessedness. Now the workings of Reason and Nature were seen as one and the same thing. William of Conches had foreshadowed the new attitudes by calling Nature the Vicar of God. The classic Latin poets helped. The Stoic concept of Nature as a living Whole was found in the *Thebaid* of Statius; and Claudian had much effect with his personification of Nature with five functions (including the ordering of elemental chaos, the making of marriages, the uttering of complaints at trespasses on the true order of things). The two Latin poets of the century who most fully formu-

23. Garden or Earthly Paradise. (Benedictictbeuern MS)

lated the new positions were Bernard Silvestris and Alan of Lille, of
the school of Chartres. This school brought to a head medieval Neo-
platonism and saw Nature as playing the central role in the universe;
they held that man could understand and interpret the natural and
moral order resulting from this situation.

Bernard in *De mundi universitate* (1145–56) strove to get outside
theological questions, to accept and experience the world as real and
concrete in its own right. In the Chartres system the Persons of the
Trinity were identified with the neoplatonic emanations. Bernard
shows awareness of this position but does not want to make it explicit.
Nature *plangens* (complaining or lamenting) calls on Noys (Nous) to
put the universe in order, provides bodies for the souls produced by the
World-Soul, makes a journey into the heavens, and joins the souls of
men (supplied by Urania) to the bodies fashioned by Physis; in her work
she emulates the order of the heavens. At the end of the first book
Nature is shown producing bodies out of matter as *artifex*, craftsman.
Man is a union of opposites, of the created and uncreated, the sensible
and the intelligible, of the male and the female, of heaven and earth,
of paradise and the earth-sphere. For Bernard, Nature unites all the
opposites in the living man.

He depicts the sexual organs "fighting with death, to restore nature
and perpetuate the race." The penis battles with Lachesis and skilfully
renews the thread cut by the Fates. Nature resumes her role as *pro-
creatrix*, since it is she who forms the seminal fluid through which the

ancestors are revived in their children. She herself survives, streaming into the world as she flows out of it.[4]

Alan composed two poems, *De planctu naturae* (1160–72) and *Anticlaudianus* (1181–4). Nature complains that she made man as the mirror of the world. Venus, appointed as subvicar of the lower world, at first followed her instructions, properly using the hammers and anvils provided, obeying the grammatical constructions prescribed for marital coition, and working hard to amend what the Fates cut. But she grew tired and committed adultery with Antigamus (Anti-marriage), bearing Jocus (Mirth, the opposite of Cupid). Thus appeared *Venus monstrosa*. The two opposed Venuses were by this time a common enough idea: Chaste Love against Lechery; but Bernard puts the pair together in one figure.

We say that the legitimate Venus is *mundana musica* [music of the world]: that is, the equal proportion of worldly things, which some call Astraea and others call Natural Justice. For she is in the elements, in the stars, in times, in animate things. But the shameful Venus, the goddess of sensuality, we call Concupiscence of the Flesh because she is the mother of all fornication.

For him the cosmic kiss of Nature and Genius represents the eternal Ideas meeting with Matter through intermediate Images or Iconiae. Here is the mystical union of Form and Matter, and there is an implied analogy of Matter and the Virgin. Alan merges in one the Genius-figures of Bernard Silvestris: the Cosmic Genius, Pantomorphus, and the twin genii residing in the male genitals to preserve the human race.

His allegorical method is more than a method of exposition; it expresses the very method of Nature's own narrative discourse, the integument that veils (and protects) a truth accessible only to those whose reason can penetrate below the surface. Nature says that the poetic lyre resounds with falsehood in its surface-shell (its literal meaning):

> but expresses inwardly to those who hearken
> a deep hidden meaning; the reader who discards
> the outer shell of falsity discovers
> the sweet kernel of truth that's hidden within.

Alan develops further his ideas in *Anticlaudianus*. Some thinkers had been suggesting that the *opus restaurationis*, the work of restoring the universe, was in effect a return to the condition that existed before the Fall. They implied that the idea of sacred history should give way to one of cosmic process as an emanation from divine unity and a return to it. They blurred out the Christian notion of the relation of Nature and Grace by identifying the cosmic and the providential order. The re-creation of fallen man becomes a return to paradisiac conditions, the ideal state and the true nature of man, which is seen as much as the point of the starting-off of the cosmic movement as the place where sin was born. In such a view, Grace is present in man and does not need an intervening God; man has only to use his own efforts to rediscover it.

Alan seeks to define the *novus homo*, the new man who achieves a state of perfection. He uses the theme of the cosmic journey of Prudentia. Reason aids her as far as the fixed stars, then Theologia takes over. Prudentia presents the petition of Natura and the Virtues to God, who sends Noys to find the Idea of the Perfect Soul. God then creates that soul and puts his seal on it. After a psychomachia, a world-battle of Alecto and her Vices against Natura and the Virtues, evil is defeated and a new golden age arises. Both Man and Nature are restored, largely through Reason, Prudence, Concord. Some commentaries take the Perfect Man to be a symbol of Christ; but we could also take him to be the New Man created by the true use of human qualities. John of Salisbury thus defined the ascent or quest theme :

When Love of Reason, which concerns earthly things, ascends with Prudence to the hidden secrets of eternal and divine truths, it becomes transformed into Wisdom, which is in a way exempt from mortal limitations.[5]

There was thus a trend to see Paradise more and more as an Earthly Paradise, as the transformed earth. A passage from Claudian's *Epithalamium for Honorius* played an important role here. It describes a paradisiac meadow with a gold hedge on a mountain without winds or frosts, and with the sweetest of songbirds in the copses. There are two fountains, one sweet and one bitter; and the place is inhabited by the Loves, Fear, and Pleasure. Early Christian poets tried to link the imagery of the *locus amoenus*, the Pleasant Place, with cosmic meanings, for instance, Lactantius, Dracontius, Avitus. Alan carries the process further, by making the paradisiac scene the perfect expression of the essence of the goddess Natura who inhabits it. It thus both unites and fulfils all the various separate potentialities in the cosmos, and is at the same time their source : *forma formans* providing the patterns and actualising them.[6]

24. Garden or Earthly Paradise. (Benedictbeuern MS)

The next step is to see the earthly garden itself as a symbol of paradise. In the continuation of the *Roman de la Rose*, Genius, at Nature's bidding, gives a sermon to Love and his followers, describing the paradise that will reward all the blessed who obey Nature's Law: the Good Shepherd's Park where the inhabitants live in eternal bliss. This Park is contrasted with the Garden of Deduit (Diversion) in the first part of the *Roman*; it is a true paradise while the latter is a vain transitory delight. Andreas in his *De Amore* (1184–6) has a parable of a young man lost in a forest who sees three companies go by: ladies on horses, each attended by a lover on foot, with a knight leading the way; ladies surrounded by noisily contending suitors; women bareback on wretched nags with no attendants. The first party consists of ladies who on earth served love wisely and truly; the second, of those who gave rewards to all who asked; the third, of those who were deaf to the prayers of lovers. The first party goes to the thrones of the king and queen of love under a shadowy tree that bears all kinds of fruit, with a nectar-sweet fountain beside them, and streams winding their way in all directions among the couches prepared for the true lovers. This place is *Amoenitas*. Beyond is *Humiditas* where the streams have turned cold and made the ground swampy and treeless; here go the second party. Further is *Siccitas*, a burning desert of thorntrees, for the third. The link of *Amoenitas* with Paradise is brought out by the orders given to the mortal intruder. He is to report his vision so that it may lead to the Salvation of hosts of ladies.

By the time of the mystery-plays it has become natural for Paradise

itself to be simply described as a "gardeyn." We are in a line of
tradition that ends with the glorification of the Garden in the
eighteenth century as providing the return to the bosom of Nature,
out of a dividing and corrupting world.[7]

More or less contemporary with Bernart de Ventadour was Peire
d'Auvergne (Alvernhe). The *vida* says that he was a jongleur, son of a
townsman in the diocese of Clermont-Ferrand. He probably began as a
professional Troubadour in the 1150s. We find him in Spain in
1157–8 at the court of Sancho III of Castile, then in Languedoc and
Provence until 1170, when he was at a festive gathering at or near
Puivert (Aude). How soon he died after that we do not know. His
poems, of which we have some score, are varied: three love-songs, a
farewell to love, a crusading song, a *sirventes*, a literary manifesto,
pious songs in a profane style and some poems seriously pious. He
wanted to be original. "My racking care is to sing a song in a way like
no one else's. No song's worth while if it recalls the songs of others."
No poet before him wrote a perfect poem. "I know the practice well.
I hold both bread and knife, and so can satisfy the people." (Such
boasts were made with tongue in cheek, made as jokes and yet meant
to catch the attention of listeners.) "Without filling-up phrases one
should be pleasant in speech." Each word "acts as herald for the
labour" that lies behind it; so the poet who wavers in his intention
and in his product "turns listening into a puzzle for the whole household." Then he goes on to insult his opponents and ends with such an
emphasis on Joy that he seems to be making fun of the motif. He is in
fact an advocate of the closed or difficult style which had been growing
up as the first stock of Troubadour themes seemed to be exhausted.
While he exploits the ideas of courtly love, he is the first Troubadour
who also turns in the direction of orthodox Christianity. He thus
shows a questioning note with regard to both theme and form, and
preludes the more thorough discussions that were to come up in the
1170s and 1180s. He had been influenced by Marcabru but quite
lacked that poet's prophetic force and concentration.[8]

In a *tenson* with him Bernart de Ventadour replies to his declaration
of conventional love-attitudes:

> Peire, if two years or three
> the world was moulded to my plan,
> I assure you ladies wouldn't be
> then wooed by us or any man.

> Into such hopeless pangs they'd fall
> they'd honour us so much, you'd see,
> they'd woo without being wooed at all.

That is perhaps more what we'd expect from him than from Bernart with daydreams of winning some great lady's embrace. But in any event Peire can at times sing the courtly song in something of Bernart's vein, but without his compelling intensity :

> With noble joy the song must start,
> rhyming fine words together well,
> and there's no fault in all its art . . .

But he doesn't want some unsuitable performer to take it up and turn his melody into a bray.

> O I did penance but no sin.
> It's wrong if forgiveness then I miss.
> For long now have I sought to win
> forgiveness that she will not give.
> Bad luck is mine if thus I live.
> The man devoid of hope is lost.
> So, that my hopes won't go amiss,
> in the Lord's name I loudly appeal.

In *Cui bon vers*, after his usual brag, with an attack on mockers and sniggerers, he becomes grave. "I wouldn't give you a pair of nuts, no, not a bushel of Spanish coin, once the mouth finally shuts and the priest sprinkles holy water on." Death confronts man with the God on the Cross.

He is a poet of transition, uncertain where he is going. Meaning seems to be lost, so the quest for meaning is itself the meaning of poetry. "The seasons call on me to pluck a *vers clus*." "I like to sing in tightened *clus* words, such as one hesitates to mock." There is both an attempt to hedge the courtly themes round with a certain obscurity, and a confused sense that there are indeed deeper meanings which have not yet been grasped. The idea of an esoteric system underlying the obvious sense of the words may be compared with the idea of the Double Truth with which the later Averroists were accused. Peire, in a poem that imitates Marcabru, depicts himself as closed in a castle from which he can defy his enemies as long as he is sure of the fidelity of the gate-keeper (the bodily senses and appetites). He ends: "May God find me a love that I can't trust : one that deceives me in proportion to my attachment; for it's at the hour when all its promises are shown as lies that I hold myself as saved." It seems he is again confronting the issue of death, which throws him back on the church. We seem to see a recognition that the aims of courtly love are essentially opposed to all the positions of the church.

Something of the same attitude to meaning is found in other poets affected by *trobar clus*. Marcabru's pupil Alegret states:

> My words seem madness to the fool
> if there's a double meaning there...
> Who contradicts then what I say,
> let him come forth and I'll declare
> how I could put into my song
> two words with diverse meanings...

And Bernart de Vensac darkly comments:

> A song of truthful words I compose.
> For the intelligent it will be
> a matter of dispute; for those
> less wise a clear uncertainty.

Trobar clus was defined as a method which managed *entrebascar lis motz*: to entangle or interlace the words or stanzas. We might take this to refer to developing in turn two different ideas in alternate stanzas; but we can better interpret it in the more general sense of mixing things up, inverting them, setting them topsyturvy; the verb is still used in the Blaisois for "turning upside-down, head-to-tail." It could then mean among other things the covering-up of religious ideas with profane terms, the use of religious terms to define human love. The word is used by Bernart Marti, Raimbaut d'Orange, Giraut de Borneil. Raimbaut sings: "I entangle, thoughtfully thoughtful, rare words, dark and highly coloured."

Bernart Marti was a poet who like Marcabru attacked False Love. If a woman gives herself to more than two men (husband and lover) she is guilty of harlotry. But he also has Bernart de Ventadour's sense of the physical being of the beloved: "She seems so slim, so plump and sleek, under her linen shift, that when I see her, by my faith, I don't at all envy king or count, so much I enhance my pleasure when I hold her naked under the figured veil." "If she granted me my desire – to embrace her clothed or naked – I'd ask for no other wealth. I'm of more worth than an emperor if I draw near to her lovely body under the cloak of vair." "Whether I'm sleeping or awake, when she takes off her cloak, I feel that my heart stays with her." "When in her dwelling I nakedly hold and caress her flanks, I know no emperor who may win more worth or own more of pure love." "In sweetly kissing me she makes me a gift of what ennobles me."

Still, love in the end is resolved into lying and lechery. That's no reason however to deprive oneself of its joys. Lovers in turn can deceive the lying ladies. What does it matter if he himself hears unpleasant rumours, even well-founded ones, as long as his lady calls him "friend and lord" when he enters the house? He, who has been "plucked like a gosling," also attacks the men of law who in a few phrases can "turn a dog into a bitch and turn sense upside-down." In yet another poem he looks back on the prosperous days when he wasn't obliged to follow another man. Now nobody bothers to notice him, or he is treated like a booby. Moral: if in youth you get some property, look well after it. "But I am like the whetstone which makes iron cut but cannot cut itself."

Another poet of the same period is Peire Rogier. His *vida* says that he was born of a noble Auvergine family and became a canon: a detail confirmed by a reference in Peire d'Auvergne. Then he turned jongleur. For long he stayed with Ermengarde of Narbonne, also with Raimbaut d'Orange, then he went to the Castilian court and to Toulouse under Raimon V, ending his days in the Premonstratensian Order of Grandmont. He must have started his career before 1160, and one of his Narbonne poems can be dated 1167–76. He is no exponent of *trobar clus* but aims at an easy witty style. He declares himself satisfied with the intimate joys gained by a carefully hidden love. Passion without hope still gains him more joys than sorrows. He uses dialogue to enliven his songs and represents courtly love with an urbane bantering spirit robbed of all intensities and perplexing depths. Thus he tells us how to succeed with a lovely lady and guarantees the efficacy of his method:

> A lover will not trust, if wise,
> witnesses who expose her ruses;
> he shouldn't credit his own eyes.
> Whatever she says that she's been doing,
> believe at once and don't be curious.
> I've known fine chaps who suffered much
> through pressing rights. They ended ruing
> the ways that made their ladies furious.

Thirty affronts, in short, I'd choose
rather than honour by which I'd lose
the one I love. My nature's such
I want no honour that's injurious.

Peire d'Auvergne in a poem in which he describes twelve Troubadours given to self-praise, "even for the most dreadful verses," begins with Peire Rogier:

First Piere Rogier I name,
first on him I lay the blame.
With loads of love-songs, up he's turning.
Better to carry, as his trick,
psalter in church or candlestick
on which a great big candle's burning.

At the end Rogier mentions himself as owning such a voice that he sings the high notes and the low, "and before the people gives himself much praise." So he's the master of the whole lot, "if only he'd make his words a bit clearer, for hardly a man grasps what they mean." He thus completes the joke by adding himself as a boaster, together with the criticism made of his songs.

We have not tried so far to set out any precise definition of Courtly Love. J. Bédier made a useful summary of points. "What is specific to it is the conception of love as a cult which is addressed to an excellent object and is founded, like Christian love, on an infinite disproportion between deserts and desire: as a necessary school of honour, which gives worth to the lover and transforms the *vilain* into the *courtois*: as a voluntary bondage which conceals an ennobling power and makes the dignity and beauty of passion consist in suffering." Not that this statement is complete. Thus it ignores the concept of joy which includes that of suffering. But it sets out some key-points. We see that in courtly love are elements from Christianity as well as from the feudal system; but the idea and its practice cannot be reduced to these components. The Troubadour gives the latter new meanings and orientations by including them in a new unity, by using them to provide emblems of the stages in the struggle inherent in human development, and in the quest for a fuller understanding of the life-process. Courtly love in a sense provides the scaffolding for a new consciousness of the structures of human experience; but it is the new consciousness, not the scaffolding, that ultimately matters – however necessary the scaffolding was in the historical circumstances.

VI

Troubadours and Jongleurs

TROUBADOURS and jongleurs were closely related. The jongleurs were the traditional minstrels and must have varied much in their musical and singing skills as well as in the sort of songs they chose. Some sought to please the lords and their courts; others were closer to the common folk and frequented markets and fairs, shading off into the many kind of entertainers with their various tricks, displays, recitations, acrobatics, plays, mimes, jugglings. Not that any hard and fast line could be drawn between the two types. On the one hand there was a tradition of entertainers and mimes going back to Roman times; on the other there were multifarious folkforms of song, dance, play, which must have fed and extended the tradition. From the seventh to the tenth centuries more and more church texts attacked all the performers. The Council of Clovesho in 747 distinguished *poetae, citharistae, musici, scurrae*: apparently poets who recited or sang their own works, minstrels who sang the works of others, clowns, tumblers, buffoons. John of Salisbury declared that patristic writers wanted jongleurs to be excommunicated as a result of their profession. They were repeatedly called the ministers of Satan, corrupters of youth, the scum of humanity; they had no hope of salvation and were classed with epileptics, magicians, whores.[1]

The conflict of the religious and the secular attitudes is brought out by what Adam of Bremen in the later eleventh century tells of Archbishop Adalbert of Hamburg.

He delighted, when reclining at meals, not so much in food and wine as in witty talk or in the tales of kings or in out-of-the-way doctrines of philosophers. When dining in private – though he was seldom alone, with no guests or royal legates – he whiled away the time with tales or fantasies, but always of sober language. Lutanists were rarely let in, though at times he felt them necessary for soothing his anxieties. But pantomime players, who tend to amuse most people by their obscene motions, he completely shut out from his presence.

One Christmas (about 1066) he and his clergy tried to quiet the loud drinking-songs that the Saxon Duke Magnus and his companions "howled in their cups" by joining in antiphonally with church chants. But he failed, "shut himself in his oratory, and wept bitterly."

The lords and warriors could sing of wine and war. We have noted how many could chant the *laisses* of the *chansons de geste*. Of the jongleur in the *Chanson de Williame* we hear: "In all France was no singer so good, in battle no bolder fighter was found, the *chansons de geste* he could sing." What seems to have happened at the court of Guilhem IX was the fraternising of some of the more accomplished nobles with the more talented of the jongleurs. As a result was born the Troubadour, who may be called the jongleur raised to a new level of composition and performance, setting before himself new and complex standards in the form and material of his songs. Many elements came together to produce this result; but without the jongleuresque tradition on the one side and novel factors brought into the tradition by noble amateurs of song as Guilhem on the other, we cannot imagine the poetry of the Troubadours.

Riquier in 1274, near the end of the line of Troubadours, wrote: "Jonglerie was invented by men of sense and was provided with some favour to divert and honour the nobility by the play of instruments." He is thinking of the kind of jongleurs that frequented Guilhem's court. As for the Troubadours, Raimbaut d'Orange remarked that "one has never seen the like, not in this century, nor in that which is past." He thus puts the origins back two or three generations. It is realised that the Troubadours represent something new. Yet in the same passage Raimbaut speaks of Guilhem as a jongleur. We see how closely the two types of singers were linked and merged, yet strongly differentiated.[2]

The name *trobador* came from a hypothetical Latin *tropator* (verb *tropare*), and meant discoverer. The Old French form was *trovere*, which survived as *trouvère*. What was found or discovered may well have been the musical form; but as music and words were inseparable, a verbal structure was still implied. The southern term for jongleur was *joglar* (Old French *jogler*), derived from *jocare* (by *joculare*); it implied someone who performed tours-de-force or tricks of skill, with poetic recitation a lesser part of his repertory. Still during the twelfth and thirteenth centuries the term jongleur went on being used for acrobat, juggler, master of beasts, buffon, mountebank, as well as for singer. Guiraut de Calanson about 1232 cites the jongleur Fader's

25. Anglo-Saxon Gleemen. (Cotton MS)

skills: he made dangerous leaps, juggled with apples and knives, imitated the songs of birds, played with marionettes, jumped through hoops. Song and music are not mentioned. Guiraut de Cabrera reproaches his jongleur Cabra for his ignorance of the poems he should know; Bertran de Paris lists the poems that the perfect jongleur ought to know. But the Troubadours here are probably merely aiming at strong effects or showing off their own knowledge.

A Troubadour might take one or more jongleurs round with him to sing his songs, though Troubadours also sang themselves. Troubadour and jongleur both used instruments to accompany their singing. Poets who couldn't sing in public must have been few, especially in the early days. Guilhem IX sang his own jests to his companions. Raimbaut d'Orange, a great lord, about 1160, was amused at being called a jongleur. Arnaut de Mareuil had his jongleur Pistoleta, but still sang his own verses, for a contemporary joked at the way that he always had tears in his eyes as he sang. Bertran de Born mentions his jongleur Papiol ten times, but also refers to two others, Guilhem and Mailoli. Cardenal's *vida* says that he "took round his jongleur who used to sing his *sirventes*." G. de Borneil "had with him two singers who sang his songs."

The importance of good singing is shown by the way in which Peire d'Auvergne and the Monk reproach Troubadours of their time, some of whom were nobles, for singing in a ridiculous way, as a beggar would, as a pilgrim, as an old woman carrying water. Peire says that Guillem de Ribas chants his poems with a raucous voice: "his way of song is such a curse, there's not a dog could do it worse, and he turns his eyes up like a silver image" of crucified Christ, showing the whites – while Grimoart Gausmar, though a knight, tries to pass himself off as a jongleur. The method of singing, the tone of voice, not the quality of the songs, is what is jeered at.

The Troubadours were careful to teach their jongleurs; and instructions or recommendations to them are common, especially with the earlier poets. But at least some Troubadours were afraid that if they trained their jongleurs too well, they would turn them into Troubadours on their own account. Raimon de Miraval remarks: "It's to my own hurt I teach and show to others what makes up my own glory. So well I've taught Guilhelmi now, he thinks he can direct himself, without me aiding him at all." At times the Troubadour assumes a superior and sarcastic tone in telling the jongleur of his duties. At the same time the Troubadours prided themselves on their special skills, as we have seen. Here are some more passages. Marcabru declares:

> Now my song grows, improving still.
> Marcabru weaves with subtle skill
> the theme and melody until
> you cannot take one word away.

Alegret says: 'I skim the words I mean to use. The good from out the bad I choose." Raimbaut d'Orange boasts that, since Adam ate his apple, no Troubadour has written a song "that's worth a turnip next to his." He challenges any contradictor to put on his armour.[3]

In some of the Biographies we meet the term *escola*. Guilhem IX, we saw, referred to his Workshop. G. de Borneil is said to have spent all winter learning at the *escola* and all summer going from court to court. But he had a library and considered himself a scholar; the phrase may only mean that he studied. It is hard to believe that there were any definite schools in which the rules were taught and the nature of the genres of song was fixed. But there may have been schools in a more informal and transitory way. The Troubadours who were so keen that the jongleurs should perform their songs with full understanding and expression must have had periods when they worked with the latter; and when groups of Troubadours or of jongleurs, or of Troubadours and jongleurs together, met at some important court with periods of leisure, it is hard to think that they did not discuss the problems of their art, even with all the rivalries, badinage, and boasts. G. de Borneil was doubtless not the only Troubadour who spent the winter in some sort of reconsideration of his art.

Eblo II of Ventadour seems the one lord who maintained a group of singers with a particular point of view, though we have none of his poems. Marcabru and Bernart de Ventadour mention him, and Cercamon dedicated to him a *planh* on the death of Guilhem X in 1137. Marcabru states: "Never shall I enlist myself in Lord Eblo's style (*troba*), for he holds a senseless opinion that's contrary to nature." It is clear that he looks on Eblo as an exponent of the False Love that he detests. Bernart states: "I'll never be a Troubadour (*chantaire*) or of Lord Eblo's school," *escola*. His lady is inexorable despite his poems and music, and he'll never succeed with her. It follows that Eblo's school of singers have lower aims and do get out of women what they want. They seem to be carrying on the lewder side of Guilhem IX with rejection of the courtly code.

Certainly in the later period Troubadours did come together in contests. An Italian novel, using Provençal material, declares that at the court of Puy the knights and ladies "composed fine songs and four experts [or judges, *approvatori*] were charged to put aside the best ones." We cannot take this evidence very seriously, but we do know of Puys. The earliest known to us was that where the Monk of Montaudon acted as judge; but the event was a tournament, with competing poets in a minor role. It seems to have gone on for years, as other Troubadours refer to it. It was held at Velay in the region under Robert I of Auvergne; he was a patron of Troubadours and may have founded it. Later on, as north France began imitating the Troubadours and the taste for their poems spread to the bourgeois. Puys were held in many towns: Arras, Amiens, Rouen, Abbeville, and so on. One occurred in London in the thirteenth century; its records survive in the Guildhall. Its main purpose was to hear songs and crown the best ones. At the Puys much attention was paid to verse-form. There was nothing like them in the early days of the Troubadours in the Midi, but there may have been informal gatherings of the kind suggested, which could have grown into Puys.

Later Troubadours, we know, agreed to take on pupils, no doubt for payment. Uc de Saint-Cire "had learned much of his knowledge from others and willingly transmitted it to others in turn." He does not seem exceptional.[4]

Thus in some way the gap between Troubadour and jongleur was

26. Musicians carved at Beverley Minster. (Minstrel's Pillar)

closed, but it was continually widened again. A jongleur might come from low down in the social strata. Bertran d'Alamanon sings: "You've been a footboy long, then raised to the *sirven*'s rank, then jongleur you have turned." (This passage has been cited to prove that the *sirventes* was at first a song composed by a *sirven*, a servant, in honour or profit of his master: but such an origin seems unlikely.) Generally the jongleurs are treated as shameless creatures. The Friar Minor Ermengau comments: "They give themselves up day and night to the vanities of the age, to all folly, all sin. As long as they're offered robes and deniers, they feed people on tricks suitable for deceiving fools. They are slanderous, badly taught, disloyal, liars, debauchees, drunkards, true pillars of taverns." He adds that they are lousy. A treatise on rhetoric compiled about 1275 links them with beggars, ribalds, lowborn whores. Churchmen kept a strong sense of a demoniac character in mimes and singers. Alcuin had said, "God does not want the demon to establish himself in a Christian house;" they must not be admitted. Minstrels were refused communion as Ministers of Satan. Those however who recited heroic tales were exempted from blame, and later there were companies of jongleurs enrolled in the service of the church, composing sacred canticles and mysteries. For long, as a retort to the attacks by churchmen, the mimes and singers had mocked their maligners. An episcopal *capitulum* of 789 lays down sharp punishment and exile for actors aping the garb of priests, monks, or nuns. King Edgar in 967 complained that the scandals of monastic life were often the subjects taken by mimes who sang and danced in the market-places.[5]

The generosity of Richard Lionheart was often contrasted with the meanness of Philippe Auguste of France; but the latter was acting on the principles laid down by the church. The *Gesta Francorum* tells how he saw the minstrels and jongleurs given great gifts and wearing gay costumes; and he swore that no minstrel would have clothes from his hands; rather he would clothe Christ or pure men. "For it was no other to give to minstrels" than "to offer to fiends." The *Penitential* of Thomas de Cobham, bishop of Salisbury, who died in 1313, shows the horror of the church for entertainers, but makes the distinction mentioned above:

There are three kind of actors, *histriones*. Some transform and transfigure their own bodies by base contortions and base gestures, or by basely denuding themselves, or by wearing horrible masks; and all such are to be damned unless they abandon their calling. Others, again, do no work, but commit criminal deeds, having no fixed abode, but haunting the courts of great men and backbiting the absent opprobriously and ignominiously in order to please others; for the Apostle bids us take no food with such men as this; and such men are called wandering buffoons, for they are good for nothing but gluttony and backbiting.

There is also a third kind of actors who have musical instruments for men's delight; and such are of two sorts. Some haunt public drinkings and wanton assemblies, where they sing divers songs to move men to wantonness; and such are to be damned like the rest. But there are others called jongleurs, *joculatores*, who sing the deeds of princes and the lives of saints, and solace men in their sickness or in their anguish, and do not those innumerable base deeds which are done by dancing-men and dancing-women and others who play in indecent figures, and make men see a certain show of phantasms by enchantment or in any other way.

These latter can be saved. A jongleur asked Pope Alexander (III?) what to do, and said he knew no other trade. So the pope permitted him to carry on as long as he dropped "the base and wanton practices." To give goods to buffoons or jesters was to commit a mortal sin. Minstrels in tales are shown as living wildly and recklessly. A tale of the thirteenth century (doubtless going much further back) tells of a minstrel of Sens, "a man of very lowly estate, whose clothes were seldom without patches. I don't know what his name was. Anyway, he often lost all he had at dice. He often had to pawn his harp or his boots or his tunic, so that when the cold winds blew he had nothing to wear but his shirt. Don't think I exaggerate. He often went barefoot . . . The tavern was his favourite haunt, the tavern and the brothel. He was the pillar of both establishments . . . He would have liked every day to be a holiday." The devil caught his soul as he died and he was put in charge of the fire under the cauldron in hell. One day the devils went on a world-raid and he was told to look after hell itself. St Peter, with long beard and well-combed whiskers, came along, lured him into dicing, and won all the souls. On their return the devils beat him and threw him out. He escaped to paradise. "Now cheer up, all you minstrels, rogues, lechers, gamblers, for the fellow who lost those souls at dice has set you all free." The despised minstrel becomes the saviour of the down-and-out.

In fact the Troubadour Gaucelm Faidit lost all his property and became a jongleur. He was so avid for food that he grew fat beyond measure. Guilhem Figueira "was not the man to frequent barons and respectable folk, but he was much at home with ribalds, whores, and tavern-haunters." Guilhem Magret could never put harness on (own a knight's equipment), "for all that he gained he dishonourably lost in play or drinking." A series of *coblas* show us a troop of jongleurs, some of whom were well known poets, drunkenly slanging one another and exchanging blows. Things are thrown about, dry bread blackens the eye of one man, a cream-cheese bursts on the head of another, a carafe would have split the head of a fourth but for his thick hair. Augier has his jaw cut by a sword and almost loses an eye. Péguilhan (who himself became the subject of similar jeers) asks: "If this spendthrift Figueira had perished through one blow or another, to whom would he have left his brilliant qualities?" Bertran d'Aurel replied by giving a list of his vices and naming the comrades who seem most worthy of receiving the gift. In dialogues sung by two jongleurs wounding insults are exchanged; Guillem Rainol abuses Magret; Taurel and Falconet do the same at the Montferrat court.

> "The woman you dote on – she's a tart, wellknown:
> you're the best-suited couple on the earth."
> "And you, beneath Cremona's walls, have shown,
> Taurel, precisely what your lance is worth."
> "The marquis' gifts won't heavily weight your bag.
> Go trotting gaily off upon your nag."
> "To trust your patron's liberal ways be loth.
> We lodge under the same poor signboard, both."

B. de Rovenac recalls to a knight, fallen to the level of jongleur, the mishaps of which, through folly or vice, he has been the victim. Albert Malespina reminds Raimbaut de Vaqueiras of a recent misadventure, then describes the time when, as a wretched jongleur, he rambled on foot along the roads of Lombardy looking for any chance-quarters.

Raimbaut in turn reproaches Albert for his betrayals and lists the lands he has lost through folly or cowardice. Ricaut de Tarascon alleges grave wrongs and pretends to challenge Gui de Cavaillon to single combat. The great lord replies with buffooneries that express his scorn for such an unworthy opponent. Bertran de Gourdon and Peire Raimon exchange insults, then turn to hyperbolic compliments, then fall to insults again. They appeal to personal experience as to whether the trade of robber or that of jongleur is more ignoble or less uncomfortable.[6]

Much of the abuse is mere word-play used to amuse the listeners and show the singer's ingenuity; but all the same there are elements of reality showing all too clearly through the formulas. We meet mock-letters of recommendation or introduction; genuine ones were at times carried by jongleurs. They have been called, probably incorrectly, *sirventes joglarescs*. Under pretence of showing off the talents of his client, the Troubadour makes fun of him. Thus Bertran de Born recommended Folheta:

> Your voice is raucous and crude. Your skin
> dark as that of a Saracen.
> Only pointless tales you can spin ...
> I'll do what you want most thoroughly
> as long as you keep away from me.

G. de Puycibot described Gasc:

> Jongleur, you ugly vicious fool,
> serf of each vice, misshapen too,
> stranger to virtues, yet you ask
> a *sirventes*. Well, I'll do the task
> and make it abhorrent. Then it's true
> the thing's appropriate for you.

Cardailhac was one-handed; indeed the jongleur was often a cripple of some kind. Here we find recommendations by G. de Borneil and the Dauphin d'Auvergne made up of rambling jests that deal with the matters the jongleur is not to undertake. The insults were not malicious; they were merely meant to raise a laugh. We can imagine the effect on the listeners of a jongleur announcing that he had a letter of introduction from some famous Troubadour, and then reciting a farrago of indignities such as the above poems. Bertran de Born says that the jongleur's device was: "Better shame and profit than honour and loss." Not easily discountenanced, a jongleur might attack a court

27. Reception of the Minstrel. (Wright 366)

where he had had a bad reception, as did Manfredi Lancia in a *sirventes* on Matfré Lanza:

Unpleasant his welcome, harsh his voice. That's how he lives.
Not the least touch of grace in the way he eats or drinks or gives.

In the later years there were large numbers of singers using the Troubadour tradition. Péguilhan, comfortable at the court of the Malespina, depicts them descending on the place and "devouring bone and skin." They cry: "I'm a jongleur, give me something!" And he comments: "We're done-for if God doesn't bring order into things." Garin le Brun advises young women in thirteenth-century Italy: "Welcome gladly jongleurs and poets who converse of love and sing *sons* and *lais* . . . Give them gifts so that they'll delight in speaking well of you. At least show a friendly face, and then, even if you don't give anything, they'll make your name known afar, even in places that you know nothing of."[7]

Yet, with all the differentiation of jongleurs from Troubadours, the two terms are often confused. The same person is described by both of them. Peire d'Auvergne in his satire begins "I'll sing about those

Troubadours who make their songs in many *colors*." But Briva the Limousin he calls a jongleur, the most beggarly man between Benevento and here, with the looks of a sick pilgrim when he sings. Grimoart Gausmar is "a knight who tries to pass himself off as a jongleur" – so "God damn anyone giving him clothes of motley and green," since, when his costume is seen, there are hundreds who'll want to turn jongleurs. And Bernart de Sayssac is described as if he were a poor jongleur. "He goes round begging little gifts. I haven't thought him worth a bit of mud since he begged En Bertran de Cardalhac for an old cloak stinking of sweat." The line between a weak Troubadour and a capable jongleur was clearly thin. Hosts, when drawn into an exchange with Troubadours of *coblas*, made no effort to hide their low opinion of them, and the Troubadours replied as rudely. The marquis Lancia tells Vidal that he looks on him as the most cowardly and foolish man he has ever met, and hopes that he'll be treated as he deserves. The count of Rodez tells Uc de Saint-Cire that he recognises him as a spy, that he won't give him the equivalent of a dice-throw, and that he'd like to see him off to Spain or the Devil. Yet the very fact that such insults were hurled by both patron and singer shows a certain equality and fellowship. At times the exchange ends amicably. Nobles like Raimbaut d'Orange or Alfonso of Aragon treat G. de Borneil with respect, as if on an equal footing. Even humbly-born Troubadours could rise high. We have noted the career of Bernart de Ventadour. Raimbaut de Vacqueiras and Sordello were sons of poor knights; Elias de Barhols was son of a merchant, come to the court of Provence with veille on his back, but in time he was the accepted poet of two countesses. Peire Bremon, called *Ricas Novas* (Fine Stories or Joyous Tales), was probably in the service of Alamanon or Sordello; three of his *sirventes* abuse Sordello and he wrote a sort of parody of Alamanon's lament for that poet.

In later years we find a disinclination to carry on the rather nomadic life of so many of the earlier Troubadours. As the tradition lost its vitality in the thirteenth century after the Albigensian crusade had destroyed the basis on which it had thriven, there was a tendency to stress the literary aspects of the Troubadour and to separate him as much as possible from the performing jongleur. The very term jongleur became an insult. Bremon cast it in Sordello's face when he wanted to hurt him. Finally there came the appeal by G. Riquier to Alfonso of Castile in 1274 for a precise ruling as to the usage of terms. In a poem of 860 lines he declared that in a properly organised society each class must have its defined office with a name describing it. There were six classes: clerics, knights, bourgeois, merchants (lower than bourgeois proper), artisans, villeins or peasants. Each class had sub-divisions apart from the bourgeois. Thus, clerics included cardinals, bishops, abbots, priests, and so on; merchants included drapers, mercers. Then, turning to his own group of singers (which he does not fit into any of the six classes), he argued that it was a scandal for the single name of jongleur to cover both the vile mountebanks, *baladins*, who spent in taverns the money gained by scraping on some instrument in public places or in showing animals, and the Troubadours who had received the gift of poetry from heaven. Among these there were many kinds. Some rhymed *coblas*, *dansas*, *servientes* "without any salt," while others, endowed "with sovereign knowledge," wrote "verses of authority," which would survive them, which could inspire virtue and immortalise fine actions. As for himself, if he must go on being dishonoured by the name of jongleur, he would prefer to renounce his work and gain his livelihood some other way.

A *declaracio* was put out in the king's name (though Alfonso was in France) with the date July 1275; the style is close to that of Riquier himself. After praising Riquier, setting out some historical views, and suggesting some etymologies, the document observes that Spain does not suffer from the described ills; for there four categories of performers are found. *Bufos*, as in Lombardy, is used for those exhibiting animals and playing instruments in public places; *joglars*, for those whose better manners permit them to appear at courts, recite tales, or sing songs composed by others; *trobadors*, for those who own the art of composing *coblas*, *baladas*, and so on; *doctors de trobar* for those who write songs and verses of authority, who can reveal the good way in both the temporal and the spiritual order, illuminate obscure passages in their own works, and rise finally to the *sobiran trobar*. These last deserve the title of *doctor* since they "indoctrinate the ignorant."

But from the early fourteenth century the art of the Troubadour was to die out in the Midi, and the question of terms was irrelevant. Much verse was indeed written in the fourteenth and fifteenth centuries in *Langue d'Oc*, but it was the work of non-professionals working in other disciplines: for instance, the dull products of the first school of Toulouse (about 1305–40) and the pieces crowned from 1324 by the Consistory of the Gay Science.

But here we are anticipating events. We must return to the story of the Troubadours while their tradition was still very much alive.[8]

VII

Raimbaut d'Orange
and
Bertran de Born

RAIMBAUT D'ORANGE was lord of Orange and Courthezon
(Vaucluze) and a patchwork of lesser holdings in Languedoc and Provence. We have thirty-nine of his poems, all about love, dated
1162–73. He is the first known Troubadour from Provence, though the
poets had for some time been taking that region into their circuits.
Many documents deal with him, but they are wills, records of acts of
homage, and so on, and tell us little about him personally. While still a
minor, he was left an orphan under the protection of the lords of Baux
and Marseille (vassals respectively of the courts of Toulouse and
Barcelona). He seems to have been much in need of ready cash and to
have preferred the pleasures of court-life to political activity and war.
Though lacking Guilhem IX's broad energies, he liked to share his
verses with "companions" treated as equals. His death in 1173 was
perhaps caused by the epidemic overtaking Europe that year with
people "coughing out their souls."[1]

   He tried to get variety into his treatment of love by using technical
inventiveness and humour, by ringing changes on the themes of separation and instability, of troubles through the zealous or the *losengiers*.
He juggled with words and walked the tightrope of rhyme.

> For you from three ladies I turned away.
> Paragons, but for you, were they.
> Now singing I go on my way
> and with such courtly follies I stray:
> "O, he's a jongleur," they all say.

Probably it was of him that Peire d'Auvergne wrote:

> Ninth comes En Raimbaut. He
> puffs his own poetry,
> but of his rhymes I don't like any;
> No warmth or cheer they evoke.
> He's like those piping folk
> who sidle up and beg a penny.

He often breaks the accepted structure of the *canzo*, using a mixture of verse and prose, or letting go in a flow of eloquence that looks to the medieval Latin epistle. Or he uses the motifs of courtly love as the starting-point for elaborate but crude jests. Thus he mocks at the orthodox purity of the distant lover as being the result of castration, of the loss of "those objects which a man holds most precious." But often his ingenuity functions at a lower level. He works afresh over stale material, using complicated stanzas or rare rhymes, or he plays about with series of related imagery or with word-games. He thus represents strongly the search for novelty and experiment at all costs: the phase in which many of the poets seek originality without driving force. From this phase there comes, no doubt via Latin literary theory, the idea of three levels of style: the closed or difficult, *clus*; the rich or ornate, *ric*; the clear, light or easy, *leu*. At his best Raimbaut feels that the play of art, the experimentation with form, is itself an adventure into new modes of thought and feeling. To keep his spirits up he indulges in the usual brag, claiming that he excels in both *trobar clus* and *trobar leu*.

> I'll teach you suitors to be wise
> and win the women with your praises.
> Who does all things that I advise
> will gain each girl for whom he tries,
> at once. And may he go to blazes,
> or hang, who thinks he better knows.
> But cheers for him who'll still repeat
> my trusty system of deceit.
>
> O would you gain a woman-prize?
> O would you gain the pretty pieces?
> Put menaces in your replies
> when they're discourteous. No sighs,
> and if their impudence increases,
> adroitly punch them on the nose.
> Pride against pride! Down to your feet
> bring them. An easy life you'll meet.

28. The Infantes of Carrion beat their newly-married wives. (Cronica del Cid, 1498)

There's one more way to get a rise
and gain the girls with the best faces.
Brag loudly and the others despise.
Sing rotten songs with shameless eyes.
Make all the faults appear as graces,
and praise the weak point that each shows.
Make sure the house that's your retreat
looks like no church or churchman's seat.

You'll do well with this scheme of lies.
But me a different method pleases.
All love whatever my heart denies.
No more than sisters may girls devise
a way that gets me down and teases.
Humble and true, rejecting blows,
my tenderness will be complete.
Women most gently I'll entreat.

But you, be sure, do otherwise.
Folly's the path my loving traces . . .

In a poem breaking out into prose he begins by saying that he doesn't know if he should call it *vers*, *estribot*, or *sirventes*, so he'll claim "that no one ever saw the like of it made by any man or woman in our century or in the one before it."

> You tax me as a madman in vain.
> From what I've started I can't refrain.
> Don't blame me, for I must explain:
> A penny is more than the round skies.
> All that they cover I despise
> except what's lying here under my eyes,

and I'll tell you the reason: if after I started this thing off I failed in it, you'd take me for a fool: for I much prefer six deniers in my hand than a thousand suns up there in the heavens.

And he ends:

> My Don't-know-what I finish here.
> That name is right, I hold it dear,
> and for my choice the reason's clear.
> No man's made such a thing before.
> Let those who like the words they hear
> learn and recite them all once more,

and if anyone asks them who made it up, they can say: a man who can do anything, and do it well at that, when that's his wish.

He is insisting on the value of the unique moment, the unique form that embodies it. He uses an otherwise unknown folk-theme to describe the odd uses to be made of the odd product. "Lady, you can do as you please with it, as Dame Ayma did with the shoulder-bone that she stuck wherever she thought fit."

In *Ar resplan* he uses a complicated system of rare rhymes, grammatical rhymes, and so on, to reflect the extremely complicated movement of his thought. The key word is *enversa*; everything is inverted, turned upside-down, paradoxical. Winter bursts into spring, thunder becomes a song; the bough is both green with renewed life and a chastising switch. The same words recur as rhymes, but with changing meanings.

> Now radiant gleams the flower inverted
> along the cutting crags, on hills.
> What flower? It's snow and ice and frost
> that stings the flesh and hurts and cuts.
> Thus, perished calls, cries, birdsongs, whistles
> I see mid leaves and boughs and switches;
> But green and merry I'm kept by joy
> while withered I see the wretched and base.

But all this I have so inverted
like pleasant plains appear the hills
and blossoming seems to me the frost,
and warmth across the coldness cuts.
Thunders for me are songs and whistles,
and decked with leaves seem all the switches.
Securely I'm enclosed with joy.
Nothing I see for me is base –

Save for a stupid people inverted
as if bred up upon the hills,
who do me service worse than frost;
for with his tongue each of them cuts,
mutters lowly and utters whistles.
No use are sticks or threats or switches;
rather they feel convinced by joy
in acts which others brand as base.

To hold you in my kiss inverted
I fail, though not by plains or hills
thwarted, and not by ice and frost :
By lack of power from you I am cut,
lady, for whom I sing and whistle :
Your lovely eyes I feel as switches
which chasten me with so much joy
that my desires don't dare be base.

I would have gone like a thing inverted
questing in valleys, crags, and hills,
wincing like someone whom the frost
torments and tears and bitterly cuts :
I wasn't put down by song or whistle
more than unruly clerics by switches;
and now, praise God, I'm at home with joy
despite the slanderers false and base.

May then my verse – since I invert it
so it's not hindered by woods or hills –
find out a place where there's no frost,
where cold has lost its power to cut.
To *midons* sing it, sing and whistle,
he who can sing it nobly, in joy,
for the song won't suit a voice that's base.

Sweet lady, may love unite us, and joy,
despite the sundering thrust of the base.
Jongleur, I feel the less of joy
since I can't see you. So you seem base.

The first four lines of each stanza end with grammatical variations of *enversa, tertres, conglapis, trenca*; then come *siscles* and *giscles*, and *joys* and *croys* – words that rhyme but express opposites: whistles and switches, joys and baseness. Raimbaut is saying that everything in the world is topsyturvy, with values falsified, perverted, inverted – what is base being accepted as good. He wants to turn things round the other way – "to hold you in my kiss inverted" – but he fails, not because of the world of nature, but because the ruling perversity among men is too strong. Yet he still hopes that through the power of joy he will achieve his aims and find fulfilment in his love: which in turn implies harmony with nature, the frost effectively transformed to blossoms. Such a poem may indeed be said *entrebascar lis motz*; the upside-down interlacing of the words reflects the theme of conflicting values. To the world the poet is *enversa*; the world is *enversa* to him.

On fully exploring this poem we then find that it is as revolutionary in its effects as Guilhem's *Enigma*. It does not merely state that the world is not what it seems; it defines this falsity, this gap between existence and people's ideas of it, in the form and imagery of the poem itself. It thus simultaneously expresses the false consciousness which is generally accepted as reflecting the truth of things, and the inversion of this inversion, which represents the struggle to realise the true nature of human process, of which love is the apex. This struggle always involves the relation of human beings both to one another and to nature. The last stanza expresses the poet's quest for the resolution of the conflict, which is possible only for the noble and joyous singer, the man who has fully dedicated his life to love and who will follow out the way of love despite all obstructions and diversions. Guilhem's *Enigma* and this poem by Raimbaut d'Orange lift us to a level of consciousness which cannot be paralleled in any previous works. For they present with the utmost sharpness the problems of following out truthfully the conflicts and contradictions of experience without losing faith in the resolution through love – a resolution that involves a new depth of union with nature. They thus not only found Troubadour poetry in its fullness, and imply all the poems directly derived from the Troubadour tradition, which carries on with changes and adaptations to the sixteenth century and later; they in effect stand out as representing crucial moments in creating the new European consciousness, the problems of which are still with us, urgently, today.

The serious side of *trobar clus* then represented the awareness of the problems posited by Guilhem in a wider sphere of reference. The weaker side revealed the mere playing about with paradox for its own sake. *Entrebascar* was justified when the poet sought to depict the "inverted" state of things in the world and the vision that set them right-sides-up again: that is, asserted a true humanity in face of the upside-down values and emotions of the false consciousness. We may note Raimbaut uses the feudal term *midons* (which Guilhem IX also used); the lady is his lord, a male term. In Portuguese courtly love, the lady was addressed as *senhor*, not *senhora*.

In *Una chansoneta fera* he defines life as precariously set on a fine balance that sways one way and another. "If there's delay, remember that a man can't save himself from cobwebs in the heart. My life's so delicately balanced, I'm full of joy, then I despair and think: I've won her to my loss."

> A little song now with good will
> I'd make, a simple thing to say;
> but I'm afraid it brings my death.
> That the sense is well hid, I'll see.
> She'll understand it all with ease
> though built upon this sort of rhyme.
> In incoherences revealed,
> the things I'm feeling will be heard ...

"By the falling light of the stars, no other woman's beauty may rival hers."

> When I lie down and eve is still,
> Lady, all night there, and all day,
> I muse on service with each breath.
> Though beaten, with torn hair, I lay
> I'd think of you yet all the time.
> My heart would leap, my heart be filled
> with love in rapture undeterred ...
>
> My heart's uplifted by this faith.
> Already I stand here, gazing still
> to where I once beheld her face.
> God, pray defend me so from death,
> and Lady, grant me life until
> I hold you close, without chemise.

He seeks a complete concentration of desire, as if it will save him from time and death; but such a concentration cuts him off from the world, from the woman herself, and he is swung back into the thing he fears, into the incoherences of time, where he is at the mercy of pain and loss. Somehow, he hopes, the inturned trance of devotion and the scattering moment of the embrace can be harmonised.

His existential sense of the moment in which the whole breadth and depth of his conflicts and aspirations are grasped appears again in *Ara.m so del tot*. He is so completely absorbed that his memory is almost gone, he has forgotten both joy and sorrow alike. "He owns so great a treasure," he feels nothing except that "God is ruling him." He could have gained his beloved only if God had set her in his way and put a good heart in her. He carefully hides her identity, despite the urge to speak her name. If someone mentions her, he feels that he is in Paradise; even to hear the name of the castle where she lies is a very great grace. Before he became her thrall, he was unaware that he was worth anything; now, looking at her ring or kissing it, he fears nothing. "If a man holds this to be foolishness, he knows nothing of love and how it lives." In another poem he says that slanders cannot take away the love that God brought about "with great power" when he chose him, the love that "voids all evil" from the lovers and does not end with old age. The idea of the length of time is replaced by that of fullness, of a concentrated realisation that brings all the moments of time into a single moment: "Through the utterance of one syllable all that pertains to love will be recognised at one and the same moment."

God here appears as the fate of love, its innermost force and not something external. "God has paid me back to my pleasure. He was well able to tell honey from wax, tell them apart and decided which was better, on the day he had her preferred for me." To a friend of his lady, whom he calls Joglar, he writes, "I desire your success, and God desires it a thousand times as much." For God is that in him which wants the total self-dedication to love. "Lady, you hold my heart captive, so sweet my bitterness. God help me. *In nomine patris et filii et spiritus sancti*. Lady, what will this be?" And so he feels that he has on his side all the powers attributed to God; even the miracles can be worked on his behalf: "May God if he please make me attain to joy in what I ask of her, as quickly as he made wine from water." More, since his lady shares his love, she too in her way is God. He says that he often laughs; his heart laughs even when he's asleep; and *Midons* sends her laughter on him with such sweetness that it seems God's laughter

29. Lovers and Flowers. (Benedictbeuern MS)

sounding. "So her laughter keeps me more in joy than if four hundred angels, who were to make me joy, laughed for my sake."

Again, he says that he doesn't sing for money, but for the joy he feels when anyone repeats a poem of his about her. "Then I think I'm possessing God or her of whom I wish to stand in awe." But having put her so high, he feels that God is his rival lover. Only with a great effort does God hold himself back from taking her up to himself with a kiss. "But he doesn't want to take her from me or do wrong." So Raimbaut needs to hide the love which has perfected him, or other ladies will try to get him in their spell; he pretends that he is scared. Having thus become God's rival, he is in a sense the Devil, the Prince of the Earth. Thinking of Satan who tempted Christ in the desert, he makes God his own offer. "May God who fasted forty days, through whom my world became converted, grant me as gift or loan just her alone, not one thing more. In the balance I leave him the world and a thousand times more in return for her who takes all falsity from me." Note that he calls the world "mine," not "yours or ours." He is bargaining with God as the principle of Otherness so as to stop him from intruding and breaking up the perfect balance of union between him and the lady. Note too that the lady represents the truth, the vision that sees reality in its fullness and that has enabled him to grasp the world in its complex state as *enversa*. The same point comes up in a poem where he calls on God who "made earth and water, hot and cold, clergy and laity," to cast down all those whom his lady doesn't protect; for he loves with a "true will" while they use the veil of false words to harm and destroy lovers. He as lover stands for the activity that tears down the veil and reveals reality.

In one sense then the lady is mother and wife of God. He swears "by my head on which her chrism is set." He twice uses the tale of the penitent thief in praying for his lady's grace and pardon. But she is Natura as well as Mary. "God kept heaven and the firmament for himself companionless. That is a sure statement; for he has sweetly left *Midons* so that she holds sovereignity, *signoriu*, on all sides, for everyone must serve her and obey her desires. Each man who sees her, as he goes, *s'enten* into her." He intends himself into her, sets in her his *intentio*, his aim. *Al partir* suggests that the vision is at the moment of death; each man then realises, through her, what has been the humanly guiding principle in his life.

We shall see later that the Troubadours commonly used a sort of parody, blasphemous in its implications, of many aspects of religion. The supreme example of this tendency is to be found in Raimbaut. Superficially one might claim that the poet is using the imagery of sensuous love to express a union with the divine, as one finds in the mystics; but the exact opposite is the fact. He uses imagery of divine union to express the deepest aspects of human love; only some such idiom can do justice, he feels, to the meanings that he is discovering in that love. Here indeed precisely lies the revolutionary element in Troubadour poetry, the way in which it seeks to take over all the aspects of philosophy and theology which can be reoriented from metaphysics and abstraction into the clarification of the nature of human experience on earth. So what the lovers learn in their lonely rapture floods out to illuminate all aspects of the life-process. Raimbaut says that he loves through his lady all other women as long as the world lasts. For they are in her *figura*, "and that's the only reason why I'm their lover." Her *figura* is herself in her full human existence and all that she thus symbolically represents as Mary and Natura.

So Raimbaut vindicates the claim he makes, in the midst of ironic self-praise, that he has a secret of "true knowledge," which he can hand on to men. In his work the Troubadour quest reaches its rich climax, and in his struggle to grasp and define the secret, the method of *trobar clus* is triumphantly worked out. Though he petulantly cries, "Since easy verses now cast their spell, I'll do my best there to excel," his heart is in that method. We have a *tenson* in which he and Giraut de Borneil exchange views.

"Giraut, I'd like to know why you go running down the Closed Style, and what your reasons are. Explain your point, if you hold so highly what is common to all. In those terms all men will be equal."

"My lord Sir Lignaura, I don't complain at each man writing the way that pleases him. But it's my opinion that a man is liked more and held in higher esteem if he expresses himself plainly and simply. Don't misunderstand me."

"Giraut, I don't want my own writing to fall into such a muddle. Let the good praise it, whether they're humble or mighty. Fools will never praise it, for they don't recognise, and aren't concerned about, what is most valuable and worthy."

"Lignaura, if for that reason I can't get to sleep and I turn my pleasure into hard work, it appears that I'm scared of general acclamation. Why do you write if it makes you unhappy that everybody at once knows your song? That's the only way to tell if a song succeeds."

"Giraut, as long as I put together what's best, express it straightaway, and bring it out, I don't mind if it doesn't spread far and wide. A very cheap thing was never a dainty morsel. That's why we value gold above salt, and it's no different with a song."

"Lignaura, the noble and disputacious lover overflows with good counsel. Yet if my piping melody makes me feel any more strain, I'm ready to let some croaker make a mess of it and sing it badly. I consider that sort of trouble doesn't suit a man of property."

"Giraut, by Sky and Sun and the Resplendent Light, I don't know what we're arguing about, nor who it was that bore me, I'm so disturbed. I concentrate so much on a fine and natural joy. When I think of anything else, it doesn't spring from the heart."

"Lignaura, she whom I woo turns the red side of the shield to me, so that

I want to cry out: God save me! Through foolish and arrogant thoughts I've been plunged into disloyal doubt. Have I forgotten how she ennobled me?"

"I'm sorry, by St Martial, that you're leaving before Christmas."

"I'm going to a royal court, a rich and mighty one."

Giraut de Borneil was another humbly-born Troubadour. His *vida* tells us:

He was born in Limousin, in the land of Excedeuil [Dordogne] . . . He had no fortune, but he was wise, instructed, and with natural judgment . . . And he was a better poet than those who came before or after him. That is why he was called the Master of the Troubadours, and continues to pass for such among people who understand poetry and love. He was much honoured by men of merit and knowledge, and by ladies who understood the magistral words of his songs. And this is how he lived. All winter he gave himself up to work and study, and all summer he went round the courts with two jongleurs who sang his songs. He never married. All his gains he gave to his poor parents and to the church of the hamlet where he was born, and which was and still is called Saint Gervais.

He loved a lady of Gascony, Hamanda d'Estanc. For long he wooed her, and the lady, with fine words, marks of honour, and good promises, defended herself courteously from him. Never did she accord him a favour or make him a gift, except for a glove of hers. And then he lost this glove, from which came to him many evils. For when the lady knew that he had lost it, she showed a great wrath, saying that he had not taken care of it and that she would give him nothing else or ever show him any love . . .

He went overseas with king Richard and the viscount of Limoges, named Adhémar, and he was at the siege of Acre . . . Richard's death and the loss of his lady caused him so much grief that for a time he gave up songs, poetry, and society.

He had just left the good king Alfonso of Castile, who had given him a superb grey palfrey and many other gifts, and all the lords of the court also made him large gifts . . . But the king of Navarre, getting news of his fortune, had him rifled when he passed through his domains. All the money was stolen and the king himself took the grey palfrey.[2]

We hear also that Gui de Limoges, in the course of pillaging Excedeuil, took all the poet's books and equipage. His career covered the years 1138–99. He visited all the great courts of France and north Spain, but his main patron seems to have been Adhémar, with whom he went on the crusade in 1189. His latest poem that he can date is a *planh* for the viscount. Few Troubadours have left more than the seventy-six poems attributed to him, of which some forty are love-songs. His fame won him enemies, and Peire d'Auvergne describes him as a thin slight man:

> Giraut de Borneil seems to me
> a goatskin drying in the sun.
> His song is thin, all sigh and moan,
> as that of a water-carrying crone.
> If he glanced in a mirror, then
> less than nothing would he see.

He is often a poet of *trobar clus*; but he likes to assert that he avoids extremes and prefers a mixture of *ric* and *leu*, the rich and easy styles. He carried this phase of the Troubadour lyric to its climax. He was most innovatory in versification, as we find with masters of *trobar ric*, and these rhythmical virtuosities we can link with changes in musical form. As advocate of *trobar leu* he claims: "I want to make a song that my young son can understand . . . If I've ever made obscure and condensed stanzas, see, all you who hear my language, if I don't make them quite transparent." But he also defends a difficult style. To belittlers he replies: "God, you never saw a Troubadour left more indifferent by these mockeries. To base my song better, I go on a quest and I lead back, as by a bridle, fine words, well-loaded words, full of a strange and natural sense that not everyone knows how to unveil. Little does it matter that these beggars [poor in spirit], stript of value and worth, banter me; for it's they who lack power of thought." And he takes back his remark about writing so that a small boy could follow: "Certain people, who don't know much of the matter, reproach me for not making my thought clear enough for a child to understand. . . . There was a time when I took more pleasure, as I was then allowed, in these broken stanzas, these words twisting back on themselves, subtle, tightly welded, which nowadays are scarcely understood. . . . My opinion is that the best song is that which isn't understood at first hearing."

But he returns to the defence of clarity. "I find it hard to know how to start off a poem I want to make light and easy, though I've been brooding on it since yesterday: how to compose so that everyone understands it, and it's no trouble to sing. For I'm doing it purely for pleasure. I could easily make it more difficult, but a song's virtue isn't complete unless we all share in it. No matter who grumbles, I'm happy when I hear my little song sung in contention, rough or clear, and someone sings it on the way to the public fountain. "He adds, "I think there's as much good sense in keeping to the point [reason, *razo*] as in *entrebeschar*." So he decides that he wants to make a song that's light and *vil* (cheap, costing nothing), "to send to the Dauphin in Auvergne, and if it strikes Eblo on the way, let it make him understand that the difficulty lies not in being obscure but in being clear." However, with all his claims to clarity, a scribe dealing with his work in the next century could write: "A man would indeed have a subtle spirit who could understand it from one end to the other."

In the poem *A penas* in which he says that he scarcely knows how to start off an easy poem, he turns in the last three stanzas to the problem of speaking out or staying silent in fear before his lady. The veering ideas as to hidden or open style are linked with the question of declared or secret desires. He wants to speak out and praise the lady's beauty, "Then a terror falls upon me, making me change my mind and slacken in my boldness."

At the same time, the use of short lines and a rapid run of rhymes gives an effect of increased action, of quickened drama:

> "Ah how I die." "Friend tell me why."
> "Betrayed am I."
> "But in what way?"
> "I set my thoughts on her one day,
> with such fine grace she welcomed me."
> "That's why your heart's in misery?"
> "It's so."
> "Your heart's then sunken in deep woe?"
> "Worse still, I fear."
> "Are you to death so near?"
> "Nearer than you could guess."
> "But why then yield to death in your distress?"

He thus describes his lady:

> Her body is so quick and gay,
> fulfilled with many a lovely hue,
> no flower yet more freshly grew,
> no rose or any other spray.
> Bordeaux, I say,
> never had merrier lord than me
> if I were but allowed to be
> her liegeman of delight.

> May I be called a Bedlamite,
> if ever I betrayed
> the least small secret that she made
> with me, in trust, apart.
> O wrath would rouse her noble heart!

The insistent hurry of rhymes and rhythm can be allied with imagery of action:

> When barons, harrying, assail
> a castle with their fiercest powers,
> siege-engines topple all the towers,
> there's catapult and mangonel,
> the noises swell,
> so mad the onslaught all the while
> that there's no use in craft or guile,
> so terrible rise the cries of pain
> from those within, again, again,
> there's need for mercy, you'll agree,
> for men who moan so piteously –
> good noble lady, here of you
> mercy I humbly sue.

There is an *alba* or dawnsong by Giraut, which we shall consider when we come to that genre. He also wrote moral *sirventes*, contrasting the present with the good old days. Though such work was weak beside the diatribes of Marcabru or the Monk, it impressed Dante, who in his *De vulgari eloquentia* took Giraut as the model poet of moral rectitude.

The one Troubadour who was a direct exponent of feudal values was Bertran de Born. His *vida* says that he was "born lord of a castle called Hautefort, in the bishopric of Perigord. Always he was at war with his neighbours and with the count of Perigord as long as he was count of Poitou. He was a good knight, a good warrior, a good Troubadour, and shrewd and gallant. And he was the guest, whenever he wished, of the king of England and his son." But he always wanted to embroil them in war, "and he always wanted the king of France and the king of England to be at war with one another. . . . If they had the least truce, he strove and did all in his power to unmake the peace." Certainly he liked to see the great lords at war, but his poems played no major role in fanning the flames. However, Dante took at their face-value Bertran's own claims and the legend that they stimulated, and put him in hell in the eighth circle.[3]

30. Geoffrey Plantagenet. (Enamel at Le Mans, c. 1151)

Born in the early 1140s, a minor noble, he had two brothers, and shared with the elder of them, Constantin, his castle, but after a quarrel drove him out. Twice married, he had two children by 1192. Later he became a monk at Dalou and died before 1215. He was not a professional Troubadour, but used his powers as a poet to win the favour of leading lords, especially the Plantagenet princes: Henry the Young King (crowned in his father's life-time), Richard count of Poitou, duke of Aquitaine, and (from 1189) king of England, and Geoffrey count of Brittany. He seems to have begun composing late, for none of his forty works dates from before 1180, and many belong to the years 1181–95. He was close enough to the princes to have a *senhal* (a song-name) for each of them: Richard was *Ic e No* (Yea and Nay), Geoffrey was *Rassa*, Henry perhaps *Mariniers* (Mariner).

Richard dealt harshly with refractory barons so that every now and then his vassals revolted. Such a revolt came in 1182, supported in song by Bertran, who probably about this time turned out his more peacefully-minded brother. After Henry's coronation, Richard refused to do homage to him, claiming that as duke of Aquitaine he was vassal of the French king. Henry and Geoffrey joined to attack him, and Bertran was one of their supporters, In a poem he lists the members of the league, challenges Richard, and reminds Henry of the disputed castle of Clairvaux. But the war did not last long, Henry, the father, intervening to take Clairvaux himself. Bertran was outraged at the briefness of the war. He accused young Henry of halting "at his father's orders: so much he lacks all independence." But the league was revived, and young Henry and Geoffrey turned on their father, with Bertran in his song admitting that their cause was unjust. Young Henry caught fever and died in June 1183; the *planh* usually attributed to Bertran was probably by Vidal. The league broke down. Richard devastated Bertran's estates and gave the castle back to Constantin. But Bertran, somehow reconciled with Richard, regained it. Henceforth he supported Richard. War broke out over Aquitaine which Henry II wanted to go to John; Bertran called on Richard to claim the English throne. About this time he reproached Geoffrey for failing to keep some appointment with a lady:

> If but count Geoffrey doesn't flee,
> he'll get Poitou and Gascony,
> although he can't behave with ladies.

Peace was patched up in 1184, but next year Richard invaded Brittany. Then Geoffrey died in August 1186, and several months later his widow Constance bore a son, christened Arthur to please the Bretons. Vidal wrote:

> The man's mistaken who feels regret
> and blames delays as grievous error.
> The Bretons have their Arthur now,
> on whom such hopes they set.

There was a brief war between England and France in 1187, with papal legates urging peace so that another eastern crusade might go to free the Holy Land. Bertran wrote two songs, expressing disgust at the peace, but more troubles occurred in Poitou, Lusignan, Toulousain, the count of Toulouse having mistreated some merchants of Aquitaine. Bertran did not fight but expressed his pleasure at the conflicts and tried to work Philippe of France up. In fact Philippe did begin war with Richard in June 1188, but Henry II died on 6 July next year and

Richard succeeded him. Bertran reminded him and Philippe of their crusade vow:

> God they keep deceiving,
> they took the Cross but say no word of leaving.

Richard indeed was keen to go, but there was a dispute with Philippe over the castle of Gisors, and Bertran wrote a song trying to stir up feeling over the issue. Then in 1190 Richard did go east. His imprisonment on his way home is mentioned in a song by Vidal, and both French and Provençal versions exist of his song in capitivity. (The tale of the location of the prison by the minstrel Blondel de Nesle is a mere legend.) When Richard was at last freed, the Troubadours greeted a valuable patron. Bertran sang that he now hoped the troublesome barons would get their deserts; in a second song he was waiting for the king's return, the resumption of war, and no mercy for the rebellious.

Richard's other surviving poem, a *sirventes* to the Dauphin of Auvergne, was written in 1195–6. The Dauphin had been angered at Richard's surrender of Auvergne to the French in return for Quercy, and refused to help him; Richard sent him a taunting French song and he replied in like terms in Provençal. Richard expected help from Alfonso VIII of Castile (married to his sister Eleanor), and Bertran sang in glee, expecting Spaniards to arrive. As for Richard:

> At pouring out gold and silver he won't fail,
> for him good fortune is to spend and give.
> It's not securely that he wants to live:
> for he wants war as sparrowhawk wants quail.

But Alfonso, defeated by the Moors, could not come. In 1196 Richard invaded Brittany, wanting to get control of his young nephew Arthur. The *sirventes* on the war seems by Bertran's son, for he himself was now in the monastery of Dalou, where he is mentioned as a witness in the cartulary of 8 January 1196. The poet calls Brittany Bresilianda (the wood often mentioned in the romances) and declares:

> They seem to have no courage left
> and of their wits to be bereft.
> Their Arthur foolishly they all demand.
> No more I'll say, as none will understand.

He means that they want Arthur to return, both the real one and the legendary; the young count had been sent to Paris.

Bertran's love of war is an aspect of his total acceptance of the

31. Richard I and his queen Berengaria. (Statue from Rouen and tomb at Fontevrault)

feudal way of life. He did not foment strife for its own sake, as Dante thought; rather he wanted war as he considered that it made possible the achievement of the chivalric ideals, provided a stirring and splendid spectacle, and loosened the purse-strings of the kings and barons. Even in his early love-songs the actual world with its conflicts and violence keeps intruding and disturbing the courtly abstractions. Many of his *sirventes* deal with definite moments of the historical struggle; a smaller group treat the ideas of courtly and chivalric behaviour. The origin of the term *sirventes* is unclear. It has been suggested that it means a song in the service of a lord, but in any event it became the vehicle for political comment and satire. There were three main kinds: judgments on events of the day, considerations of manners and ethics, and personal invective, which included literary satire. Here is the *razo* or commentary of one of Bertran's *sirventes*:

Never for anything that Sir Bertran de Born might say in stanzas or *sir-ventes* to king Philippe, or for reminders of wrong or shame that that had

148

been done or said to him, would he fight with king Richard, but Richard rushed into war when he saw the weakness of king Phillippe and robbed and took and burned castles and burghs and towns and killed and imprisoned men. So all the barons, who disliked the peace, were very glad, and Sir Bertran more than any, as he desired war more than other men, and as he believed that through his words king Richard had begun the war, and so he called him Yea-and-Nay, as you shall hear in the *sirventes* he made.

> Now I shall sing a song, for Yea-and-Nay
> has come with plundering flames and blood is shed.
> Misers grow generous when great wars appear.
> Therefore the pomp of kings I hail with glee,
> for cords and stakes and tentpoles we shall need,
> and meadow-rows of tents will soon be shown.
> We'll meet in thousands for the field-debate
> and men to come will sing the gay affair.

> My shield would then have felt the clanging fray,
> my flag of white I would have stained with red.
> But I'll deny such play, although it's dear,
> since Yea-and-Nay has loaded dice for me.
> For Rançon and Lusignan do not heed
> my voice, and I've no wealth to fight alone.
> Yet friends at bay have never found me late,
> shield on my back and helmet on my hair.

In two further stanzas he says that he'll know Philippe is worthy of his ancestors if he has "burned a boat or drained a pond before Gisors," so as to force his way into the Wood of Rouen and besiege the town by hill and valley – "so that only a pigeon might carry a letter there." More, as war shames the ignoble, he feels sure that Yea-and-Nay in his craft won't abandon Cahors and Cajors. If only he gets the treasure of Chinon, he'll have the sinews of war. "Hard work and expenses are a great pleasure to him who's always harrying friends and foes." But then Bertran turns abruptly to his lady and ends with a *tornada* to his jongleur.

> Think of a ship, with cockboat wrencht away:
> it's whirled upon a reef with crew halfdead,
> shot like a storm-shaft while they cannot steer,
> rising and falling, hurried helplessly.
> My fate is worse. Against her ways I plead.
> She will not take me. That is why I moan.

She breaks the treaty governing my fate.
My joy and luck are foundering in despair.

Go, Papiol, and use your greatest speed.
Reach Trainac ere the feasting-hour is flown.
To Roger and his kin I bid you state
that I must stop, since I've no rhymes to spare.

Whereas the use of the spring-theme to start a poem is normally used for love, he uses it for war.

When I behold returning spring
and watch the leaves and flowers unfold,
then love reviving makes me bold,
gives me again the power to sing.
Since then that power I fully claim,
a fiery song with diligence
I'll send as gift to John, who'll wince
to read it out, grown red with shame.

Shame to his heart it sure will bring,
shame for his ancestors of old.
Poitiers and Tours he cannot hold;
Cowed from Philippe he's scurrying.
Guyenne regrets the noble name
of Richard, who spared no expense,
pouring out gold in its defence;
but John, it's clear, won't do the same . . .

In another spring-poem he turns straight from the woodlands of song to the scene of war: tents and pavilions pitched in the fields, horsemen and horses in armoured lines. "I'm happy when skirmishers put to flight both men and wealth, and after them a serried mass of men in arms. I'm happy too at heart to see strong castles closed around with siege, the ramparts breached and crashing down, and the defenders on the bank enclosed with moats and palisades." When the battle begins, we'll see "maces and swords, bright-coloured helms and shields all hacked with holes and cracked across, with many vassals fighting hard, with horses of the dead and wounded careering off without a rider."

Let every man who's nobly bred,
when in the battle-line he stands,
think only of cleaving someone's head.
To live defeated! better lie dead.

32. Great Seal of Richard I.

There's no such pleasure in food or drink or sleep as there is in hearing the yell "At them!" all around, with riderless horses whinnying in the shadows, and cries of "Help, help!" There's no such pleasure as when he sees both mighty and humble falling in the grass by the moats and the dead men with bits of silk-pennoned lances sticking in their ribs. He ends with the appeal: "Barons, put all your castles in pawn, your towns and cities, rather than halt the war among yourselves."

Again in *Ar ver*: Now is the fine season when our ships come into port, and Richard too will come. Gold and silver will flow, siege-engines will be built and put into action with walls breached and towers collapsing, and the captured enemies will be put into chains.

> I like the shields all set together
> with the bright scarlets and the blues,
> ensigns and banners in spring weather
> unfurling all their wealth of hues.

He is always harping on the need of war to make the great lords pour out their money.

> I like to see the rich men brawl.
> Good things to servitors then fall,
> to castellans. Rich nobles all
> more generously their funds release,
> more easily, in war than peace.

151

In one song he sets out frankly and passionately the implacable hatred of the feudal character for the townsfolk with their new claims and assertions. In this matter he is not in the least typical of the lords of the Midi, as we have seen, but the poem is a remarkable document of feudal class-feeling:

> My heart is joyous when I see
> the cursèd rich in misery
> for baiting the nobility.
> I laugh with joy to see them die,
> twenty or thirty, knee to knee,
> or when I watch them raggedly
> come beg for bread; and if I lie,
> then may my mistress lie to me.
>
> For swine they're born and swine remain.
> All decency they find a strain.
> If any wealth they chance to gain,
> then all the ways of fools they try.
> So keep their trough devoid of grain,
> plague them with requisitions, drain
> their pockets, and to make them sigh,
> let them endure the wind and rain.
>
> Hold fast the serf or you will trace
> the treason growing on his face.
> That lord deserves to meet disgrace
> who, with the chance to crush, stands by.
> For peasants are a rebel race
> when sheltered in a strongwalled place,
> their hearts grow insolently high,
> exposed as treacherous and base.
>
> If broken-armed they come, or lame,
> if dearth and hunger make them tame,
> don't pity or admit their claim.
> God help me, peasant-folk deny
> their fellows whom misfortunes maim.
> To give in alms they count a shame.
> Then since their miser-hearts are dry
> of pity, let them have the blame.
>
> They're usurers too shrewd to beat.
> They're puffed with pride and foul deceit.

> In impudence they all compete.
> Loud to the heavens their actions cry.
> For God and Man alike they treat
> and trample Justice in the street.
> Old Adam's part they claim – but why?
> God, with disaster may they meet!

In the direct strength of his emotion, when once his feudal convictions are touched, he stands alone, since he is in no way torn by the far more complex relationships and questionings of the Troubadours of the Midi. Among the latter the whole movement is in the contrary direction, into sharp criticism of feudal systems and above all of the oppressive church – at least along the main line that leads from Marcabru through the Monk to Cardenal. Bertran's songs, however, remained so popular that they were still sung forty years after his death, and jongleurs used *razos* that combined fact with much fantasy to introduce them.

His lady he praises for scorning the great lords and being ready to cherish with her love "a worthy vassal rather than a deceitful count or duke who would bring her shame."

> A lady fresh and finely free,
> gaily she goes, and gracefully;
> ruby-shot gold her hair you see,
> more white her limbs than flower can be,
> plump arms, breasts spread firm for me;
> a rabbit's supple loins has she.
> Then by her delicate fresh hue,
> her merit and the praise her due,
> a man may tell her at first view
> as one of whom all good is true
> and know where I adoring sue.

But even here he turns to praise war and attack lords who are more interested in hunting.

VIII

Arabic Influences

WE now pause to consider a question that has been with us from the start: how far the Troubadour system was influenced in its origins and development by Arabic music and poetry. There is no more vexed question than this in the story of the Troubadours. We may divide the matter into three main sections: rhyme-systems and stanzaic forms; specific motifs and images; general philosophic and ethical positions. There is also the questions of means of transmission, which we may deal with first. We have seen how there were many means whereby Moslem science and philosophy entered the Christian West, and how important the contacts were in stimulating western thought. Songs would move along different channels, through the courts, both Moslem and Christian, where the singers, especially the women singers, could introduce elements of music or song from either culture. The *ahdadi* were popular singers, found in town and country, while the *rûwahi* or poets proper were in the alcazars. At Seville was held a concourse of songs and poems, and the most outstanding of the composers of *muwashshah* were acclaimed. No townsman received friends or celebrated an anniversary without a gathering of singers. Things were much the same in Christian Spain as in Andalusia. From early days at popular levels there was a mixture of cultures, including songs.

At least after the conquest of Toledo in 1085 the troops of jongleurs at the Christian courts were of mixed composition. Thus at the court of Sancho IV a group of entertainers was made up of thirteen Moorish singers, twelve Christians, one Jew. A miniature of the *Cantigas de Santa Maria* in the Escurial shows two jongleurs, one Moorish and one dressed as a Troubadour, singing some sort of *tenson*, each playing a lute. In Spanish churches up to the fourteenth century they used Moorish singers. A decree of the Council of Valladolid, 1322, condemned the use in the offices "of Saracen or Jewish jongleurs, who sing and play their instruments." Moorish musicians at times played in the courts of France, England, Sicily. In the romance of *Galeran de Bretagne* a young woman is instructed in Saracen, Gascon,

33. Shipwrights at work. (Knight iii 200)

and French music or songs. The crucial period of interaction indeed for us here is the eleventh century or earlier; but the sort of contacts we can illustrate from later times certainly existed much earlier, even if not in such organised forms. Cultural exchanges and assimilations were made easy by the fact that as well as Moslems and Christians there were Mozarabs (assimilated Arabs) and Mudejars (assimilated Christians). In the wars there were many prisoners made on both sides, and interpreters and intelligence-officers, often of Jewish race, were used. The sense of a deep debt to the Arabs appears in such comments of those of Wolfram who in his *Parzival* takes Chrétien de Troyes to task for getting the story wrong; he himself claims to have righted things with the aid of Kyot of Provence "who has offered the true story" from the Arabic.[1]

We may add that in the raids and wars large numbers of Moorish dancing and singing girls were carried off, kept at courts, or dispersed. Thus in 1065 in a crusade against Spain the Christians took Barbastro, a flourishing city near Lérida. There was large-scale massacre and rape in violation of the truce, and then the Christians settled down to enjoy their gains. Ibn-Hayyan relates how a Jew called on a Christian prince to discuss the ransom of the daughter of the deposed alcayade. The prince, dressed in Moorish robes, was installed in the harem of the former ruler; he refused to let the girl go and ordered her to take her lute and sing to him. (We saw how Guilhem IX had many contacts with Spain.) Women, we may note, often had high status in the Arabic world of Spain. Some, wives or daughters of viziers of caliphs, held administrative offices. Copying manuscripts was a woman's occupation; a quarter of Cordova had hundreds of women busily making books. The manuscripts of a Fatima had a particularly high name. There were many women poets, for instance the princess Walhada, daughter of Mohammed II (1008–10), and Aisha bint-Ahmed, who also protected poets. Both the Moorish and Christian regions were largely bilingual. In the former regions people spoke Arabic and a mixed romance-dialect, which provided the basis of later Spanish. With the expansion of Castile the Arabic-romance vernacular spoken in Andalusia became Castilian.

Now to rhyme-systems and stanzaic forms. Arabic had certainly developed far more sophisticated systems than the vernaculars of the West by 1000. There were clear strophic forms known as *muwashshah* (necklace), which was invented according to tradition in the ninth century by Macaddem de Cabra and which we find copiously exemplified in Ibn Quzman's work of the twelfth century. It used the rhyme-scheme AA BBBAA CCCAA and so on. There was also the *zéjel*, a popular variant ready to take in various vernacular elements and not concerned with the decorum and dignity of the classical strophic form. The *zéjel* begins with a couplet AA, called the *estribillo*. Then come the stanzas BBBA, CCCA, and so on. The *estribillo*-rhyme was thus repeated at the end of each triplet, binding the poem together. Though we do not find the exact *zéjel* form in Guilhem IX, he uses its fundamental idea, and the forms he thus produced laid the basis on which the Troubadour lyric developed. The system seems to have gone far back in the Arabic world. Ibn-Kaldun tells us: "The Bedouins have another kind of poetry, set out in four lines, of which the last has a rhyme different from that of the first three, so that the fourth rhyme is repeated in each *baït* up to the end of the poem." The use of this principle by the Arabs and by Guilhem can hardly be fortuitous. But that does not mean that we can reduce the stanzaic innovations of Guilhem and the later Troubadours to an Arabic basis. We have seen that there were also certainly influences from the *conductus* of St Martial in Guilhem's stanzaic and rhyming systems. We are dealing with the convergence of a large number of factors, not with some single factor that started the whole thing off.

We must however allow for the influence of the *zéjel* and of Arabic music in general. That music seems more developed in its song-forms than was the kind of music used by the minstrels and jongleurs of the West up to about 1100. Apart from the cither, and the harp, all the musical instruments used in the medieval West were of Arabic origin. The *rahab* was ancestor of the rote, the gighe, the rebeck, the vielle (and so in time of the violin); and this was the instrument most commonly used. We may now recall the word *gazel* in a song of the late eleventh century cited at the beginning of this book. The meaning is uncertain, and the word has been interpreted as gossip (cognate with *jaser, gazouiller*), but it may very well represent the Arabic *zéjel* or *ghazel*. The latter interpretation certainly fits in far better with the context, and the line then means: "Turn from your secular songs, your love-songs, to the praise of the Virgin Mary." If so, the hymn shows that the term *zéjel* was already well known in Limoges.[2]

Next there is the question of specific motifs. In Arabic poetry we find many references to the enemy, the scandal-mongering whisperers, in very much the same way as Troubadour poems complain about the *losengier*. Already in a work by a poet of Baghdad, Ibn al-Mu'tazz (861–908) we read in ABAB rhymes:

> Except at night do not meet your lover.
> The night's a bawd, the sun scandal-mongers in the skies.
> How many a lover, whom the dark shades cover,
> meets his belovèd when sleep has shut the slanderers' eyes.

In another poem he writes: "On how many nights did sleep divert the blamers . . . Nothing disturbed us in the darkness there but the likeness of the stars to eyes of spies." Ibn Zaydûn of Cordova in the eleventh century writes in a quatrain ABAB:

> It's as if we never embraced, our union making a third,
> and good luck closed the slanderers' eyelids there.
> In the mind of the covering darkness two secrets stirred
> till the tongue of dawn almost betrayed our lair.

In a poem of Ibn Quzman in the Andalusian vernacular the opening triplet (in which the rhymes ABC are repeated at the end of each stanza, e.g. DDDABC, EEEABC, and so on), runs thus:

> My lovely girl drinks and gives me drink.
> No spy disturbs us, no censor of morals:
> is it not better so?

The Arabic use of the motif seems definitely to link on with its use by the Troubadours. Attacks on spoilsports or intruders are common enough in love-poetry anywhere; but the slanderers have a specific role in the presentation of Troubadour love-experience that strongly suggests Arabic influence. The *losengier* is close to the *washi* of the Arabs; the *gradador* of the wife to the *raqib*.

Other similar themes in the two bodies of poetry can be traced: the cruelty of the beloved, the submissive worship of the lover, and so on. Some Arabic poems express the relation of lover to lady as that of a servant and even make the man address his beloved by the masculine pronoun of lordship. "To a free man submission is good when in the service of love," says a caliph of Cordova. But we cannot claim that here we feel the same specific link as with the slanderer. Still, it is of interest to look at the *Dove's Neck-ring* of Ibn Hazm. He was born in 994 at Cordova in a family recently converted from Christianity to Islam, and he produced his treatise on love and lovers in 1064. Here we find many elements of courtly love. Among the thirty chapters we meet such titles as: Love-messages, the Role of the Eyes in the Birth of Love, Loyalty, Fidelity, the Submission that a Lover owes to his Lady, Proofs of Love, Slanderers, the Good Offices of a Friend. We meet the theme of love for a Distant Lady whom the poet has never seen but whom he has heard of. Ibn Hazm tells of the poet Ibn Harun-al-Raschid, well known in the literary annals of Moorish Spain, who met his beloved only once near the Gate of the Druggists and then dedicated to her the love-poems of the rest of his life. We find Ibn Hazm discussing also the effects of separation and the nature of spiritual union. No kind of pleasure, he insists, "so powerfully affects the soul as union with the beloved, especially if it comes after long denial and continual banishment. For then the flame of passion waxes exceeding hot, and the furnace of yearning blazes up, and the fire of eager hope rages ever more fiercely."

Further Ibn Hazm realises the unity of opposites in a way that closely resembles the dialectic of Troubadour poetry.

Opposites are of course likes, in reality; when things reach the limit of contrariety, and stand at the furthest bounds of divergency, they come to resemble one another. This is decreed by God's omnipotent power in a manner that baffles entirely the human imagination. Thus, when ice is pressed a long time in the hand, it finally produces the same effect as fire.

We recall Raimbaut d'Orange seeking to express the mysterious moment of deep transformation: "Blossoming seems to me the frost, and warmth across the coldness cuts." And Bernart de Ventadour:

"Such is my love and such the power of joy and sweetness in its dower, each icicle seems to me a flower, and the snow is greenery."

Ibn Hazm in his later *Philosophy of Character and Conduct* goes on to discuss the problem of overcoming, resolving, or driving out contraries, and his account suggests strongly the psychology of the Troubadours:

Yet each of these actions is in turn an inescapable hotbed of new anxieties; unexpected obstacles to its realisation raise difficulties according to the occasion . . . loss of what was gained, inability through misfortunes to reach a happy conclusion, unpleasant consequences that come with satisfaction, fear of competition, criticism of the jealous, theft by the covetous, aversion to seeing what we desire in the hands of an enemy, slanders, and the like.

Yet through all the complex zigzag and entanglement of joys and fears there is a drive onwards to what he calls Supreme Goodness.[3]

In the *Diwan* of Ibn Quzman, with its 149 pieces, we find also the attempt to define love in terms of contraries:

The bitterer it is, the sweeter it is to me. My life departs but my love does not wish to leave. The whole world ages from day to day, my love does not age. (cxxxii)

O joy of love, in you is life, in you is death. Since my eyes have met yours, I die and no pain equals that which I see inflicted on me. (cxv)

He also uses the opening with imagery of spring, the dawn-theme, the brag that his poems are the finest ever composed. He claims that true love expands only in adultery, and that beauty inspires the lover to bear any burdens. "What heart would be equal to sustaining the weight if beauty did not give the spirit the strength and the life? The very ones that are his victims give thanks to him and sing his praises." He wrote several political pieces, for instance on the battle of Fraga in 1134 when Alfonso I of Aragon, ally of our Guilhem IX, was killed by the Almoravid Emir.[4]

In making these comments one is not at all claiming that the Arabic mixture comes together precisely in the Troubadour form. We find the idea of love as an ennobling power, but Ibn Hazm, in dealing with the Signs of Love, is mostly concerned with the attempts of the lover to impress the girl before he gains her. Al-Ahnaf compares his submission to his lady to the relationship of child to father, slave to mistress, serf to queen; but Ibn Hazm suggests that such long-suffering submission is based in the frailty and weakness of women.

Let no one, say, please, that the lover's patience with the beloved's ignoble acts is a baseness of the soul, for he would be making a mistake: since we know that the beloved is not his compeer or equal in strength, so that she should be repaid for her wrongs according to her deserts.

He talks of the union of souls as far finer in effect than that of bodies, but has no elevating ideas of women. In the Andalusia of the eleventh century women had a relatively free position; the poets often addressed married women. Still, most of the love-poems are for girls or slaves. The Old Arabic word for slave-girl had lost its pejorative sense.[5]

But then the Troubadours include both Rudel with his worship of the distant lady and Raimbaut d'Orange who advises a punch on the lady's nose. However, though many elements of courtly love are present in Arabic poetry in various degrees of development and combination, we cannot claim that they cohere in the definite and dynamic form of courtly love in the Troubadours. But in denying that we can look for a complete answer to Troubadour origins in Arabic poetry, we are not denying that poetry made important contributions to the Troubadour tradition founded by Guilhem IX, both in form and content.

The interspersing of verse-passages in a prose narrative, as in the romance *Aucassin and Nicolette*, seems to come from the Arabs. Here is a passage from the biography of Ibn Zaidun in the *Dhakhira* of Ibn Bassam of Santarem (1081–1147):

Abu'l-Walid said: "When fate granted the meeting and destiny provided help, she wrote to me:

> Expect my visit when the darkness comes.
> The night I think is best for hiding all.
> If the full moon felt like me she wouldn't rise;
> if the star, it wouldn't move; if the night, it wouldn't fall.

And when the day wrapped up its camphor and the night spread out its ambergris, she came with a waist like a wand and buttocks like heaps of sand. She lowered the narcissi of her eyes towards the roses of shame. We turned to a braided grove and tempered shade, where the pennants of the trees rose on high and the links of the streams flowed together, the pearls of dew were scattered and the robe of wine was gathered.

When we had kindled the fire of wine and it took vengeance on us, each of us admitted love and complained of what was in the heart, and we lay that night, picking the camomile of lips and gathering the pomegranates of breasts. And when at morning I left her, I said to her in parting:

34. Playing with bears. (Knight iii 197)

A lover who bids you farewell bids farewell to patience,
losing that secret he trusted you with in play.
He gnashes teeth for not going some steps further
when he walked down to see you on your way.
O equal of the full moon in her radiance,
did I moan for the short nights when with you I lay?"

We now turn to the question of general philosophic views. Here we
need mainly to consider Sufism with its quest for union with the
divine. In its early forms it was ascetic, deeply aware of sin and afraid
of punishment, seeking to empty out the self through mortification and
purification. In the ninth century it became much fuller. Union with
God was sought through knowledge and love, and the ascent to union
was defined by a number of stages or steps. There was a strong
pantheist element in the concepts, probably through influences from
Greek philosophy, Neo-platonism, and Gnosticism – perhaps also Persian Manicheanism and Christian mysticism. The idea of the transforming act of union, of deification, was first set out by Abou Yazid Bistami
(died 875), with Al-Hallaj as one of the leading exponents. Al-Ghazali
(born 1058) was the thinker who attacked the pantheism of Sufism
and reconciled the system with orthodox religion. Sufism stressed the
concrete immediacy of the moment of experience. Al-Junayd said:
"Sufism is the preservation of the moments: that is, that a man does
not consider what is outside his limits, does not agree with anyone but
God, and only associates with his proper moment." Al-Kalanadhi, disciple of a friend of Al-Hallaj, tells us:

Sahl said: "Whoso loves God, he is life; but whoso loves, he has no life."
By the words "he is life" he means that his life is agreeable, because the
lover finds delight in whatever comes to him from the beloved, whether
it be loathsome or desirable: while by "he has no life" he means that, as

he is ever seeking to reach what he loves, and ever fearing that he may be prevented from attaining it, his whole life is lost. One of the great Sufis said: "Love is a pleasure, and with God there is no pleasure: for the stations of reality are astonishment, surrender and bewilderment."

Al-Hallaj saw suffering as a sign of election: "I desire you, I do not desire you for the rewards [of the chosen]; no, but I desire you for the anguish [of the damned]. All the goods that were necessary for me, yes, I have received them but for Him who would rejoice my ecstasy by torments." Bayazid of Bistam (died 874) put the matter in terms of the following imagery:

Desire is the capital of the lover's kingdom. In that capital there is set a throne of the torment of parting, and there is drawn a sword of the terror of separation, and there is laid on the hand of hope a branch of the narcissus of union; and every moment a thousand heads fall by that sword. And seven thousand years have passed, and that narcissus is still fresh and blooming, never has the hand of any hope attained thereto.[6]

The concept of the quest for perfection or fulfilment, with a psychological analysis of the movement of hope, fear, defeat, success, in Islamic mysticism as in Christian, has many close analogies with the concept of the lover's quest in what we may call the Troubadour experience. No records exist of Iberian Sufism before the twelfth century, but we cannot doubt that Sufi ideas had long been know to Moslem thinkers in Spain. If we turn to Avicenna's treatise *On Love*, we find an Aristotelean rather than a Platonic basis. The doctrine advocating the suppression of the lower parts of the soul as the price of reaching perfection is supplanted by one of an harmonious hierarchical order of the parts of the soul. This sort of attitude had already appeared in *On the Essence of Love* in the *Encyclopedia* of the Brethren of Purity, in which all kinds of love are accepted as having their place and their type of unification. Embracing, kissing, and copulation are types of unification in accordance with the capacity of the animal soul – the desire for the preservation of the species being part of the nature of most animals. All love – which never ceases its action in the souls – is "a perfection given by God's grace for the purpose of leading the souls toward good aims." Avicenna sees love at work in simple inanimate entities, in vegetative forms, in animal souls, as well as in divine souls.

One will never find the wise – those who belong to the noble and learned, and who do not follow the way of those who make greedy and avaricious

35. Pointed Arches (arcade in the Sanctuary) of the Mosque of Ibn Tulun, Cairo, built 876–9 A.D. and covering 6½ acres. (M. S. Briggs, *Architecture*, 1947)

demands – to be free from having their hearts occupied with a beautiful human form . . . Three things follow from the love of a beautiful human form : (i) the urge to embrace it (ii) the urge to kiss it and (iii) the urge for conjugal union with it.

The third urge is specific to the animal soul alone and must be controlled. But the other two urges are not in themselves blameworthy. "The soul of the lover desires to reach the object of his love with his senses of touch and sight, and thus he delights in embracing it. And he longs to have the very essence of his soul-faculty, his heart mingles with that of the object of his love, and thus he desires to kiss it."

This point of view is sympathetic to imaginative activity. Avicenna says that the animal soul in man can be much affected by the rational soul, so that "man applies his faculty of imagination toward noble and more than ordinary matters, so much so that the activity of his imagination often almost resembles that of the pure intellect."[7]

We see that these positions have close resemblances to certain aspects of the Troubadour idea of love. It has been argued that *Fin' Amors* involved the Avicennan notion of the permissibility of embrace and kiss but denied the lovers the final act of coition; and this attitude may indeed have been present in the ideas and practices of some Troubadour-lovers. Bernart de Ventadour for example might hope for some sight and even touch of the beauties of his Eleanor, but he can hardly have hoped to get into her bed. Also the joy and anguish of going so far and no further could be viewed as a kind of test or ordeal in which the body was both accepted and dominated, an *ascesis* of love. (We must recall that the term asceticism came from the disciplines and privations of athletic training.) But it is clear also, from the works of the Troubadours, and from the discussion of courtly love by Andreas, that the aim of the lovers was essentially to enjoy one another in all ways. The Troubadours took over from the mystics the idea of love as the one great ennobling force, which drove man up through the stages of self-fulfilment; but for union of the lonely soul with God they substituted the union of two earthly lovers in the fullness of their spiritual and physical existences. Islamic and Christian mysticism had many common roots. As we saw, the inner movement of Christian thought in the eleventh and twelfth centuries involved a feeling of the need to find a personal relation to deity and to move through various stages into a living union with what was felt to be perfection. There is no reason for us not to believe that elements from both Islam and Christianity contributed to the Troubadour concept of love, its trials, stages, and constant struggle towards the highest possible level of human integration.

There is yet one other matter connected with the cultural contacts between the Moors and the romance-speakers. It has been found that many Arabic and Hebrew strophic poems of the eleventh and twelfth centuries ended with lines in romance-dialect. The sophisticated poems, amorous or panegyrical, sung at the Andalusian courts, had this end-piece appropriate to the woman-singer. Usually these pieces were simple and direct, quite different from the poem to which they were attached. It seems clear that the Arabic or Hebrew poet used the small romance-song as his starting point, the basis of his own invention. For instance, an Arabic poet took a romance-love-song (often a well-known one) and built out of it his own more elaborated work. Thus al-Tutili (about 1126) takes a romance-triplet in which a girl cries that her lover is sick with love and needs a doctor. He uses the same rhymes in a more sophisticated triplet about fire and water mixing, and uses a refrain on this system after each stanza (AAAA, BBBB and so on). There are five stanzas in all. In the last stanza he ends:

> I've been abandoned sick and wasting away,
> but then she sings, half serious, half in play:

and he cites the originating triplet in which the girl speaks and which was called the *jarcha* (refrain, literally departure: compare the Troubadour's *tornada*, turning-away). The interesting thing is that the *jarcha* is always in its romance-form a folksong for a woman, a *Frauenlied*, a *winileoda* or *cantiga de amigo*. Here are some examples in which to keep the primitive simplicity of the short lines I do not attempt rhymes:

Tell me what I must do / I wait for my lover / through him I'll die.

What shall I do, mother, what shall I do? / My lover is there at the door.

O beautiful dark one, apple of my eyes / who can bear your absence / my darling one?

O God, how can I live / with these agitated feelings? / Before he greets me / he bids me farewell.

Fair son of stranger / you've drunk with me and lain on my breast.

O lovely dawn / tell me where you come from / for I know you love another / it's not me you love.

The other characters met in the *jarchas* are: a merchant, who will be the girl's messenger; a soothsayer, whom she asks to tell when her lover will come; and a jeweller. "The merchant of necklaces, mother, will lend me no jewels. My lord shall see a white neck, he shall see no adornments." If the lover is given a name, it is that of someone apparently well-known in the community.[8]

The evidence of the *jarchas* for an influence from the folk-levels of the romance-dialects on the Arab or Hebrew lyrics is thus of great

importance in showing (a) that there was no simple one-way movement of ideas and forms from Arabic to the romance-tongues and (b)
that women-singers played a key-part in the exchanges, particularly at
the early phases. But the *jarchas* did not themselves create the forms
of *muwashshah* or *zéjel*, though scholars, in their eagerness to deny the
role of the Arabs in helping to bring about Troubadour poetry, often
write as if we have proof that they did. Certainly we can now surmise
that romance-forms of song did play their part in the creation and
development of the Arabic forms. Even if we consider that the latter
forms based their rhymes and metres on *jarchas* which were normally in Arabic vernacular, in romance-dialect, or in both, we still have
to give the Arab poets much credit for the expansion and elaboration
of the song-forms, which in turn would have reacted back on the songs
of the romance-vernaculars. Interestingly we have evidence for a jongleur in pre-Arab Spain. Saint Valerius tells of an Ethiopian priest,
Justus, who among other things sang lovesongs to the lute and who
must have used the local vernacular. Such evidence as we have then
suggests much interaction from early times, but does not deny the
Arabs a role in the complex development of the simple forms, *jarchas*
and *refrains* into such song-forms as *muwashshah* and Troubadour lyric.
What seems sure is that there was a great and lively body of popular
songs all over the West, Christian or Moslem, which underlay the developments on the upper levels. Here many of the ideas gathered into
the system of courtly love, such as the supreme importance of love as
an experience, were to be found in clear but often embryonic form.[9]

IX

Arnaut Daniel and other Troubadours including Women

A VIDA tells us that Daniel was of the same country as Arnaut de Mareil, and was born in the castle of Ribérac, of noble parents. He studied to be a cleric but became a jongleur. "He liked to write songs in rare rhymes, so his poems are not easy to understand or learn. He loved a great lady of Gascony, the daughter of Lord Guilhem of Beauville, but it is not thought that she ever gave him pleasure in the matter of love." There is a story about his sojourn at King Richard's court, when a jongleur boasted before him of rhyming more richly than he did. Daniel took up the challenge and a contest was arranged under the control of the king. The two poets were told each to make a song and were shut up for ten days in two adjacent rooms. Daniel was not in the humour to compose, and his competitor, having made up some stanzas, imprudently spent a night in singing them over so as to get them well by heart. Daniel listened and learned them too. Before the king he was allowed to sing first, and he sang the other man's song. The latter protested and explained, and Richard roared with laughter. Benvenuto da Imola says that Daniel, hard up, sent a song to some lords, asking them to show their gratitude for the pleasures he had given them. When the messenger returned with a full purse, Daniel said, "I see that Heaven doesn't abandon me," and took the habit of a monk. Dante chose him as the model love-poet and put in his mouth eight of the worst lines of Provençal verse ever written; Petrarch in his *Triumph of Love* makes him the *Gran Maestro d'Amor*. These were absurd overvaluations. He was merely a virtuoso of genial and often bizarre extravagances.[1]

He was a noble like Bertran de Born, whom he may have known; they share the *senhal Mielha de Be* for a lady, and Bertran may be addressed by Daniel in one piece and imitated in another. One of Daniel's poems works out a jest shared with two lesser nobles of the Quercy; another claims that he had been at the great courts. He says that he attended the coronation of Philippe II of France (29 May 1180). He seems of the aristocratic amateur line of Guilhem IX and Raimbaut d'Orange; in one piece he addresses *senhor e companhon*. Probably he was not a nomadic performer as his biographer says. His period of activity seems to be 1180–1200; he is not mentioned in Peire d'Auvergne's satire of 1170 but comes into that of the Monk about 1200. A reference to Legates of Rome suggests that he may have lived till 1210.

He wrote one coarse piece that deals with a situation like that of Chaucer's *Miller's Tale*; his seventeen other known poems are of a very different kind. He was proud of his craft-power and fifteen of his poems have his name in the *tornada*. He repudiates the idea of singing for gain as the jongleurs normally did. "Those who blame me for too often singing would have the right to do so perhaps if it cost them anything. But what stirs me is solely the pleasure, not the thirst for gain."

> A tune with words I've lightly blended
> and fashioned with dexterity.
> A proper song will soon be made
> when with my file I've had a try.
> O love will make my poem please
> and gild it smoothly to declare
> the lady who is virtue's bride.
>
> Now daily is my spirit mended.
> I'm rarefied, so fair is she
> to whom my open worship's paid.
> All hers, from head to foot, am I.
> The wind will vainly strip the trees
> while love within my heart I bear.
> I'm warm, though winter howls outside.
>
> A thousand Masses I've attended
> and lamps and candles burn for me.
> Helpless, to God for help I've prayed;
> her power alone I can't defy.
> I've watched her sweet vivacities,
> her gracious limbs, her yellow hair –
> and "Take Luserna back!" I've cried.

Luserna (Lucerne) was a fabulous city in Spain.

36. Marriage at the Church Door. (Reinach, *Grandes Chroniques de France*)

So much of love my heart's expended
that now I dread my love will be
the reason why my love's betrayed.
She drowns me deeply from on high
in never-ebbing miseries.
She's such a usurer, in her snare
craftsman and workshop both are tied.

I do not seek for something splendid,
the Roman throne or Papacy,
if far I still must roam, dismayed
at losing her for whom I sigh.
One kiss of hers would bring me ease.
Unless within the year she'll spare,
I'll die and she'll be damned for pride.

Although my sorrow's never ended,
I love her inexhaustibly,
and rhyming words come still to aid
the solitude in which I lie.

A ploughman's toils were light by these.
In Monclin's love and mine, I swear,
no ounce of difference may be spied.

Arnaut am I, that hoard the breeze,
I am the ox that hunts the hare,
the man that swims against the tide.

With his lack of original matter, he elaborates form, multiplies inner rhymes or breaks his verses into short lines, rejects familiar rhymes and draws on all vocabularies, makes up words, alters the usual forms, varies suffixes. Dante, impressed by the structural unity of the poems, called him "the finest smith of his maternal tongue," the vernacular. However, Daniel claims that he doesn't adopt the *clus* style, but is "easy, gracious, fine, light, and simple," though the Monk reproaches him for not being all that and he himself admits: "He colours his song with a Flower whose Fruit is Love; the Seed is Joy and the Scent Preservation-from-Ennui." He does not like "violets that quickly wilting are seen: rather laurel and juniper always green." Despite his protestations about simplicity, the *tornada* of the poem given above, noted by both Dante and Petrarch, shows that his aim is that of *trobar clus*. "Arnaut am I, that hoard the breeze . . ." (This poem seems written in 1191 when both the imperial and the papal thrones were empty.)

Here is an example of the way in which he uses broken lines or internal rhymes. There are no rhymes in the first stanza, but each of the following stanzas rhymes with the seventeen end-points:

The cold north wind
              strips all the woods the breeze
of spring
              has clothed with tufts and leafy green,
the joyous
              birds
              don't sing among the branches.
That's why I sing
              by words
                  by gestures too
I force myself
              to please
                a host of men
in praising her
              who cast me from on high.
I'll die of it
              unless she ends my pangs.

His most tormented form is the *sestina*, where the same end-words are moved around in the stanzas according to a set scheme. Words that are hard to work into a poem are chosen: nails, uncle, enter, rod. Such words are used to create an ironic tension, which fails, as it is meant to fail, to break the mood of obsessed emotion:

> Desire, that's learned to enter
> my heart, defies the scratching beak or nail
> of slanderer whose lying taints the soul.
> Then since I may not thrash him with a rod,
> I'll seek a nook denied to prying uncle,
> I'll find love's joy in orchard-nook or chamber.
>
> When I recall the chamber
> where, sadly I'm aware, no man may enter
> and all are harsh as brother or as uncle,
> my body quakes to every tingling nail,
> I'm like a child that sees the lifted rod,
> and fear she's overthoughtful of the soul.
>
> O there, in flesh, not soul,
> I'd be, if she'd secrete me in her chamber.
> I feel it more than blows of any rod
> that where she is I'm not allowed to enter.
> I cleave to her as finger to its nail
> and simply laugh at warning friend or uncle.
>
> The sister of my uncle
> was not more loved by me, I pledged my soul.
> For close as finger to the growing nail
> I'd press, if she would nod me to her chamber,
> since love, which in my heart has learned to enter,
> can bend me as a man a pliant rod.
>
> Since sprouted Aaron's rod
> or nephew came from Adam's loins, or uncle,
> such love as my unfaltering heart feels enter
> has surely never netted flesh and soul.
> Whether she's out of doors or in her chamber,
> my heart is there, the distance of a nail.
>
> I'm fastened with a nail
> upon her, close as bark adheres to rod.
> She is my joy of palace, tower, and chamber.
> Now less I love each parent, brother, uncle,

and double bliss in heaven I've earned my soul
if there a faithful love helps man to enter.

Here Arnaut sends his song of Nail and Uncle
by leave of her whose Rod commands his Soul,
to Desirat, whose Chamber will virtue Enter.

The sister of his uncle would be his mother. In the poems he is saying that passion is absurd, so by insisting on its absurdity he makes it all the more obviously passion; that the emotions of love are a continual repetition of the same elements put together in new forms, in the hope of reaching a stable point of sense. The *sestina* seems his invention. The dry branch that puts forth leaves, we may note, is the Virgin; so, by linking her with Adam, he covers the two epochs of the Old and New Testaments.

A different poet is Peire Vidal, who started his career in the early 1180s. Here we meet a mixture of publicist and lover. He "was of Toulouse, the son of a furrier, and he sang better than any man in the world, and he was one of the most foolish men that ever lived, for he believed that all things that pleased him, or that he wished, were true. And song-making came more easily to him than to any man in the world, and it was he who made the richest melodies and talked the greatest nonsense about war and love and slandering of others." He was concerned, not to refine or complicate form, but to build up his poetic personality. With nothing of *trobar clus* in his work, he moves restlessly about, mixing love and politics, details of his wandering life and his imaginary affairs, with touches of humour.[2]

He began at the court of the local count Raimon V, then, after some disagreement, moved into Provence, where he had Barral de Baux as protector. Next he appeared in north Spain, at the court of Alfonso of Aragon. Raimon died in 1192, Barral in 1194, Alfonso in 1196. About 1193 Vidal was in the Carcassone district, singing of Loba. He made trips into north Italy, performing at the brilliant court of the marquis of Montferrat, also making the round of the lesser courts of Lombardy and Piedmont as well as of Provence, Languedoc, and Spain. In the later 1180s he had gone on pilgrimage to the Holy Land (under pressure from Raimon V, he suggests); in 1198 he offered his services to the king of Hungary, who was Alfonso's son-in-law. He supported Boniface's projected crusade in 1202, and about 1204 he was at Malta, celebrating the deeds of a Genoese admiral. Then he fades out.

He parodied the Troubadour brag, calling his poetry imperial: a term used for splendid, unique – and so finds himself promoted to the rank of emperor. He feels insulted that his lady has left him for a simple count, and a red-headed one at that. He pretends to be a mighty warrior:

The adventures of Gawaine – I've had them all and lots of others. All on my own I've taken prisoner a hundred armed knights, and I've captured the accoutrements of a hundred others. I've made a hundred ladies weep and filled with joy the hearts of a hundred others...

Sire Drogman [*senhal* for an unknown lord], if I ever had a good warhorse, would be in a bad way. They fear me more than the quail does a sparrowhawk. They wouldn't give a denier for their lives, so well they know I'm bold, fierce, and ferocious...

If I had a good warhorse, the king [Alfonso] would be able down there, near Balaguer, to live quietly and sleep in tranquillity, for I'd keep the peace of Provence and Montpellier, and I'd stop brigands and second-rate knights from ravaging the Autavès and the Crau.

Such a character begot many tales.

It was true that a knight of Saint Gili cut his tongue because he gave out that he was his wife's lover. And Sir Uc del Baux had him cured and healed. And when he was cured he went over the seas, and from there he brought back a Greek woman who was given him to wife in Cyprus; and he was given to understand that she was niece to the Emperor of Constantinople, and that through her he ought by right to have the Empire, so he spent all he could gain in making a fleet, for he thought to go and conquer the Emperor. And he had himself called Emperor and his wife Empress, and he always took about with him fine steeds and fine arms, and an imperial Throne. And he thought himself the best knight in the world, and the most loved of ladies; and he fell in love with all the good ladies he saw, and prayed them for their love, and they all said they would do or say what he wanted, so that he thought he was the lover of them all, and that every one would die for him – and they all deceived him.

He fell in love with Azalais, wife of Barral. The husband was very friendly with him, "and they called each other Rainier." When he grew angry with Azalais, Barral "always made peace and made her promise all he asked." Then one day, when Barral had risen and Vidal knew the wife was alone in bed, he went into her room and kissed her mouth as she lay asleep. "And she felt the kiss and thought it was Sir Barral her husband and smiling she arose; and she saw it was the fool Peire Vidal, and began to cry out and make a great clamour. And her maidens came from within when they heard it, and asked, What is this? and Peire Vidal ran away." Azalais tried to get Barral to punish Vidal, but he took the whole thing as a joke. However, she kept on searching for Vidal and uttering "great threats against him." So Vidal went across the seas with king Richard.

There he remained a long time, and there he made many good songs, re-calling the kiss that he had stolen, and he said in one song that he had had from her "no reward save a little knot of ribbon – and yet I had, for one morning I entered her house and kissed her like a thief on the mouth and on the chin." And in another place he said: "I should be more honoured than any man born if the stolen kiss were given to me and fairly acquitted." And in another song he said: "Love beat me well with the rods that I gather, for once in her royal castle I stole a kiss from her which I remember well – alas, so wretched is he who does not see the one he loves."

At last Sir Barral prevailed on his wife to forgive Vidal, who then re-turned to Marseille, "and was very well received by both of them." Grieved at the death of Raimon V, he dressed in black, cut off the tails and ears of all his horses, and had his own head and the heads of his servants shaved, though beards and nails were uncut. He carried on long as a crazed man. King Alfonso came to Provence and found him "thus sad and sorrowful, and clothed like a man sorrowful and crazed." The king and his barons begged him to cease mourning, and "to sing and rejoice, and to make a song that they might take back to Aragon." And at last he did as they asked. "The king had arms made for himself and for Peire Vidal, and he was very pleased, and he made that song which says: I had given up singing for grief and sorrow."

And he loved the Loba of Puegnautier, and my lady Estofania, who was of Cerdagne, and now again he fell in love with lady Raimbauda de Biol, wife of Sir Guilhem Rostanh de Biol [in Provence]. Now the Loba [She-Wolf] was of the country hard by Carcassone, and Peire Vidal had himself called Wolf for her sake, and he wore the arms of a wolf, and in the mountains of Cabaret he had himself hunted by the shepherds with mastiffs and greyhounds, as one hunts a wolf. And he donned a wolfskin to give the shepherds to understand that he was a wolf. And the shepherds with their dogs chased him and treated him so cruelly that he was carried away for dead to the house of Loba. When she knew that this was Peire Vidal she began to rejoice greatly over the folly that Peire Vidal had done, and to laugh much, and her husband as well. And they received him with great amusement, and the husband had him put in a place apart, as well as he could, and sent for the doctor and had him tended until he was healed.

We can see how these stories arose out of his poems. The term imperial led to the story of his political ambitions. The wolf-story seems to have been devised to explain some lines in a song where he declares himself ready to play the role of wolf to prove his love; but behind it there may also lie folktales connected with wolf-fraternities. At Jumièges in Normandy, at the time of the midsummer bonfire, the man called the Green Wolf (who wore a long green mantle and tall green hat) was chased by his comrades till they caught him and pretended to throw him into the flames.

He gives the trite themes his own slight twist of humorous variety. "I haven't yet ever died of love, nor of anything else, but my life is worse than death . . . Soon we'll grow old, my lady and I, and if we lose our youth, that'll be a sorry thing for me, but much worse for her." In a lighter way he uses Marcabru's thesis of False Love.

> Barons, I utterly defy
> false slanderers to damage me :
> so worthy is she for whom I sigh,
> so inborn her nobility.
> There's no deceit. I love with all my will.
> Whether or not she's mine, I love her still.
> Such is her beauty and merit that it's plain,
> if a king loved her, honour he would gain.
> Wealthy I feel if only yes she'll say.

> Solace and song now men deny,
> gifts, court-life, hospitality.
> Love-services neglected lie
> unless the lovers false we see.
> He gains most who betrays with practised skill.
> I'll say no more, but, be it as it will,
> he should at once have perished through disdain,
> that scoundrel who taught lovers how to feign.
> He set the example of the lying way.

> But happy ever more am I,
> Lord Barral now has sent for me.
> May fortune raise him, and God on high,
> that I am what I am. For see,
> From Lombardy and Catalonia spill
> love-letters, thousands daily, I've my fill.
> Daily my merit swells, and I don't feign,
> The king is nearly dead with jealous pain,
> while with the ladies at will I dance and play . . .

He knows a hundred ladies who'd have him if they could. But he's never been a braggart or talked much about himself; instead he kisses ladies and unhorses knights.

> Wherever I go, I hear the cry:
> "Look, there's Vidal – look, that is he!
> Fine love and courtship, yes, he champions still,
> and for his lady shows his jousting skill,
> tourneys and fights he loves with might and main,
> more than a monk his cloisters. Off again!
> It's sickness for him in one place to stay."

In *Ab l'alen tir* we feel a genuine love for Provence:

> I breathe – and I inhale the air
> that blows, I know it, from Provence.
> I love whatever's coming thence.
> When good things of it men declare,
> I listen smiling, and I seek
> to draw them on. To hear them speak
> its praises cheers me all the while.
>
> No peace is half so sweet as there
> between the river Rhône and Vence,
> bounded by sea and the Durance,
> with pure joy shining everywhere.
> A nobler folk you'd never find.
> With them I left my heart behind,
> with her who makes the grieving smile.

He lived long enough to presage the disaster coming on the Midi:

> The Pope and the false doctors bring
> our holy church to such confusion
> that God himself is sorrowing.
> With sin and folly and delusion
> they make the bands of heretics grow.
> They were the first to sin, and so
> what can we do but imitate? –
> though I won't be their advocate.

"And all the trouble comes from France, from those who were once the best." The French king has abandoned the Sepulchre; "he buys and sells and haggles still, like peasant or burgess is he." Richard Lionheart is a captive; the Spanish Christians fight among themselves and send

37. Rose Battle of Ladies and Knights. (Louterell Psalter)

fine warhorses to the Moors. Then he passes on to praise of Loba. His diagnosis of the ills of his world was all too true.

Raimbaut de Vaqueiras, also of lowly origin, was born in the Vaucluse region. He visited the court of Hugues I des Baux, in his home area, but his career was mainly connected with north Italy. He knew the court of the Malaspinas there, but most of his time was spent with Boniface I of Montferrat as patron. He took part in that lord's expeditions, including the Sicilian campaign under the Emperor Henry VI, the siege of Constantinople, and various battles in Greece; and he probably died at his side in 1207, during the fourth crusade. In the Sicilian campaign Boniface knighted him for his service as a soldier. Among other poets who visited Montferrat were Peire Vidal and probably Conon de Béthune (with whom Raimbaut exchanged a *partimen* in Constantinople). Though lacking any strong individuality, Raimbaut was a talented and capable poet, and his great importance lies in the fact that it was he who gave the first strong impulsion for the integration of the Provençal lyric in Italian culture. His influence spread out from Montferrat to Malaspina, Este, and Savoy, and from the courts into the towns.[3]

In a *tenson* between him and the marquis de Malaspina, the latter remarks:

> I've seen you a hundred times in Lombardy,
> like a poor jongleur tramping out at heel.
> Short of cash, unhappy in love, you'd be,
> more than content if you could get a meal.
> What state did I find you in once at Pavia?

In a *tenson* with a woman who talks in the Genoese dialect, she opens each of her stanzas by calling him jongleur: "Jongleur, you're a bore . . . Jongleur, you talk like a fool . . .' And she ends by telling him to seek a patron from whom to get a horse, "poor jongleur that you are." She is rude all the time, while he politely woos her. "Am I not your liegeman and your serf?"

He has a clear effective style:

> When love had chosen us, in all men's sight
> I showed my triumph and found nothing daunting.
> A peacock, proud of his rich plumage, white
> and red and green, from out his yard goes flaunting,
> superbly vain; but looking down below
> he sees his feet, is humbled suddenly.
> Happy because my lady smiled on me,
> I strutted on – then came the crashing *No*.

In an *alba* or dawnsong the lover calls to a friend who is watching in a tower, telling him to watch well. In the fourth stanza he turns to his girl to bid goodbye.

> Lady, goodbye,
> I can no longer stay.
> Though I may sigh,
> I yet must go away.
> How sadly I descry
> the quickly rising Dawn
> brighten the sky
> and summon up the day.
> Our kisses to betray
> intends the Dawn, the Dawn, O yes, the Dawn.

In an extravaganza of 135 lines Raimbaut depicts a rebellion of the women against the supremacy of his Béatrice, who, alone, defeats them. The poem with its rushing rhythm thus opens:

> The ladies of the land
> with jealous malice filled
> wage war on every hand
> and a strong town they build.

> Flat be the site or hilly
> a city there will stand
> with tower on tower.
> So high the honour is
> of Béatrice.
> Belittled at her side
> they want to break her pride.
> Her power, with banners raised, they're all defying,
> with fire and war against her they go crying,
> powder and smoke they recklessly send flying.

Christine de Pisan in the late fourteenth century may have had this poem in mind when she wrote *La Cité des Dames*, a city wholly built and inhabited by women.

Guilhem de Cabestanh was a knight of Rousillon, who lived till at least 1212. He plays the humble lover:

> Lady, the day when first on you I gazed,
> when you were pleased to show yourself to me,
> all other loves were from my heart erased,
> my hopes in you were closed eternally.

He asks only that she takes pity on him and "merely agrees to call me friend." In his work the vagaries of the *rima cara* lead to the bring-ing-together, for instance, of the Nile, Christ, sycamore, hyssop, and amethyst. But his main claim to fame is the fact that the legend of the Eaten Heart was attached to him, earning him the attention of Petrarch and Stendhal. One *vida* says that in his home-area was the lady Sere-monde, wife of Sir Raimon de Castel-Roussillon, rich, wild, and proud. He made songs on her and "she loved him more than anything in the world." Her husband noticed, laid snares for the poet, killed him, cut off his head, and tore out his heart. Then he had the heart roasted and served to his wife. "After she had eaten, he told her what it was. And she, on hearing it, lost her sight and hearing. And when she recovered her senses, she said to him: Lord, you have given me so fine a dish that I'll never taste another one. He took his sword and ran at her. She fled to the balcony and threw herself out."[4]

Another version adds that the king of Aragon, suzerain of the lord and of the poet, had come to Perpignan. He arrested the killer and put him in a dungeon, where he died. Then he had the lovers buried at the door of Perpignan church, with the episode of their deaths carved on the tomb, and founded a yearly service in their honour, to which he invited the knights and ladies of the region. There are two further versions. In one, the lady's sister tries to turn the husband's suspicions on to her herself, but only succeeds in making things worse, and precipitating the disaster. In the other, the husband shuts up his wife and the poet composes a song which only serves to bring the husband's wrath upon him.

We know however that Raimon and Saurimonde de Peralada were married on 26 March 1197, a year after the death of king Alfonso, and the lady outlived her husband, marrying at some time before 1210 another man, her third husband. The legend may have arisen through tales told about some tomb-carving at Perpignan. The poet may be the Guilhelmus de Cabestan, whose name is found at the foot of an act of 1162; he names Raimon as his protector in two *tornadas*. The tale of the Eaten Heart is also told of a harper in Brittany and of the minnesinger Reinmar de Brennenberg (thirteenth century). It comes up again in France about the Châtelain de Coucy, and in Spain in the late seventeenth century.

Raimon de Miraval was lord of the place of that name, in the Carcassonne region, and was active 1180–1213. A tale is told of him, G. Faidit, and Uc de Saint-Circ. A Troubadour sighs for a noble lady; a woman friend of the latter pretends to take pity on him and lures him on with vain hopes, offering him a compensation, *esmenda*, on condition that he renounces the old love and publicly pays her his homage; he falls into the trap, but when he asks for his promised reward he is laughed at as a lover who can't be trusted. In the version told of Raimon a married woman, Ermengarde de Castres, promised to console him for the troubles he has had with Azalais de Boissezon if he repudiates his wife Gaudairenca. He handed Gaudairenca over to a knight who had been wooing her and who duly married her. But Ermengarde married the knight Oliver de Saissac.[5]

Arnaut de Mareuil, a cleric of lowly birth, belonged to a castle called Mareuil in the bishopric of Périgord. As he could not get a livelihood from his learning, "he went off through the world. Hazards and chance led him to the court of the countess de Burlats. He knew how to sing well, he read romances well, and was agreeable in his person. He fell in love with her and made his songs on her, but didn't dare to admit that he was the author, so he made them pass as the works of another. However, his feelings became so strong that he at last confessed them

38. Shooting with Crossbow at small bird. (Royal MS 2B vii)

in a poem. And the countess didn't reject him, but listened to his prayers." She gave him an equipage, with permission to sing about her. But king Alfonso also loved her and he grew jealous. He objected so strongly to Arnaut that the countess dismissed him. Arnaut then went to the court of Montpellier.[6]

> Whiter than Helen's self is she,
> no opening flower's so warmly bright,
> she's unsurpassed in courtesy,
> sincere her words, her teeth are white,
> gentle her heart with nothing ill.
> Fresh is her skin and gold her hair.
> Let God protect her. It's His will
> that she's so ravishingly fair.
>
> In pity let her set me free
> from tests and tremours in my plight,
> give me a kiss most graciously,
> then more, as I shall serve aright.
> And a short voyage we shall share
> and all my hopes at last fulfil,
> advancing onwards slowly where
> her grace and beauty lead me still . . .

But his main work was not songs but five letters or salutations of love in couplets, in which he fervidly pours out all the commonplaces of adoration. He'll die, embracing "your noble body, charming and precious, kissing your eyes and mouth, with such sweetness that one kiss will be worth a hundred." He dreams day and night always of kissing, embracing, caressing her. "Were such a dream a lasting thing, I would not envy count or king."

Gaucelm Faidit, says his *vida*, was "of a bourg named Uzerche in the bishopric of Limousin. He was a townsman's son and sang as badly as it's possible. And he made many good *vers* and *canzos*. He lost all that he owned at dicing." We noted above his reputation as a great drinker and eater, his bulk. "For more than twenty years he roamed the world before his songs were welcomed or accepted. And he took a whore for wife and for long carried her with him to the courts of the great. She was named Guillaumette Monja. She was very beautiful and informed, and became as big and fat as he was." The marquis of Montferrat, Boniface II, "gave him money, clothes, equipage, and covered him with honours, and his children as well." He was the most prolific of the poets of the little court of Marie de Ventadour, and counted among his patrons Raimon d'Agout and Hugue IX, count of the Marche. In 1202 he went on the crusade.

In the tales about him he is said to have first loved Marie, who in-spired many of his best songs; but he ended by displeasing her and was thrown out. He next wooed Marguerite d'Aubusson, but she did not treat him well, being in love with Hugue de Lusignan. She is said to have given Hugue a rendez-vous in the poet's house. When they arrived he was out, but Monja welcomed them. On his return he was enraged to hear how the lovers had been aided by his wife. He also loved a lady whom he called Bel-Espoir, Madonna Jordana, but he found a rival in Alfonso II, who calumniated him so that he had to go off. He left for the Holy Land with Boniface, and wrote a pleasant poem on his return home.[7]

> From the great gulf of sea,
> the ports' weary delays,
> the perilous beacon, see,
> I'm home. To God the praise.
> Now all my misery,
> the suffering days I spent,
> I'll tell. For God has heard my plea.
> O never happier could I be
> than thus returning joyously
> to Limousin whence I went
> with lingering lament –
> great is the favour shown to me!

"A little garden here at hand outdoes great splendours seen afar in another land." The princess has welcomed him home with gifts, and he sees many festivals and gallantries to sing. "The springs and the clear streams, they all rejoice my heart, the meadows and the vine-yards here." In *Lo rossinholet* he tells how he listens to the wild bird and is stirred to sing a song, "something I thought I'd never hear again." In 1195 he wrote a *planh* on Richard Lionheart: "The king is dead, the bravest king I've seen, the bravest earth has seen this thousand years." Its popularity is shown by the many copies and variants. He also composed an *alba*:

> Beside his girl the lover lies
> and loves her while the moment flies.
> He kisses her and then he sighs:
> "You darling thing, ah must I go?
> Eastward I see the daylight glow,
>   *O!*
> *I hear the watchman and he cries:*
>   *Arise!*
> *Up, I see the day announced*
>   *by dawning skies.*

The refrain is repeated after each stanza:

> My darling thing, if, cheating spies,
> no light of dawn could ever rise
> to take poor lovers by surprise,
> what joy within our hearts would grow,
> what kisses endlessly would flow . . .
>
> My darling thing, no man denies
> a parting lover almost dies,
> I know that truth beyond surmise,
> I'm agonised that it is so.
> Ah God, how quick the night hours go . . .
>
> My darling thing, the day defies
> our love, but I remain your prize.
> By God, be faithful and be wise.
> My life to your embrace I owe,
> you are the only one I know . . .
>
> Though far I go, my heart replies:
> I'm still the captive of your eyes.
> To break me down my longing tries.
> Therefore I'll come when starbeams show.
> Without you I am dazed with woe.
>   *O!*

> *I hear the watchman and he cries:*
> *Arise!*
> *Up, I see the day announced*
> *by dawning skies.*

Eblo, Peire and Gui were brothers and co-seigneurs of the town of Ussel; Elias was their cousin. Gui seems the youngest brother; he renounced his seigneurial rights when he took over two canonries. Eblo and Peire are first mentioned in 1190, and the last reference is in 1240; Peire and Gui were dead by 1245. Gui, whose earliest dated piece is about 1205, wrote songs, pastorals, *tensons*; the others are known only in dialogue-songs. Gui stopped being a Troubadour on the order of the papal legate in 1208. Such poets felt the problem of striking out into new territory. Though poets like Vidal or Raimbaut de Vaqueiras had vigour enough to make effective use of old themes and now and then to achieve original notes, and poets like Arnaut Daniel devised new technical complexities, what we see in the later decades of the twelfth century is mainly the considerable expansion of the tradition in method and in audience. Gui d'Ussel comments:

> More often songs I should compose,
> but it's a bore each day to cry
> that Love has made me moan and sigh.
> There's nothing of interest in such normal woes.
> I need new words. Quite well the melody goes,
> but I strike nothing not already said . . .

He says that he'll try to get an air of novelty by putting the same old thing in a different way.[8]

Women played a central role in the Troubadour system; they were patronesses as well as heroines of love and song, and they also wrote songs. Some twenty women Troubadours are known. Some names may be misreadings or inventions; but some are certainly genuine, and we find women taking part in *tensons*, *partimens*, or *coblas*. Gui d'Ussel addresses a domna na Maria, who must be Marie de Ventadour; Elias Cairel, a domna Isabela; Lanfranc Cigala, a Guilhelma. Two ladies argue about marriage and celibacy as Carenza and Alaisina Iselda. We reach firmer ground with Azalais de Porcairagues, the Lady of Castelloza, Clara d'Anduza, a Toulousan Lombarda, Tibors, even Gormonda de Montpellier, Almois de Châteaubeuf, and Iseut de Capieu. The best-known however is countess Béatrice de Die, though we cannot

much trust her biography. She is confused with other countesses de
Die, and even her name Béatrice is uncertain. "A beautiful and noble
lady, the countess de Die was in love with Raimbaut d'Orange and
composed many fine songs about him."[9]

In Gui d'Ussel's *tenson* Marie declares:

> Honour to her lover a woman should pay
> as friend but not as lord. That's what I say.

The Lady of Castelloza expects of her beloved "only the succour and
joy that will come in sleep." Clara d'Anduza, who is said to have loved
Uc de Saint-Circ, is steadfast:

> My love of you is censured all in vain.
> No oath could change my heart, I surely know,
> no, nor my love, which cannot cease to grow,
> nor my desire, my longing sweet with pain.
> Ah, any man, although my enemy,
> I'd cherish if he spoke good things of you.
> Should he betray – no matter what he'd do
> afterwards, never grace he'd get of me.

We see from these examples that the women tended to be more
straightforward and positive than the men. They had indeed a difficult role to play as both lady and poet. How could they reflect in turn
the complicated parts of supreme and distant goddess, of base and
treacherous cheat? In the poems by their lovers they set hard or impossible rules and tests that must be accepted if they were to remain
benign, let alone yielding. But instead of trying to enact the goddess-
rôle they concentrated on the more truly human aspect, on equality
in love. Thus the countess of Die set out frankly her emotion.

> O great is my unhappiness
> through love of an untruthful knight.
> For times to come, I tell the plight
> I've earned through loving in excess
> For he indignantly has fled
> and says I'm niggard of my grace.
> That fault as mine I do not trace
> whether I'm dresst or stretched abed.
>
> For the encounter I would bless
> if naked-armed I held him tight
> and pillowed on my breasts at night
> I gave him joy with my caress.

Floris loved Blancheflor, it's said,
but more I love his comely face.
He in my heart alone has place;
for him my soul, my life is spread.

Dear gracious friend, I here confess
if you succumb, returned from flight
to clasp my body warm and white,
I'll kiss you, rescued from distress.
Here, to its end, will love be sped.
My spousal body I'll unlace
if you'll requite my frank embrace
and prove all disobedience shed.

Again, in six stanzas of complaint, she declares: "I'll sing what I
would never wish to sing." She has never failed in love. "Recall the
way in which our love began." Yet "I am no less deceived now and
betrayed than if I'd not the least slight charm to show." She ends:

Now with my merits I won't try to woo.
Not with my noble birth, my beauty too,
and most of all, my heart that's always true.
That's why this message-song I send to you.
Tell me, dear, gentle friend, why I'm denied,
why you're so cruelly harsh in all you do.
Is it from malice that you act, or pride?

In a *tenson* she argues with Raimbaut d'Orange, who is far away in
his own house:

Béatrice:

Much worry, friend, and weary care
you're causing; but it seems to me
this endless misery that I bear
through you, you scarcely feel at all.
How then yourself a lover call?
If all the pangs are mine, I say
unequal parts in love we play.

Raimbaut:

Lady, love's character you declare.
When man and woman in bonds we see,
each takes the joy and the despair
that to his lot, or hers, may fall.

39. The Garden of Pleasure. (*Le Jardin de Plaisance*, c. 1500)

> The bitter miseries that maul
> the heart, I claim with truth today,
> are wholly mine in every way.

He blames the *losengier*. "If I am not beside you now, blame the loud braying of those asses." She replies that he claims to be more concerned about her good name than she herself, and he says that he fears the harm which the jealous ones can do to their love. "What you lose is merely sand beside the good that I am losing." She is unconvinced. "I wouldn't wonder if your thought has turned towards another woman, since now to you it no more matters what is my thought of you." He swears that he is still true, "or may I never bear a hawk on wrist or meet fine weather for my hunts." The jealous ones are to blame. They end:

> *She*: Friend, I then will trust in you,
> if only you will still be true.
>
> *He*: Lady, I cannot but be true.
> I'll think of no one else but you.

The tales say that she married Guilhem of Poitou, but loved Raimbaut. This Guilhem would be the count of 1158–89, or his grandson, who died about 1227. But each man was count of Valentinois, not of Die. The first married a Béatrice, daughter of Guigue IV, Dauphin of Viennois, but Guigue could not have handed on to his daughter a title he never bore and which was unused from 1168 to 1307. And the Raimbaut can hardly be the famous poet, though he may be a nephew who lived in the first half of the thirteenth century.

Béatrice's poetry may be paralleled among the Arabs. For instance, Ouallada, daughter of the Caliph of Cordova, after her father's death set up a literary circle and lived untrammelled by the conventions of Moslem women. Ibn Zaïdun, born in 1003, wrote love-poems to her, in which we find the theme of the slanderers, submission, desire and longing, sorrow in separation. "In affection lies enough reason for equality."

> If you had wished it, we'd still share a deathless thing,
> a secret lasting when others, unveiled, are lost.
> You've sold your share in me. But always I shall cling
> to mine in you, though life should be the cost.
> Let that suffice. If here my heart you loaded now
> with what breaks other hearts, I should obey you still.
> Scorn: I'll endure. Delay: I'll wait. Be proud: I'll bow.
> Leave me: I'll follow. Speak: I'll listen. Order: I'll accept your will.

But the affair soon ended in mutual recriminations of infidelity, he with a black slave-girl of hers, she with a rich townsman. Her poems have Béatrice's frankness. A quatrain of hers was cited earlier from the biography of Ibn Zaïdun. After the break she vilified her lover: "You have been called the Man of Six Qualities: a description that you'll never get rid of till you get rid of life. You are a sodomite, emasculated, a fornicator, the vilest of beings, a coward, a thief." However there is no need to invoke any directer Arabian influence in Béatrice's work; she is a natural product of the Troubadour tradition.[10]

There were many *jongleuses*, whom the texts show to have been dancers, acrobats, singers, musicians; but we do not hear of any composing poems, though the *vida* of Miraval mentions that his wife Gaudairenca could compose and that she "made dances" (songs, not choreographic exercises). We hear of a *jongleuse* who, in 1317 when Edward II was keeping Whitsuntide at Westminster, approached the king's table and set there *quandam literam*, which may have been some sort of composition. Our poetesses however cannot be considered as moving about like the Troubadours. They all seem ladies of more or less noble birth, accepted in their world. But there was a further role played by women, at least in the origins of Troubadour song, that we will consider in the next chapter.

X

Folk-songs and
Popular Bases

WE saw how large was the part played by women-singers in the world
of Arabic poetry, and how the *jarchas*, though used by male poets,
originated as lyric songs of women. Certainly women's songs, especially
connected with the spring, were an immemorial part of folk-culture,
and the church had steadily condemned all such *cantica, amatoria,
obscoena, turpia,* and the *chori fœminei* or *mulierum,* as obstinate
returns to diabolical paganism and devil-worship. One of the *jarchas*
runs: "The trysting-time [Easter] has come, but it has come without
him, ah how my heart burns for him." Charlemagne in 789 issued a
cartulary ordering that "no abbess should presume to leave her convent without our permission, nor allow those under her to do so ... and
on no account let them dare to compose *winileodas* or send them from
the convent." *Winileodas* are songs-for-a-friend. The Anglo-Saxon
Wulf and Eadwacer gives us an idea what the *winileodas* were like,
and some lines of it suggest the *jarcha.* "Wulf, my Wulf, I am sick with
longing for you, with the rareness of your coming, the grief of my
heart, not the famine I live in."

The *jarchas* are close to the *refrains* of Old French, in the twelfth
and thirteenth centuries. These are short pieces, usually from one to
four lines. They are certainly fragments of dance-songs. They seem to
have been part of a narrative, into which the chorus at set intervals
brought the *refrain.* These repeated choral parts would have impressed themselves more strongly into the memory than the impro-
vised narrative sections; they were, so to speak, the nodal points
around which the other parts revolved. We must recall also that the
use of liturgic dances is attested up to the thirteenth century, and that
in early times it was the women who danced at festivals. There must
have been many May-songs in the Midi, though we have only one ex-
tant (preserved in a single French manuscript). We have however some

40. Girls Maying in the fields. (Wright 289)

half a dozen dance-songs, two of them songs of the unhappily-married woman, both anonymous and late. (We know of a man conducting a *carole* with a *refrain* who in June 1272 was killed in a brawl, in the bourg of Pairac.)[1]

> *I'm pretty and sad, and I'll tell you why:*
> *I hate my husband and that's no lie.*
> O I've a lover. I'll tell you my case.
> *I'm pretty and sad ...*
> I'm small and I'm young, and I set the pace.
> *I'm pretty and sad ...*
> I need a husband who's no disgrace
> and playfully sends time laughing by.
> *I'm pretty and sad, and I'll tell you why:*
> *I hate my husband and that's no lie.*
>
> May I be damned if I bear his embrace.
> Of love for him I haven't a trace.
> O I'm ashamed when I see his face
> and pray in my heart that he soon will die.
>
> However I'll tell you another thing.
> I'm loved by someone who likes a fling.
> And that is the hope to which I cling.
> I'm loved by someone I won't deny.

Now all of my doubts have taken wing.
He's come for a long time whispering.
So I'll let him dance in my wedding-ring,
for I know the fellow for whom I sigh.

Therefore I made this ballad I bring.
O sing it afar, let the music ring.
O sing it, you highborn ladies, sing.
I know the fellow for whom I sigh.

Each stanza has the repetition of the *refrain* as shown in the first. An interesting point is that we have here the same rhyme-scheme as in the Moslem *zéjel*: AABBBA. However we cannot date the song with any precision or base arguments upon it, though we may claim in a general way that it reinforces the lesson taught by the *jarchas*, that there seem to have been early exchanges between Moslem and Christian, between Arabic, Hebrew, and the romance-dialects. This point is further reinforced by the fact that many English carols have *zéjel* forms, which seem well suited for songs of the round-dance. But it is a matter of sheer conjecture and we are thus brought back to some early date, say in the eighth and ninth centuries when romance and Arabic forms met.

The emphasis on the singer's youth and freshness suggests that the husband is old. A spring-song of this sort suggest the struggle of the Old and the New Year for the earth-bride; and we can imagine a mimed form in which the jealous old husband tries to break through the ring of dancing girls to get at the singer, but is repelled, while the young man gets through. Here the turning to the noble ladies, *domna enseg-nada*, shows a far from primitive performance. Caroles of the twelfth and thirteenth centuries in the north often had a mimetic element in the dance; many dealt with the cuckolding of a jealous old husband by his wife and a young man. One of these, *La Belle Aelis*, was very popular in the thirteenth century, to the rage of preachers. A Dominican sermon treated it as an allegory of the union of Jesus and his disciples, with the seductress, Aelis, representing the Virgin Mary, plucking flowers of charity, chastity, and so on. Jacques de Vitry told his congregation in parodic verse-couplets how "when Aelis had risen and adorned and admired herself, Mass had already been sung, so the Devils carried her off." The intrusion of the devil into the wooing-dance gives a homiletic model for Dances of Death, a playform close to the carole of the stolen bride and performed in some of the earliest cases by Franciscans. There is a German ring-dance of Mary Magdalene in the *Carmina Burana* Passion-play (about 1200). The *Interludium de Clerico et Puella*, a wooing dance of the late thirteenth century, seems a show offered by professionals perhaps at a feast. The clerk woos a reluctant girl and wins her through a bawd's aid. Such a wooing by a clerical seducer was common in medieval verse and especially in Middle English dancing songs.[2]

We have another southern *balada* in the same form as the one translated above. The *refrain* runs: "My lady's smiles have killed me with desire; her lovely eyes have filled me with love and fire." The language is that of the pleading courtly lover. Again a song by a distant lover has the *refrain*: "Love is a sweet thing I'd agree, if more of my lady I could see." The rhyme-scheme is AABBA. An anonymous dance-song is again put in a man's mouth:

> O in my heart I keep
> a thought that smoulders deep
> where no one else may pry;
> and should a gust of memory sweep
> the embers where they lie,
> the least thing seen can make me weep.
> Across my mind the miseries creep.
> Without her, what am I?
> *O, I must see her soon or I shall die.*
>
> But love is far away
> and grief is near, men say
> and do not tell a lie.
> For seven days a week I stray
> and every day I sigh.
> I see the death for which I pray
> since I must seek her day by day
> and still the fates deny.
> *O, I must see her soon or I shall die.*
>
> She's beautiful, I know,
> and earth may nowhere show
> her worth beneath the sky.
> The whiteness of the falling snow
> her body can defy.
> Her tints to fards she doesn't owe
> and May has roses but they glow
> less freshly to the eye.
> *O, I must see her soon or I shall die.*

41. Woman Spinning. (Louterell Psalter)

There is also a Poitevin dance in which we find a folk-queen with a jealous king. Each line of the stanza ends with a cry, *eya!* and there is a refrain: "Hey, you jealous, on your way, leave us, leave us here today, to dance together as we may."

> From his side see the king appear, *eya!*
> to stop us all from dancing here, *eya!*
> He's worried and he's full of fear, *eya!*
> someone will steal away his dear, *eya!*
> this Queen of April.

In an anonymous song of a lonely lady we again find a woman singer. It begins, "When I see the meadows grow green..."

> I sigh, I tremble all over
> all night long and in my dreams
> beside me now my lover
> lies waking, so it seems.
> How soon would he be healed
> if only it might be
> one night he was revealed
> at last come close to me...
>
> Messenger, leave in the morning.
> The voyage will be long.
> To my friend in his own far land
> carry now this song.

194

> Tell him I'm very happy
> with the words he said to me
> after he'd given me a kiss
> beneath the canopy.

There is a direct simplicity about the words, but the singer calls herself a great lady, *domna del mieu paratge*.

A Troubadour form with folk-elements is the *pastorela*. Here there is a dramatic element; a knight encounters a shepherdess and they speak together. Again we have a form that seems far more common in the north than in the south; some 130, coming up from the late twelfth century, are known in French. The setting is the countryside in spring. The knight makes advances to the girl and at times wins her with his cajoleries, promises of gifts, and so on. At times she resists, using some subterfuge or calling on shepherds nearby. The knight may then get rough treatment. There is no direct narrative; the form is a debate. Such songs could have been done by jongleurs, one of them pretending to be a woman, or by a man and woman taking alternate stanzas. The tone is mainly aristocratic. The courtly audience is amused at the encounter of knight and peasant-girl. In some forty pieces, not among those cited above, the author intrudes as witness and describes the scene with various aspects of the life of shepherds, sports ending in blows, love-rivalries, and the like. A few are idyllic, but the general note is humorous.[3]

In the south the genre is not common, and seems to be much used only near the end of the thirteenth century, as the poets look round for new material. There are, however, a few earlier examples. Marcabru, as we saw, composed one, in which the dominant role is given to the girl. She rebukes him and reduces him to silence. Marcabru uses the girl to repeat his lament over the decay of Worth, Youth, Joy. Only four pieces end with the triumph of the gallant, and only one is coarse in diction. G. de Borneil and Riquier use the form as a roundabout way of protesting their loyalty to the lady. The former complains to the girl on the first day of August near Alès that he has suffered much from a perfidious woman he wants to forget. "Demanding and flighty, that's all the highborn ladies are." And he keeps on failing to note the girl's advances. In six poems Riquier pretends to address homage to the same shepherdess over twenty years, but still cannot get her. In the first three his ardours are quenched by the thought of Bel Desport, evoked by himself or the girl; in the last three the girl sermonises more and more. In one poem she has just come back from a pilgrimage to Compostella. Complicated versification is used to palliate the extreme artificiality of the whole thing. The girl of Paulet de Marseille knows as much about the political situation as he does; they both exhort the kings of Aragon and England to an alliance. Cerveri's fourth *pastorela* deals with the struggles of Aragonese nobles against a new tax. In the later thirteenth century the moral and religious aspects increase. The shepherdess met by Joan Estève in April 1288 calls herself the Spouse of God; the one met by Guillem d'Autpol, though offered gloves and belt, reminds him that "pleasure engenders death."[4]

Whatever popular elements existed in the early *pastorela* were thus soon lost in the Troubadour forms and exerted no influence over the development of their songs. There is however an anonymous example, probably fairly early, which is simple in its form. Here the knight wins the girl by gifts.

> When the knight saw her go, he ran
>   and wouldn't let her pass.
> He took hold of her white hand
>   and laid her on the grass.
> She didn't open her mouth,
>   though he gave her kisses three,
> but when he gave her a fourth kiss,
>   "I'm yours, my lord," said she.

We see a genuine folk-formula there. Here is a quatrain from the traditional Furry Dance sung at Helston, Cornwall :

> John the beau was walking home
>   when he met Sally Drover.
> He kissed her once and he kissed her twice
>   and he kissed her three times over.

A much more complex problem is posed by the *alba* or dawnsong. Two lovers have spent the night together and now must part as it would be dangerous for them to be seen together. Usually there is a certain amount of dialogue or a combination of narrative and direct speech. In various lyric forms the genre is very widespread and ancient, the earliest known example going back to Egypt in the thirteenth century B.C., with other examples found in ancient Greece and China. We can see signs of dawnsongs in the *jarchas*, and there is an interesting dawnsong in Latin with a Provençal *refrain*, in a late tenth-century manuscript :

42. Woman Carding. (Louterell Psalter)

When Phoebus has not yet brightened in the skies,
Aurora with her slight light earthward flies,
a watchman calls to sleepers all, "Arise!"
Dawn lovelily   *on the dark sea*
draws the sun out
then passes by   *O watchman shout*
darkness we see   *cleared from the sky.*

There are problems in the text of the *refrain*, and we cannot assume
that the watchman had the same function there as in the Latin poem
to which the romance-song has been attached. In the poem there seems
no love-element. There are enemies who could be either invaders or
bandits, or even spirits of evil. The Latin stanzas, each with the refrain,
go on :

Our enemies lurk, and out they are bursting, all,
upon the idle and the rash to fall.
The herald pleads "Rise up." He gives his call . . .

The northwind from Arcturus freely blows,
the host of stars no longer brightly glows,
towards the eastern sky the Plough now goes . . .

In the stanzas the watchman calls to the drowsy; in the *refrain* he is
himself addressed, apparently by lovers (in the original use). Further,
the stanzas have their own melody, while each phrase of the *refrain*
has new notes, agitated as compared with the calm flow of the
melody. A Latin watchsong was composed at Modena in 892 when
Hungarians were menacing the area; and Christian dawnsongs, connected with vigils, go far back to Ambrose and Prudentius. The faithful spent a night of prayers together, with exhortations not to sleep,

197

and dedicated themselves on the cock-announced return of light.
Prudentius writes, with the Dawn as Christ's advent:

> Take off these beds. They stand
> for sickness, sleep and sloth . . .
> Keep watch, for I'm at hand.

He and Ambrose may have been adapting love-songs to the church's
need. Here are some more examples from the *jarchas* showing that the
dawn-theme was well known to romance-singers of the eleventh
century:

> Still ours is the dawnlight,
> soul of my joy, my brightness,
> long enough for the spy,
> my dear one, is this night.

Here the girl thinks the night will tire the spy out, so that they will be
able to embrace in the dawn. The lover can be himself identified with
the dawn; a girl tells her mother that she won't sleep in the morning
light, her lover is the face of her dawn. We find however the dislike of
dawn. A girl says: "Go away, Dawn, witch with fiery charm, when
he comes, you see our love." We are not far from such simple lyric
utterances in a brief Provençal *alba*:

> While the nightingale, early and late,
> sings away at the side of his mate,
> warmly I clasp my darling and wait
> under the flower,
> until the watchman high in the tower
> sings: Arise, you lovers, arise,
> the dawn is up and there's day in the skies.

The way in which the statement is sustained through the seven lines is
however not primitive. The other anonymous *alba* is a subtle thing.

> Deep in an orchard white with flowers of may
> the lady holds her lover closely gay
> until the watchman cries: Here comes the day!
> *Ah God, ah God, the dawn, how soon it comes.*
>
> Would God that morning never broke the night
> and left me sad with kisses put to flight.
> Would that the watchman never hailed the light.
> *Ah God, ah God, the dawn, how soon it comes.*

43. Bob-Apple. (Knight iii 197)

My darling, while I kiss, lie kissing me.
The meadow-birds are singing merrily.
All yours, despite my jealous man, I'll be.
Ah God, ah God, the dawn, how soon it comes.

My darling, with new love-play wake, then drowse,
here where the birds are singing in the boughs,
until the watchman bids us both arouse.
Ah God, ah God, the dawn, how soon it comes.

Sweet from the waters blows a little breeze:
it's from my lover, young and thewed to please,
his honey-breath comes softly through the trees.
Ah God, ah God, the dawn, how soon it comes.

Gentle the lady is, and full of grace,
and many come to look upon her face,
but in her heart one love finds loyal place.
Ah God, ah God, the dawn, how soon it comes.

The first stanza gives us the scene. Then the lady speaks. What is surprising is her frank wooing. Then in the fifth stanza it appears that the lover is not present after all. She is remembering past embraces and thinking of those yet to come. The tone, it has been suggested, is that of the *Song of Songs*, where also we find the wind as messenger. "Awake, north wind, and come, south wind . . ." The sudden change of focus in the last stanza may occur because the poet feels that he needs some objective note to get the subjective dream of the previous stanza into perspective; or he may want to stress that even after her abandonment to love the dreamer is still the respected lady of Troubadour tradition. (We can however assume that after the fourth stanza the lover goes away and leaves the lady in a reverie.)

Giraut de Borneil plays about with the motifs, making himself the watchman and a friend of the lover at the tryst.

> True king of glory, splendour, light,
> if so it please you, lord of might,
> aid my companion trustily.
> Since night fell, he has gone from me
> *and soon will come the dawn.*
>
> Sweet friend, who sleep or wake, it's right
> to sleep no more. The eastern height
> reveals the star that makes night flee.
> I marked it open steadily
> *and soon will come the dawn.*
>
> Sweet friend, I'm singing urgently
> The bird that flits from tree to tree,
> seeking the day, calls loud and clear.
> The jealous one is near, I fear,
> *and soon will come the dawn.*
>
> Sweet friend, go to the window, see
> the stars grow pale. Rise cautiously.
> Then your true watchman I'll appear.
> Else you'll be hurt, for danger's near
> *and soon will come the dawn.*
>
> Sweet friend, I've had no sleep or ease
> since you went off, but on my knees
> I prayed that Mary's Son will send
> you safely back, my loyal friend,
> *and soon will come the dawn.*
>
> Sweet friend, there by the steps your pleas
> I heard, and pledged my loyalties
> to watch on sleepless till the end.
> My song and me no ears you lend
> *and soon will come the dawn.*

"Sweet friend, so richly here I lie
I want no dawns to claim the sky.
The noblest woman ever born
is mine to embrace, and so I scorn
the jealous fool and dawn."

In the last stanza the lover at last answers his friend. The seven manuscripts however differ considerably; and this stanza occurs only in two.
In one of these manuscripts there are also two more stanzas, in one of
which the watcher calls on the Virgin Mary. Yet another text gives a
stanza in which the lover answers back: "Sweet friend, I heard your
singing clear. I'm grieved that you disturb me here, drawn back from
paradise-depths am I, where on a lily-bed I lie." The melody, trans-
cribed in one manuscript, is grave and serious, in the Dorian mode,
and was used in the fourteenth-century Provençal play about the
martyrdom of St Agnes as a lament. Its end is very like that of
Cadenet's melody, suggesting that perhaps the notes used for *alba* in the
refrains were traditional.[5]

There is an anonymous *alba* in which the lover replies furiously to
the watchman, for breaking in on his love-making. "May God the Son
of Mary curse you . . . If I could get my hands upon you, I'd slaughter
you again, again." In a late *alba* by Cadenet the watchman takes over
and claims that he is a courteous fellow; he is so sympathetic with
lovers that he enjoys the long nights, cold and unpleasant as they are
for a watchman. Whatever the dangers, he'd carry on to help a friend;
but with false lovers he'd try to disguise the fact that dawn had come,
so that they might be caught.

A distinctive mark of the Troubadour *alba* is the watchman or
gaita. It has been argued that here is a sign of Arabic influence and
that the *gaita* derives from the muezzin. True, the dawn-theme is
strong in Arabic poetry and common from the seventh century; but
there is no independent dawn-genre. At first the main themes were the
separation of the tribes and the beloved's phantom leaving the lover at
dawn. But from the seventh and eighth centuries we also meet the
themes of lovers or wine-drinkers whom dawn separates; and the two
themes could be combined. Two works, the *Book of Similes* by Ibn
Abi 'Awn, early tenth century, and the *Collection of Concepts* by Abu
Hilal al-'Askari, later tenth century, have chapters listing dawn-
imagery. The Troubadour's *gaita* however is sufficiently explained by
the prominent role of watchmen in the towers at the approaches of a
castle or fortified town. The *gaita*, with or without instrument, sang

to keep sleep away and to prove his wakefulness. At the hour of work he sounded a horn or sang out certain words that might be rhymed or assonanced. Guibert de Nogent tells of a watchman who was said to have been ferried across a stream by the devil as he was at his rounds after dark. Also of the watchman at the abbey of St Médard: "after passing part of the night over the towergate beside the fishpond, springing rattles, singing out, and blowing on a horn, as watchmen do, at last he went down to walk about on the edge of the water." There he was accosted by three fever-spirits in the form of women. (In northern France, however, the watchman occurs only in one dawn-song, where there are a pair of watchers, though two *pastorales* refer to games or dances in which someone acts a watchman's part.)

The *alba* then gives us glimpses of the way in which poetic genres of courtly love could have a complex origin in folk-themes and forms, and it is clear that under the development of sophisticated forms there was a lively background of popular elements. We cannot however reduce the Troubadour tradition to such elements. They were one important factor in a complex situation, but only one factor.

XI

The Monk of Montaudon

WE have seen how there was an expansion of poets able to use the Troubadour system effectively in the later years of the twelfth and the early years of the thirteenth century. From the start the poets had been much concerned with questions of style and technique, which in turn were linked with questions of content: what they wanted to say and the best way to say it. And the enlarged audience now wanted to understand what was going on in the new vernacular literature and what it implied. Thus we find a treatise *Razos de Trobar* by Raimon Vidal, of Catalan origin, dated between 1190–1213. Vernacular poetry lacked prestige and the tradition of scholarship that surrounded works in Latin. Raimon knows that there is a public interested in Troubadour technique and themes, but not capable of a grammarian's analysis, and he addresses this audience as well as turning to practising poets in parts of his work. Part of his readership would have had Old Provençal as mother-tongue, others not. These latter would be his Catalan compatriots, who were connected with the courts. At this phase there is no sign of middle-class cultivation of poetry in Catalonia.

Raimon aims at instructing and correcting, at times in sharp terms; but though he attempts a display of erudition and starts with large claims, he has no system in his exposition and does not deal with the language or content of the poetry. Some three-quarters of his work is taken up with grammar. What he is concerned with are the errors to be avoided; and he seems to want to help in building up a critically-equipped public which will not be taken in by the superficial and the conventional. (We may compare the protests by the poets G. de Calanson, Peirol, Elias Cairel.) He is aware of a crisis in the relation of poet and audience, the turning-point marked by the rejection of *trobar clus* and by the use of well-worn material and themes. But he fails to carry out his argument and turns to the distinction between French (the language of romances and pastorals) and Provençal (the language of *vers, canzo, sirventes*). This point serves to set off his previous point as to the correctness of Provençal and its conformity to the grammar of

44. Horse beating a Tabor. (Knight iii 197)

the learned tongue. (Catalan and Provençal were close in vocabulary, but one had an established literary tradition, the other not.) He defined the area of Provençal as "Limousin, Provence, Auvergne, Quercy, and the provinces adjacent to them." He feels that the language of a literature with *auctoritat* (one that has attained classic status in the vernacular comparable with that of the Latin *auctores*) must necessarily have canons of correct usage; and he assumes that a poet facing a linguistic problem can appeal to a living tradition definable geographically and by the canons built up.

The interest of the treatise lies in three points; (a) the Troubadour vernacular is now treated on a level with Latin, (b) the new literature has spread strongly enough into Catalonia to warrant a work such as Raimon's, (c) there is wide agreement that there is something of a crisis in the poet–audience relationship which necessitates clarification of the many problems raised by the new poetry.[1]

During this period (1180–1213) a new vigorous personality has appeared, the Monk of Montaudon. A *vida* tells us that he was born in Auvergne, in a castle called Vic (Vic-sur-Cère), not far from Aurillac.

He was nobly born. He became monk of the abbey of Aurillac and the abbot gave him the priory of Montaudon. Once there he busied himself in making the house prosperous. While still in the cloister he composed songs as well as *sirventes* on matters talked about in the country. Then the knights and barons made him leave the priory, overwhelmed him with honours, and gave him all he asked. He took everything back to his priory and was thus able to embellish the church and augment its revenues. All the while however he kept on his monkish habit. Finally he returned to Aurillac to find the abbot and show him what good he had done. In return he asked permission to obey orders given by king Alfonso of Aragon, and the abbot agreed. And the king ordered the monk to eat meat, woo the ladies, sing and make poems. And the monk did it all. As a result he held a position at Puy-Sainte-Marie [Puys-en-Velay] where he was the master in charge of the sparrowhawk. For a long time he carried on this work. After the ruin of the Puy court he went to Spain; and all the kings and barons there loaded him with honours. In the end he went into a Spanish priory called Ville-franche [Villefranca] and belonging to the abbey of Aurillac, and the abbot gave it to him. He enriched this priory and made it prosper, and he died there.[2]

Peire de Vic says that his office at the Puy court gave him the right to be shown with a bird on his wrist in the illumination of manuscripts. Just what it was we have little idea; perhaps he was in charge of festivals or was the president of some poetic tribunal. He was a man of rumbustious humour, coarse and down to earth.

> I like enjoyments and gaiety.
> Good food and gifts and jousts for me!
> I like a lady of courtesy
> who's unembarrassed, ready and free,
> a rich man spending generously,
> sharp only to his enemy –

"the man who treats me with kindliness and opens his purse without being asked; the lord who doesn't rebuke me. I like pleas made in my favour, sleep amid wind and thunder, a fat salmon to eat at high noon. To relax in summer by a spring or a stream, when the meadows are green, the flowers push up again, the birds scream, my girl comes slyly to find me. I like the host who gives me a good welcome and makes no refusals. I like the company of my darling, her kisses and all the rest of it. I'd like my enemy to lose something valuable, especially if it was I that took it from him. And when foes are all around, I like good comrades who undertake my defence and make themselves heard as they wish."

In a longer piece he tells us what he does not like: "A man who keeps talking about doing you a service and never does it; a braggart who wants to kill everyone; a horse that goes lame; a young knight who drags a buckler everywhere without taking a single blow on it; a bearded chaplain and monk and a flatterer with sharpened nose; a poor and haughty lady; a husband who loves his wife too much, even if she's a noble Toulousaine; a knight who's arrogant afar from home, but at home is given the job of crushing pepper and looking after the dishes; a coward swinging a banner; a bad goshawk at a hunt; a big cauldron with not much meat in it; a little wine in a lot of water; a blind man or a cripple met in the morning, since their company doesn't last long":

> I hate at dinnertime to sigh
> for food delayed and scorched and dry.
> I hate a priest that's learned to lie,
> a mouldering whore that will not die.
> And by Saint Delmas I'm annoyed
> at idiots giggling overjoyed.

He hates to run on an icy run or gallop fully-armed. He hates the oaths of dice-throwers, or food taken without a fire in the dead of winter, or bed with an old farting crone who lets off tavern-stinks in his face. "I dislike and I find it frightfully unpleasant to be obliged at night to call a servant to wash the pot." He hates to see a lovely woman in the hands of a ferocious husband who prevents her from offering or granting him anything; a shabby vielle-player at a fine court; too many brothers on a small bit of land. He hates a partner who puts only a sou on the table when he, the Monk, makes a good throw; two lots of fur on a single cloak; too many heirs in a single castle; meagre cheer in the house of a rich lord; shafts or square-headed bolts of an arbalest at a tourney; a short cloth on a long table; a lackey with scabby hands who cuts the roast; a heavy hauberk in which the chain-links don't hold. He hates to wait at the door in rain and storm or to see friends bickering, "and I suffer abominably at knowing they're all wrong in the quarrel." He hates an old crone with too much finery, a poor slut giving herself grand airs, a young man playing the dandy, a little cunt in a fat woman, a lord who shears his peasants too roughly. He hates to ride in a cape under a downpour and to find near his horse a hog that empties the manger; a saddle in which the saddlebow doesn't hold; a hook that won't catch; a host who in his own house makes only clumsy blunders.

> I cannot like that knight's rude part
> who takes three helpings of sauced cabbage,
> nor the gallant who lets go a fart.

His satire on painted women needs to be cited in full; even in prose its liveliness and gusto comes over, and it shows his free-and-easy tone with God.

The other day by a bit of luck I was admitted to an audience in Heaven.

45. Horse beating a Tabor. (Knight iii 197)

Rightly the holy statues were making complaints against women who paint themselves. I saw them present their protest to God. If we're to credit them, the ladies make the price of paint rise by engrossing for their own embellishment a product to which the Holy Images have the first right.

God remarked to me without beating about the bush: "Monk, I learn that a great wrong is being done to my statues and their rights harmed. Go quickly, run for the love of me and tell the ladies to stop it. Let nobody pester my ears any more on the subject. If they won't renounce their little game, I'll go in person and scrape their paint off."

"Lord God," said I, "you should show more judgment, more moderation. It's in the nature of ladies to repair by paint the beauty of their complexion. What's that got to do with you, and what have the statues to complain about? If they keep it up, it's my opinion that women won't make them the least offering."

"Monk," replied God, "your arguments are bad and false. My creature has no right to embellish itself without my order. What would be my superiority over women if, no matter what I do to make them old, they can always stay young merely by anointing and polishing themselves?"

"Lord, you make your comments from high up in Heaven, like a being who hovers far above things. I see only one way to convince women that they should give up painting. Agree to let them stay beautiful till they die, or suppress paint itself, so that nobody can find the least bit of it anywhere in the world."

"Monk, it's not proper for a woman to enhance her charms by paint and you go miles too far when you put up such a case for them. Despite your backing, they must not assume a borrowed beauty which leaves wrinkles in their skin and which besides they lose as soon as they piss."

"Lord God, who paints well sells well. So they do it with great care and they use a thick hard material that doesn't yield at the first piss. Since you don't want to prettify them with your own hands, let them at least do it with their own. You should rather permit them the wish to make themselves beautiful without having to touch them."

"Monk, all these painting preparations tend to make them get a blow in the lower part of their bodies. Do you think they feel comfortable when a man holds them all bent-over under his love-making?"

"Lord, let them all go to the fires of hell. Never do I manage to stuff them up fully. With them, when I think I've reached shore, I have to swim more strongly than ever."

"Monk, the only thing is to let them go on painting. And since for destroying the fard it's only necessary to make them piss, I'll send a malady on them that keeps them pissing all the while."

"Lord, make all the women piss that you will. Only, in your grace, spare Lady Elys de Montfort, who never seeks to do up her skin and doesn't wake the complaints of any church-statue."

There is a mixture here of cosmetics and of astringents used for tightening up the vaginal orifice. In yet another piece the debate goes on. Finally each woman is allowed to use fard for fifteen years. Then in a *tenson* we find that the women overstep the limit and compose pastes "with camphor, narcissus, sarcocol, borage, and powdered silver" until an advanced age.

> So much of red, so much of white,
> they plaster chins by day and night,
> and plaster faces.
> No bit of clear bare skin you'd spy
> in any places.
> Beans soaked in ass's milk they try;
> on their old leathery skins they ply
> the foul confection,
> and swear by the great gods on high
> it's their complexion.

The Monk's rhyming adroitness is shown by the fact that the dialogue with God given in prose above consists of nine stanzas and two *tornadas* with the rhyme-scheme ABBACDDC, the same rhymes being used throughout.[3]

In another song he discusses his career with God in the same carefree way:

> In paradise the other day
> I found myself come joyously.
> With hearty words he welcomed me,
> he whom all things on earth obey,

on sea, plain, mountain, far and near.
"Hey, Monk," he said, "why come this way?
How's Montaudon where you should be
with far more company than here?"

"Lord, cloistered there I had to stay
a year or two, and that, you see,
aroused the barons' enmity.
Far from their graces does he stray
who holds the love of you too dear –
though Randon at Paris loves my lay:
he has never hurt or cheated me.
My travels he regrets, I hear."

"Monk, what's life enclosed and grey?
Obsessed with wars, you disagree
and fight still for your priory
with neighbours day on bitter day.
But I – I'd like to make it clear –
prefer your songs and revelry.
The world is better when you're gay
and Montaudon gains from the good cheer."

"Lord, making songs along my way,
I sin, and fear comes down on me.
The man who's sinning wittingly
loses your love to his dismay.
I'll leave my troublesome career.
To avert your wrath, the world I'll flee.
Beside my psalter now I'll pray
and Spain I never will go near."

God tells him to go to his old friend king Richard at Oleron. 'Ah, how
many marks it will cost him to make you gifts, he it was that got you
out of the mess." The Monk replies:

"Lord, if no visits there I pay,
the fault's with you who carelessly
permitted his captivity.
No sense of war do you display.
If Saracens into Acre steer,
weaker before the Turks we'll be.
Quite mad is he who in fray
follows behind you with a cheer."

209

46. Bowling. (Knight iii 197)

Thus, while God tells him to carry on with his life of song and cheer-
fulness, he ends by ironically rebuking God for not looking after his
own business, which involves war and destruction.[4]

A glance at a couple of his contemporaries will bring out how they
tended to seek originality by twists and variations on the accepted
conventions rather than boldly confronting new areas of experience.
Uc de la Bachélerie (near Uzerche) belonged to the world of Faidit
and Marie de Ventadour. His six pieces consist of three *tensons*,
a *partimen*, a dawnsong, and a lovesong. He praises his lady "with no
deceit and with no false affection," claiming that "no lover yet loved
more, who loved unloved." In his dawnsong he inverts the normal
motif of the *alba* and wants dawn to come :

> This true love I would glorify.
> Under its law I'm strictly bound,
> and so that less I now may sigh
> a new tune for the Dawn I've found.
> The night has a calm cloudless sky.
> I hear a bird, and O the sound
> seems to me still the echoing cry
> of my own grief spread all around.
> I am weary of night.
> God, bring the light!
> That's why I want the Dawn.

Gavaudan wrote a crusade-song that seems dated 1195. Of his ten
pieces one is a *pastorela* in which he meets a shepherdess whom he
knows on a hilltop. "I almost fainted with the pleasure, when her
hair touched my tingling skin." She is complaisant, but he tells her
how his lady is dead or gone off. "I do not know where she is gone.

Since then no comfort can I find." The girl consoles him, "Messire, this language well I know. In deep regrets my life I've spent since sadly I beheld you go." He congratulates himself on his luck. "Things never have gone so well for us. We both are free of serving another." The girl accepts his embrace with a rejection of any sense of sin.

> Dame Eve transgressed, another day,
> the orders given her, it's true.
> He who'd reproach me now for you
> would throw his time and words away.[5]

Rigaut de Barbezieux was a poor knight of the Saintonge, active round 1170–1200. His *vida* says that he fell in love with the wife of Jaufré de Tonay, whom he called Mielhs-de-Domna, Mieux-que-Dame. He pressed her, but she said that if he was truly her friend "he would know how to be satisfied with what she had already said or done." But another lady summoned him and offered to yield herself if he would leave Mielhs-de-Domna. Rigaut told the latter the situation and left her, but the second lady then "replied that he did not deserve the favours of another woman, and that, for having left so lovely and gracious a lady, he must be the falsest man on earth." He tried to gain forgiveness from the lady he had left, but failed. "Then he went off overwhelmed with grief into the woods, had a hut built, and enclosed himself there, saying that he'd never come out unless his lady forgave him." So the noble ladies and knights of the land went to beg Mielhs-de-Domna to pardon him. "She replied that she would not do so unless a hundred ladies and a hundred knights, all in love, came before her, on their knees, with clasped hands, to ask grace and pardon for him . . . And the hundred ladies and the hundred knights in love gathered and came to ask grace for Rigaut. And the lady forgave him."

This tale-type, we have seen, was told of at least three Troubadours. Rigaut's speciality was the use of the Bestiaries for similes drawn from wild life. In his appeal to the true lovers of the court of the Puy to end his lady's anger he compares himself to the elephant which, once fallen, cannot get up unless his fellows come to encourage him with their calls.

> Just as the powerful Lion
> so raging in his wrath,
> when a young cub comes forth,
> breathless and very small,
> he gives a rousing call

that makes him rise and stir,
so I am roused by her,
my lady. I rise again,
her love drives out my pain.

But he also uses more usual rhetoric. He says that his lady's cruelty
makes him alternately fat and thin. And,

Though such great torments I have known
through you alone,
I'd rather die for your harsh sake
than from another the least pleasure take.

Rigaut is the singer who invokes the Holy Graal, or Grail.

As Percival
when long ago
he saw the Lance, the Holy Grail,
amazed, felt all his senses fail
and didn't know
what things they were at all:
so, lady, I'm your thrall.
When I behold your body's grace
I'm rooted in the place
where you bewildering gleam:
I want to speak of love, but mutely still I dream.

[XII]

Symbolism

WE have just seen Rigaut de Barbezieux using the symbolism of the
Holy Graal to express the awe he feels before his lady and we have
continually come up against the use of Christian or other symbolism
by the Troubadours; it is now time to ask more definitely what it all
amounted to. First, there is the obvious fact that from one angle the
Troubadour system represented a feudalisation of love. The lady was
called *midons* or *senhor*. *Midons* comes from *mi dominus*. Only a bad
lord refused to protect and aid his vassal with the deserved *gerredon*.
The lady is depicted as so lofty and unapproachable that the lover in
aspiring to her is like a lesser knight seeking a seat by a mighty baron.
Vidal writes: "I'll then turn elsewhere. A man is wise and earns no
blame if without vain murmurings he goes off from a cruel and pitiless
lord." (In Languedoc we saw that change of lord was especially easy.)
Pons de Capdueil writes: "A weak castle closely-besieged cannot be
saved without aid. If the lord to whom it belongs brings no aid, he
loses it by default, and it's a great dishonour and loss for him. So my
lady will lose me by her own fault if she doesn't succour me when I
cry out for mercy." R. de Miraval pretends that he holds his castle from
his lady, and his reference to a kiss no doubt implies that he holds it
through a ritual kiss or obeisance. Cardenal writes: "No question of
homage, of grant, of gift of my person, abandonment of my liberty,
my heart put in pawn."[1]

But the poets do not use the feudal idiom for submission because it
lies ready to hand. The love-relation is explicitly substituted for the
power-relation, the property-relation. Feudalism is mocked at. The
continual claim of the lover for acceptance and for possession implies
equality between him and the lady, and the breaking-down of feudal
hierarchy. In the working-out of the relationship there is a ceaseless
dialectic between submission and freedom, power and equality.

If we look at religion we find again the use of feudal metaphors.
We saw how in the pre-Anselm formulations the relations of God,
Devil, and Man were set out in feudal terms. St Odilo as a young man

H   213

– he later became abbot of Cluny – entered a lonely church and offered himself to the Virgin with a token of serfdom hung round his neck and with God as his witness. Peter Damian (988–1072) states that his brother Marinus, layman, also offered himself with a rope round his neck at an altar to the Virgin as a serf. St Gerard of Brogne went every second year to Rome "with ten shillings hanging from his neck and offered himself as a serf to his Lord." The crusaders of 1099, entering Jerusalem, went to the Holy Sepulchre to offer their head-money to the Lord. The pattern of feudal connections, of overlord, vassals and sub-vassals, found a clear reflection in Cluniac organisation.

Again here we find in such attitudes both a carrying of feudal ideas to their limit and a transformation of them. The man who dedicated himself as a serf to Mary or God felt that he was gaining freedom from the world, from the very system of which he used the imagery. He did so even if the next moment he reverted to acceptance of the feudal system and its hierarchy. The contradiction of freedom and submission was deeply felt. The jingle ran: *Lex poli* was not the same as *lex fori*. Heaven's law was not the State's law. Men were aware of this deep conflict, the opposition of feudal division and apostolic unity, even when they fiercely defended the former. But just as the heretic rejected the divided world and tried to live on the apostolic system, the Troubadour kept always before him love's need for a true unity and equality, even when he was desperately entangled in the living conflict where division reasserted itself. Where he differed from the heretic or the orthodox lay in his steady effort to secularise the conflict and see it as worked out wholly in earthly terms.

The church, we saw, was committed to an anti-sensuous position in which sex was essentially evil or contaminated, whatever excuses had to be found for it as propagating the human race and thus providing the society which the church felt itself called upon to dominate and castigate. Yet, in order to define the living unity of the church, ecclesiastics felt it necessary to fall back on the imagery of Christ copulating with the body of the faithful. The same imagery was used to express the union of the devotee with a discipline of knowledge that he wished to master. Abelard cites Heloise as saying: "They refused for themselves all fleshly pleasures so that they might find rest in the embraces of no lady except Philosophy."[2]

The cult of the Virgin, already noticed, is relevant here. Its importance lay in the way it represented the breakdown, at least to some extent, of the rigidities of fear underlying earlier world-views dominated by the concept and image of God's Judgment. She was defined as a human character who could really temper justice with mercy, even with whims of sheer kindliness. As her cult grew, there was an order of secular knights, *La Chevalerie de Sainte Marie*, which took her as patron, and poets made songs in her honour, often using the terms of secular love-lyrics, for instance Gottfried von Strasbourg: "You are a potion sweet of love, sweetly pervading heaven above." The *Ave Maria* was composed in the twelfth century.

The adoration of the Virgin thus satisfied some of the attitudes that went into the Troubadour system with its worship of the Lady. The origin of the Marian cult and Troubadour poetry were more or less contemporary. There were no direct interrelations at first, though the two trends met in the common stream of twelfth-century thought and feeling. The positions set out by Tertullian in his address to women still had much strength:

Do you not know that each of you is an Eve? . . . You are the Devil's Gateway. You are the Unsealer of the Forbidden Tree. You are the first Deserter of the Divine Law. You are the one who persuaded him whom the Devil was too weak to attack. How easily you destroyed Man, the Image of God. Because of the Death which you brought upon us, even the Son of God had to die.

Augustine had made the modifying point that it was through a woman the Incarnation came about; but it was only now that that point was at all strongly taken into the main stream.

It is of interest that as the vital Troubadour tradition broke down, the poets turned more and more to the Virgin, at times paraphrasing the *Ave Maria* or imitating Latin liturgies. We find the old concentrations of love on the Lady turned towards the Virgin. The poet expresses the devotion of a knightly servant to her. The Virgin is all beautiful and amiable; she lifts the worshipper up to perfection and never lets down his hopes. With a minimum of retouches the old conventions are used. G. Riquier and Bernart de Panassac are examples of the turn to Mary. The Dominicans, who had been the Inquisitors destroying southern culture, were great propagandists of the Marian cult; and the poems on her multiply after 1250. Near the beginning of the fourteenth century the system of her seven sorrows, seven joys, her plaint at the foot of the Cross, has been worked out. The same process changed the dawnsong of lovers into one of religious symbolism. The night is the

47. The Ladder of Perfection. (*Hortus Deliciarum*, Whicker 160)

darkness of sin, the dawn is the day of Christ. Peire Espanhol exemplifies this sort of thing.

One effect of the social forces begetting the Marian cult was a certain humanisation of God. In both cases we can see an upsurge of deep pagan elements kept alive at the popular level, linked with fertility-cults and their offshoots. In the Virgin the Earth-mother reasserts herself, and God too is swayed over to acceptance of sensuous love. In *La Lai de l'Oiselet* the wise Bird declares: "This truth then is recalled by me: God and Love do well agree. God loves honour and courtesy; and Love they please most thoroughly. God hates disdain and Falsity. Love holds them base in every way. God hearkens to those who truly pray. And Love won't turn from such away." Such statements, made by the early thirteenth century, would have been unthinkable a century before, except perhaps in a defiant *refrain*.[3]

In making love of woman a supreme good, whether or not the goal was physical consummation, the Troubadours ran against all medieval preconceptions. It was as if they took up Peter Lombard's dictum and said that if all passionate love was adultery, then adultery was the best form of love. It was assumed that married love could not bear the significances that the Troubadour system demanded. In feudal thought marriage, to begin with, had no connection with love; it was essentially a matter of status, property, and the continuation of the family. Andreas, expounding courtly love, explained why marriage could not provide the basis of that love's ethic. He cites Marie de Champagne, who insisted that true love could exist only between unmarried persons. A husband and wife were legally bound to loyalty, while in true love there must be no legal compulsion, there must be only the free and sustained choice of the lovers. This judgment was given in a Court of Love.

Andreas expounds this position under three heads. First, the embraces of married couples involve no furtiveness or secrecy, and secrecy was a necessary aspect of true love. The essence of love is desire. Love is not mere pleasure, comfort, acceptance of a good thing already gained and habitually enjoyed. It is a never-satisfied searching and longing for a good that is not yet possessed in any stable sense. In married love the relation is fixed and stable, so that there is no quest or forward drive for new horizons. Secondly, love by its essence involves jealousy, *zelotypia*, which is not a good thing for a married couple. The jealousy of true love is not seen as a base suspicion, as would be doubt of a wife's fidelity; it is a pure jealousy. If lovers felt the base suspicion, they would be *amicus* and *amica*, not *amantes*. Pure jealousy is an aspect of the instability inherent in a ceaseless and unsatisfied quest. It is a questioning vehemence of desire and devotion, which keeps on needing to test the situation to ensure that it is not breaking up or losing its drive, and that the beloved is indeed all that is felt or assumed, not an illusory idol. It is also a consuming anxiety about her wellbeing, to the exclusion of everything and everyone else. It is compared with the jealous love of a God who is himself a jealous god; this jealous love is described by the pseudo-Dionysius and is an essential aspect of desire, of quest. It provides the bitter and joyous discipline urging the lover on to perfection.

Thirdly, there is an aspect of love connected by Andreas with the analogy of friendship and kinship. Between friends, and between husband and wife, there is or can be equality, a settled relationship that makes no further demands. But between lovers there is inequality, as between father and son; and this inequality is an essential aspect of love and its instability, its ceaseless striving which is also a conflict. Even if the lovers have an ultimate ideal of equality, in the working-out of their relationship there are unbalances, uncertainties, a continual breaking-down of symmetries. Such a condition is the price paid for growth.

These formulations by Andreas come late and represent a fixation of ideas that had been built up in a dynamic way by the poets themselves over generations; but they point correctly enough to the reasons for the stress on love of someone else's wife. Love is seen above all as a quest in which all the comforts and conventions of settled life are discarded: a deepening penetration into life, which in the conditions and ideas of the time could not be imagined as happening in marriage. But we must not therefore see the Troubadour love-system as attached by its nature to adultery. The social conditions bringing about that connection did not encompass the whole impulse behind the love-system, though they partly limited its application. The impulse had roots in popular elements that were not concerned with problems of feudal marriage and saw love as something with its own inherent rights of freedom. The Troubadour expressions then, however in some respects limited by feudal concepts of marriage, radiated out influences that broke through those concepts and looked to a much wider and deeper idea of love.[4]

It is from this angle of the quest, with a dialectic of give-and-take, of union and separation, conflict and resolution, that the Troubadour system merges with certain aspects of Sufism and of Christian mysticism as it had been developing through Anselm and Abelard. If we go far enough back we find that both the Arabian and the Christian traditions had roots in Greek philosophy, especially the Neo-

48. The Ladder of Salvation. (Wall painting, c. 1200, in Chaldon Church, Surrey)

platonism of Plotinus, and in Gnosticism. Perhaps in particular through the treatise of the pseudo-Dionysius with its strong pantheist elements, there were common factors in Arabian and Christian mysticism of the eleventh and twelfth centuries, in the concept of the quest for God and the stages by which union was achieved.

Early in the monastic system there had been set out the idea of a progressive movement upwards, imaged in terms of the ascent of Jacob's Ladder. To go up represented humility; to go down, pride. But at first the steps were defined as signs or tokens or humility, not as stages of growth. With the second half of the eleventh century came the various social malaises that stirred a desire for the life of a hermit: an acute inner conflict with a new need for solitariness. Even the old Benedictine orders were affected, for instance in Anselm. In his account of the Ladder he recasts the twelve rungs mentioned in the Rule and turns the Ladder into a Mountain; the rungs become seven steps, which are set out in a more logical order, with greater stress on the inner life. The corporate element in monastic life is played down and the steps are seen as concerned with the individual who struggles alone with himself, through self-knowledge, grief, confession, persuasion of guilt, acquiescence in judgment, suffering or punishment, love of punishment. The searching of the soul appears again in the Cistercian system, with an idea of progress in self-knowledge leading up to God. St Bernard wrote a treatise on St Benedict's twelve steps of humility. He increased the logical coherence and saw the stages as moving from self-knowledge and self-contempt to neighbourly compassion and on to perfect contemplation of the truth.

Such schemes, though limited to questions of individual development and leading away from the earth to an abstract principle of being and authority, were permeating the thought of the epoch, applied in various ways. Thus in the medieval Tower of Knowledge we see the boy led by Philosophy first to Donatus on Grammar and Priscian on dialectic. Above, on the battlements over the door, is Aristotle (logic), Cicero (rhetoric), Boethius (arithmetic). Higher still are Pythagoras (music), Euclid (geometry), Ptolemy (astronomy), Plato (physics), Seneca (ethics), with Peter Lombard (metaphysics and theology) on top of everyone else. The importance of the Troubadours is that they first sought to draw down the scheme of development, of a quest through stage after stage, into earthly life and to secularise it.[5]

Inevitably there were many elements of confusion, many limitations, in this process of secularisation, this withdrawal from other-wordly goals. Still only a few chosen spirits go through the process, which in turn is limited to the experience of love. But the important thing is that the first crucial step has been taken. Again, the concept of a hierarchy of powers is rejected, though the scheme of courtly love is still much entangled with contemporary notions of power and submission. There was a strong general idea in the twelfth century that supremacy of will, whether one's own or another's, was an evil thing. How was one to escape from the oppression? Society showed the serf as the pure example of a person subjected to another's will and thus losing his nature as a human being and turning into a mere thing, a chattel. Bracton in the thirteenth century saw the serf as someone always at the will of another; he did not know one day what he would do the next. Yet in a sense the ascent into liberty was into an area more fully defined by law; the knight did not obey fewer laws than an ordinary freeman, but more. To live entirely a *vita voluntaria*, where a man had to will each detail, was not freedom. Ivo of Chartres tried to persuade a canon, who lived according to the Rule of St Augustine, not to be hermit; life lived according to a well-known rule was higher and more free. The highest law of all, the highest freeedom, was that by which a man stripped himself of the goods of this world and subjected himself to a rule of poverty and obedience. A man under that rule at last overcame the conflict of will and selfwill.

The Troubadour, secularising such attitudes, saw himself as moving to an ever greater freedom the less he asserted his own will, the more he accepted that of the lady, which was seen as a rule emanating from pure beauty. Thus his union with a higher level of life (a higher level of his own self) was assured; he leaped into a new dimension where the dichotomy of law and freedom, rule and will, was overcome. But in fact this position, which hypostasised the lady and destroyed her individuality, was all the while contraverted by the conviction of equality in love, by the acceptance of her as a real person who was also struggling forward. It represented a metaphysical carry-over, which all the same was necessary at this stage as the poet sought to realise fully in human life the dialectic which had been previously handed over to the lonely soul and God. Entangled with the metaphysical notion of the lady was the realisation of her as a person in her own right; and it was this recognition that love was the union-and-conflict of two differing persons struggling towards the same goal that gave the novelty and the richness to the Troubadour dialectic. She was the other, who must be taken into the self without her distinctive existence being denied or flattened-out.

Because of the dual existence of the lady as both perfection and an imperfect human being who shares the quest, the stress in Troubadour experience is on the phase leading up to union, in which uncertainty, jealously, distance, cannot but rule. Love seems to have its inner unpredictable law. "Love can descend," says Bernart de Ventadour, "wherever it may please her." The lover declares his love without any claim on the beloved. "In love man has no dominion; who seeks it there serves woman basely. Love does not want what is unfitting." The lady remains inscrutable. "She does not make known her desire; rather she hides all the more from her lover what she would wish if she wished to be honoured still and so more prized there where longing constrains her" (attributed to both Bernart and Daude de Pradas). Thus he is loved and not loved; he makes his plea of hope and his lament; he suffers and endures in steadfast faith. Even if he gains a kind word, a touch, a sight of her beauties, a kiss, an embrace, and finally complete union, yet his happiness is threatened by a world of evil-speakers and malicious spies. Separation may be forced upon him; the beloved may fall into caprice; there is ceaseless fear as well as joy.[6]

We may say then that in so far as the Troubadour insists on the perfection of his lady he moves towards the mystical or metaphysical position In so far as he carries out with her a drama of union and separation, in which she is treated as in no way essentially different from himself, he is breaking down the metaphysical element and creating a true dialectic of human process. In the former case the sub-mission to the lady becomes masochistic and love is an *ascesis* of cruel tests and ordeals. Daude de Pradas thanks Love for an inexorable mistress. In the decadent Troubadour tradition, as poets of northern France take over the motifs, the stress on suffering grows. Poets such as Gace Brûlé, Gautier d'Epinal and Blondel de Nesle like to depict themselves as ecstasiated saints. The metaphysical side leads on further to Dante and Petrarch. Here we see what is essentially a turning up-side-down of the vital aspects of the Troubadour positions.

We have seen how Raimbaut d'Orange used religious imagery to define human love in its fullness. We can here look at further examples of the same sort of thing in poets who are using the method with less comprehension and intensity. Cabestanh says that when he prays he has his lady, not God, before his eyes. Vidal thinks that God gave his lady more perfections than he kept for himself. Daude de Pradas, though a canon, sings:

> Now in my heart a living thought comes clear –
> and there it's been deep founded by my eyes –
> I wouldn't want to be in Paradise
> since then I couldn't hold my only dear
> in whom reign Youth and Beauty and all things
> in which Love's used to find its pleasurings.

Raimon Jordan prays to God: "And if I tell you my joy in her, don't hold it against me as a thing of pride. So much I want her and desire her, I wouldn't so strongly beg of God to take me into his paradise as I beg of him to grant me the chance of lying with her one night." Ber-nart de Ventadour calls on God only to help him with his lady, to put a curse on faithless lovers or those who betray love's secrets, and to keep him, Bernart, always in love; also he uses God's name as witness to his love. Arnaut Daniel likewise sings:

> I hear and have a thousand masses said,
> and lights of oil and wax I burn for this:
> that God may grant me fair success with her
> where effort fails or goes amiss.

Guilhem IX writes: "I praise God and Saint Julian I've learned now the sweet game so well I'm skilled above all other men." The Monk

49. A Demon Tourney. (Louterell Psalter)

and Cardenal address God familiarly, even contemptuously. Peire d'Auvergne recognises the opposition of Christianity and courtly love:

> For in the world I've had my pleasure
> till I'm a sinner past all measure.

Pujol laments that two girls have become nuns: "Saint Pons will make me utter an impiety: he has taken the two jewels of Provence." He goes on: "By night, by day my spirit is moved to ride away with all my soldiers, straight to Saint Pons – good sense or folly – and burn the nuns discovered there. I suffer penance since Huguette has entered the order. You've deprived me of all joy, lovely Huguette, you and your sister." Rigaut de Barbezieux, as we saw, compares his lady to the Holy Graal. Gavaudan, lamenting his dead lady, asks for her to be raised to the innermost heaven among the angels; and in the last two lines he sees himself as her witness, her martyr, not God's. "A martyr he'll be made by grief. Nothing can bring him now relief." Pons de Capdueil insists that his Azalais, dead, should be enthroned above all other women in paradise, among lilies, irises, roses, while "joyous singers, the angels celebrate her." She thus takes over the place of the Virgin Mary.[7]

As Troubadour influences spread, directly or indirectly, we find more and more the secular use of religious symbolism. Chrétien de Troyes takes over a great deal of the religious vocabulary and turns it to the use of sensual love. Love is adoration. In Gottfried's *Tristan* of the early thirteenth century there is a Cave of Lovers described as a richly adorned church with its saint's shrine. In the centre is "the nest of crystalline Love" with design and proportions explained after the

modes of the Gothic world. Here Tristan and Iseult faithfully obey
Love's precepts. What is brought out is a sense of a deep gap between
Christian doctrine and Christian duty or practice.

The Troubadours, however, were men enough of their world to
express a normally pious fear at a strong impact of death. We saw the
turn in the last poem of Guilhem IX, and similar sentiments are found
in Peire d'Auvergne. Guillem de Saint-Leidier deals with transub-
stantiation, Marcabru and G. de Borneil pause to meditate on death,
and so on. But these passing moments of orthodoxy only emphasise
the strength of the main secularising trend.[8]

Though the Troubadour system of love took care not to meddle
directly with any dogmas of the church, it was at root heretical,
though the church failed to take in this point clearly at the time. When
Andreas wrote his *Three Books on Love* (1174–86) he felt compelled
to draw attention to the incompatibility of Christianity and courtly
love, while at the same time setting out the ideas of the latter with
full sympathy. He used the method of the rational dialectic. Most of
his work consists of a set of dialogues. The Troubadour ethic, he shows,
is based on nature, declaring that it is of man's nature to love. Love
in turn copies nature. The poets seek to show that human fulfilment
occurs through accepting nature and the impulse of love that all men
share. The cleric who loves women, against his church's teaching, is
thus vindicated. What love forbids is only what is contrary to nature.
A defect in nature brings love to an end. Our human nature is not what
we share with the animals; otherwise the wanton, the promiscuous,
even the peasant would feel the drive of desire into even deeper and
fuller hopes and aims. Human nature is thus what separates man from
animal nature and enables him to see that love is not just a random
response or impulse, but the greatest and only steadfast good. "The
rule of Love shows us that neither woman nor man in the world can
be considered happy or well-bred, nor can he do anything good, unless love inspires him."

We saw earlier how a woman raised the question in one dialogue
that love was undeniably offensive and injurious to God. The answer
was that her remark was true enough, but in effect earthly life would
be useless and pointless if men acted in accord with it. It was wrong
for lovers to refuse to practise mixed-love and enjoy copulation.
Copulation was true love and as such was the praiseworthy origin of
all good things. "Besides, it does not seem at all proper," comments
Andreas, "to class as a sin the thing from which the highest good in

this life takes its origin and without which no man in the world could be considered worthy of praise." Yet in his third book he turns to the religious view and condemns courtly love as wholly evil and the source of evil, composed of errors and vices, opposed in every respect to the love of God which the church held to be the sole source of virtue and of the good. Nothing could more strongly underline than does this volte-face how impossible it was to reconcile the Troubadour system with the church.

But Book Three did not save Andreas. His work was condemned on 7 March 1277 by bishop Stephen Tempier of Paris as teaching "manifest and execrable errors." It was seen as setting out the doctrine of the Double Truth. This year 219 propositions were condemned, covering the whole range of science, philosophy, logic, theology. What was being attacked was not so much a formal system of ideas as a state of mind that came to be associated with the work of Averroes. The union of dialectic (reason) and faith, which the earlier thinkers had hopefully postulated, had kept on showing signs of strain, with the rationalists unconcerned as to the way in which they undermined dogma, and the church feeling that rationalism was a crafty enemy. Though the doctrine of the Double Truth was seldom enunciated, it had come more and more to operate. Avicenna's system had in effect got rid of any creator god, stressing that matter was eternal and itself the principle of multiplicity, and that there was a single active intellect for all humanity. Al-Ghazali (1058–1111) saw the danger of a universe held together by inexorable laws, and tried to restore freewill to a god enclosed in the necessities of his own nature. But Averroes, commenting on Aristotle and accepted by western thinkers by about 1250, had even more deeply broken the unity of faith and reason. The philosophers, to save themselves from the church, had to avoid drawing the final conclusions of their positions and develop the idea that certain truths could only be entrusted to the fully instructed and initiated. They thus laid themselves upon to the charge of teaching two sets of truths. (Esoteric tendencies had developed in *trobar clus*, but these were based, not so much on a wish to hide certain doctrines, as on a sense of trembling on the edge of deeper truths than the poets could rationally formulate.)

In condemning Andreas' treatise the church was in effect condemning courtly love and the Troubadour system. It was denying that there would be any compromise between a system looking to earthly love as the source of all good and its own system of other-worldly sanctions. Courtly love was thus essentially shown to be a heresy.[9]

XIII

The Albigensian Crusade

BUT there were more obvious heretics in the Languedoc, more im-
mediately dangerous to the church, than were the Troubadours. These
were the Cathars and Poor Men of Lyon. And one of the complaints
of the papacy was that the leading churchmen, not only the nobles,
were too lax in combating them. One of the main aims of Innocent
III's programme for reform was the deposition of such ecclesiastics as
Archbishop Berengar of Narbonne; he was attacked as having only one
god, money, and for letting his clergy become usurers, doctors,
lawyers, even jongleurs. Bishop Hugh of Auxerre was as greedy, but
he persecuted heretics and so was not attacked. The Council of Avignon in 1209 accused many bishops of caring more for money than for
souls, and among the practices they were forbidden was the use of
musicians for entertainment at meals. In the next four years several
of them were deposed.[1]

Let us glance at the Cathars. Attempts have been made to work out
how many Perfected existed in the early thirteenth century, but they
vary greatly. Perhaps there were a thousand or a thousand and a half;
and there were even less Waldensians. Still, the effect of these devoted preachers was considerable. The main area dominated by the
Cathars was along the Toulouse–Carcassone axis. They were particularly strong in the plain called Lauragais with its small fortified
towns. Here a large number of the knightly families were heretics.
Everywhere in the medieval world there were disputes between nobles
and ecclesiastical landlords; but in Languedoc, because of the conditions we analysed earlier, the nobles were specially given to invading
church rights and claims. The ecclesiastical records depict them as
ruthless aggressors looting abbeys, turning monasteries into fortresses,
despoiling bishops. The counts of Toulouse and the Trencavel
viscounts were in continual trouble with the church, though they went
on protesting their orthodoxy. Raimon VI insisted that he was a good
Catholic, though the clerics declared that he kept Cathars round him to
provide the *consolamentum* if some accident happened. Raimon Roger

de Foix persecuted monks while his wife and sister became Cathars, though he refused to make gestures of veneration for the *Boni Homines*.

The lesser rural nobility seem the class most strongly affected by the heresy; they hated the church because of its reclamation of tithes that they had once enjoyed. They fought against the Catholic crusaders, though perhaps more out of a dislike of the enemy than any strong attachment to the Cathar cause. The families were often closely linked by intermarriage, and it seems that the womenfolk did much to draw the men into action against the Catholics. Women were particularly attracted to Catharism, in part because the heretics did not single them out for condemnation as the church did. All flesh was equally evil in Cathar eyes and adultery was not worse than marriage. Often the women in a family were Cathars, while the men, out of personal loyalty, defended them. A poor knight, asked by bishop Fulk of Toulouse why he didn't drive heretics off his land, replied, "We cannot; we have been reared in their midst; we have relatives among them and we see them living a life of perfection." But at times the question divided families.

Of peasant reactions we know little, and in towns the situation varied. Some towns were rather orthodox, for example Montpellier and Narbonne; others had strong heretical groups. Of the leading families in Toulouse some were accused of Catharism; others seem to have been orthodox. When Fulk later set up a White Confraternity on the city action against usurers and heretics, a Black Fraternity appeared in the bourg; but whether the latter represented a political reply or direct sympathy with heresy, we cannot say. Among the workers the weavers had a name as heretics, perhaps because, roaming about, they could serve as missionaries. Certainly in the Midi we find that heretics and their sympathisers in the towns often had textile or other workshops, and that they travelled round as merchants or craftsmen. The crusade aroused sustained opposition in the towns; but here a strong emotion was the fear of losing their independence, together with hatred of the Dominican inquisitors and their ruthless methods. Apart from persons or groups ready to give direct support to the heretics they were clearly large numbers who respected them and had no wish to see them persecuted and murdered. How far the heretics had succeeded in making people realise the deep gap between the church's professions and its practice is shown by the common saying: "I'd rather be a priest than do that."

50. Dominican or Black Friar, and Franciscan or Grey Friar. (Knight iii 268)

St Bernard had come preaching in 1145; and there had been another mission in 1178. When a papal legate with abbot Henry of Clairvaux came, Henry said that they were jeered at in the streets. One heretic was flogged and exiled for three years to the Holy Land, his town-house was razed, his property sequestered. Henry failed to get Roger Trencavel II to free the bishop of Albi whom he had captured in a brawl. Two heretics, brought under safe conduct, were held to incriminate themselves when they refused to take an oath as something sinful, and were excommunicated. All these proceedings were mild. But at the Lateran Council of March 1179 the use of force against heretics was approved. They and bandits were to be hunted down, and any men who hunted them were offered indulgences. The abbot of Clairvaux gathered an army and in 1181 besieged the castle of Lavaur. The Trencavel viscount who held it sued for peace. Church legislation went on urging action, but nothing much was done for twenty years.

In January 1198 came the election of pope Innocent III (Lothar of Segni, a Roman aristocrat). For the next eighteen years he fought hard to strengthen papal power. In 1199 he defined heresy as treason, as lèse-majesté against God; and for five years he tried to reform the clergy of the Midi by removing the lax dignitaries, winning over the nobility, and arranging for preachers to resist the heretics. He mainly used Cistercians as preachers. Of the first pair one was his own confessor. They had the right to excommunicate heretics and lay contaminated land under interdict, while ordering the confiscation of the property of heretics or their protectors. Then more authority was given. In 1203 two more Cistercians took over, with the abbot of Citeau added, and monks were to be called in to supplement the preaching of the three legates. Churchmen of the area disliked these intrusions. The bishop of Béziers was suspended for refusing to excommunicate the consuls of his town. A case against the bishop of Narbonne dragged on till 1212, when he was deposed; but quicker action was taken against many other prelates. The secular authorities refused to co-operate with the legates. The papal efforts had little effect on the situation.

In 1204 the pope realised that he would never get far unless he was able to call in military support from outside the Midi. He began to work on the king of France, hoping to get him to intervene. But he had little success for some time. In 1206 there was a new preaching campaign under three Cistercians and the bishop of the Spanish see of Osma with his sub-prior. They acted on a new system perhaps devised by the pope. Trying to beat the heretics at their own game, they dropped any effects of luxury and went around barefoot. In 1207 twelve Cistercian abbots with accompanying monks were drawn in. A series of open debates was held with heretics in large and small towns. At Montréal the argument went on for fifteen days, at Servian eight. At times a panel of judges, Catholics and Cathar sympathisers, presided. The orthodox had some small gains.

But the pope had now decided that military action was the only way by which he could win. He had kept on appealing to the French king with alluring pictures of the lands to be gained, but Philippe Auguste was entangled in conflicts with England and keeping an uneasy eye on Germany. Now in 1207, with the missions breaking down, the pope resumed his pleas and Philippe tried to get him to arrange a two-year truce with England, arguing that he could not afford to keep two armies in the field, one against king John, one against Languedoc, and that the pope must agree to a money levy on the clergy and barons of France. These conditions were met. Then in January 1208 the legate, who had excommunicated count Raimon VI in the previous year, had an interview with him. Raimon's excuses for failing to carry out papal policy were apparently not accepted and there was a quarrel. Soon afterwards a knight attacked the legate as he was about to cross the Rhône, and killed him. The causes of the murder are obscure and it seems more than unlikely that Raimon had any hand in it. But the pope assumed that the knight had acted at the count's orders, though later he reduced the charge to one of suspicions of complicity. Raimon however made the mistake of not trying to find and try the killer.

The pope now felt that he had the pretext for demanding a crusade against the heretics, with offers of land for the invaders. The French king was at first against such action unless Raimon had been convicted of heresy, then he agreed that some five hundred of his knights might take the cross, though he would not let his son join in. The crusade offered many inducements to knights and nobles hungry for land. The land to be grabbed was close at hand and did not involve any long journeys eastward, and the war of loot and seizure brought with it relief from penances for sins. In Italy the pope had been putting pressure on the towns to bring in legislation against heresy; in France he had been active in prosecutions at Nevers and La Charité-sur-Loire; and he sent warning letters and commissioners to the Rhineland.

The war thus started lasted from 1209 into the 1240s. Here we can only briefly tell its story, the military ups-and-downs and the periods of truce. First came the invasion and conquests of 1209–15. In the French army gathering in June 1209 under a papal legate were the duke of Burgundy and many counts, with archbishops and bishops bringing contingents. In the first phase most of Languedoc passed into the hands of the crusaders and the fourth Lateran Council confirmed Simon de Montfort in possession of what had been the lands of the count of Toulouse and the Trencavels. In the second phase, 1216–25, with the death of Simon, the southerners seemed near success, then in the third, 1226–9, the French king made a powerful intervention and turned the tide.

We may glance at a few important moments. In July 1209 Béziers was attacked and stormed. The crusaders cut down everyone they met. The church of Ste Marie-Madeleine was packed with refugees from the bloody streets; the crusaders set fire to it and burned everyone inside. The massacre went on till the pillaging footsoldiers were driven out by knights; they fired much of the town including the cathedral. The legate wrote that in this "miraculous" event some 150,000 people had been killed by the crusaders who "showed mercy neither to order nor to age nor sex." His figures may have been a mere guess, but the shock of the slaughter to Languedoc was acute; a contemporary said that the

51. The King's Dream: the Ecclesiastics. (John of Worcester MS)

killings were deliberate, meant to terrorise resisters. Carcassone, with wells dry and sickness raging among the refugees, at last surrendered. The viscount had refused safe conduct for himself and eleven companions at the cost of abandoning all the others in the city. Now the inhabitants were driven out, "bearing with them only their sins." Many other towns, dismayed, gave in. Toulouse was attacked but succeeded in its resistance, though Simon now had German crusaders as well as French. The church had drawn in warriors from the Rhineland, Frisia, Saxony, Westphalia, even the Balkans.

Count Raimon Roger, held as captive, had died by early November, perhaps of dysentery, but generally considered to have been murdered. An unknown Troubadour lamented his death, comparing him to Christ:

They have killed him. Never has there been such a crime, such a madness, a deed so displeasing to God, as the act of these renegade dogs, this treacherous breed of Pilate, who have killed him. As for him, he made himself like Jesus Christ who died to redeem us. Has he not passed, to save his own, across the same bridge?

A thousand knights of high lineage, a thousand ladies of great worth, go off through his death wandering here and there, and a thousand towns and a thousand servitors, who, if he had lived, would have been nobly endowed . . . Ah, God, what a loss. Do you see to what we are reduced?

Rich in lineage, rich in pride, rich in worth, rich in judgment, rich in prowess . . . in you we have lost the spring from which we return all joyous.

By the summer of 1212 the Toulousan region was more or less encircled. Then Pedro II of Aragon intervened. He had kept on offering his mediation, but was disregarded. The growing power of Simon (whose homage he had at first accepted) was angering him, and he was jealous of the intrusions of France. A Troubadour wrote a song to urge him to take action.

Go, Hugonet, with no delay, to Aragon's noble king and sing this new *sirventes*. Tell him that he is too slow in appearing and that dishonour is therefore imputed to him. It's said that the French hold his land too long and he doesn't think of defending it.

Tell him that his great valour will be tripled if he comes as a good king to exercise his rights in Carcassone; and if he finds some resistance, let him show that it displeases him – that if need be he lights fires and sheds blood, and that his machines strike so briskly the walls can't shelter our enemies.

In this way, lord, you silence the French – God's curse on them! for they shout that you don't know how to avenge your own. And so you'll revive Nobility that's lost to us so completely I see no trace of it.

It would make me happy to see along the fields the helmets glittering, the hauberks and the lances, and the many-coloured standards afloat. Yes, I'd be happy to see the French measure their strength with ours. Then it will be seen who are the bravest, and since right is on our side, the loss will surely be on theirs.

In August 1213 Pedro crossed the Pyrenees and was joined by knights of Toulouse, Foix, Comminges. (The exaggerations in the *vidas* of the Troubadours is exemplified by the claim that he invaded in order to restore to the poet Miraval the castle that the crusaders had taken.) At Muret he was defeated. The Toulousan militia, coming up to his aid, were caught by crusading knights and fifteen to twenty thousand are said (no doubt with exaggeration) to have been ridden down or drowned in the Garonne. Aragon's power to intervene was broken. Simon de Montfort went on to eliminate most points of resistance in the north of the country. The pope was reluctant to grant him full rights of possession, but in January 1215 he made him temporary custodian of the conquests. Prince Louis of France accepted Simon's position and ordered Narbonne and Toulouse to break down their walls. Count Raimon, we must remember, had never been proved a heretic and his heir was charged with no offence. The situation was complicated by the fact that the French king was taken up with plans for invading England and the papacy was preaching an eastern crusade.

On 30 November 1215 the Council at Rome deprived Raimon VI of his county and his title went to Simon, while the lands of the Count de Foix were sequestrated. Raimon VI and his son were however welcomed at Marseille and again at Avignon, where the townsmen offered them the town's governance. Offers of support came in from nobles of Provence. Raimon VI went to recruit men in Spain while his son rallied the eastern regions. Between March and June 1216 two Tarascon poets, Tomier and Palazi, expressed the loyalty of their area. They protested against the false peace, which, based on iniquity, could only beget war. They called on the lukewarm to see themselves "in Toulouse and Foix," and to consider the lot of the two counts betrayed by those they trusted. They poured scorn on the cowardly and predicted a traitor's end for that man (Guillem IV of Baux) already dispossessed of the lands he thought to usurp from a banished man. (He had gained the title of king of Arles, but most of the country had just made homage to Raimon.) They glorified Avignon which had set the example of its faith in justice, its devotion to its legitimate lords.

Does she not do better than those kinsfolk who carry on like the Algais [troops of mercenaries and brigands, dispersed after the French hanged their leader in 1212]? She alone lifts up her head and takes the good road, leading one way to Portugal, the other to Lombardy. How villainous and cowardly are the others. Avignon rears up in the midst of Provence . . . A noble and courtly people, your energy is the honour of the Provençals, always, everywhere.

Raimon's son had invested the French troops in the castle of Beaucaire, which surrendered despite Simon's attempt at relief. This, the first success for some seven years, delighted the southern fighters. An unnamed poet in a *sirventes* protests against the foul peace for which Simon is responsible – Simon who despoils, puts the world upside down, and turns towns into deserts. "If he wants in person to get his tributes in, I don't advise him to lodge at Beaucaire." The poet calls on the Provençals to make a resistance of which they have just seen the effect. "What are you doing, baron who hide like rat in hole? Don't you see what harm can fall on you for it? Come on now, up, get a move on with your arms and hands."

> By struggle many a man breaks free from trouble,
> who else would be the prey of doom and death . . .
> Come on, we're in the open! On again,
> he who has any worth! And marsh and plain

let us defend, no longer weakly swayed
by heedlessness. Disarmed and with no aid
the Frenchmen see us; but at last we've learned
the things they mean. Thank God our luck has turned
despite the men concocting the false peace.

Count Raimon was said to be crossing the Pyrenees with new troops. A French force, breaking into Toulouse, was captured by the citizens. Simon marched up, managed to get in, but was driven to take refuge in the castle, Bishop Fulk persuaded the consuls to accept a truce with terms advantageous for Simon, who exacted an indemnity while his men pillaged. Then Count Raimon entered the town on 13 September and drove the French out. In July the pope had suddenly died. The French lacked enough men to encircle Toulouse, so they camped on the south side. The new pope, Honorius III (1216–27), did his best to draw the French king himself into the war and ordered the preaching of a new Albigensian crusade.

Meanwhile dispossessed knights came in to help the defence of Toulouse. The partly-destroyed walls were rebuilt, with a moat beyond them, then wooden barricades and another ditch. Near one important gate the moat spread out into a marsh. The area between outer ditch and moat was dug with trenches, barriers were set up, and stone-throwing machines were raised on to platforms behind the walls, while stones were hauled up out of the river. The count and consuls organised the defences and raised funds for mercenaries. Militia from other towns and mercenaries were quartered on church property. Montan Sartre, the tailor, in a *sirventes* exhorted the count to resist the French.

When the crusaders advanced through the suburb of St Cyprien, they were driven back by the outposts on the western bank. Most of the fighting during the next months was along the southern walls. Prisoners were blinded, mutilated, dragged at the heels of horses, or used as targets in shooting practice. In the spring of 1218 both sides were reinforced. Simon used Flemish knights to make another attack on the bridges through St Cyprien. A sudden flood weakened the defence-works and Simon took one outer tower, but could not press the assault further. More troops joined both sides in late May and early June. Simon built a cat or movable tower. Early on June 25th an attack from two points was launched on the cat and the ramp. A catapult built by a carpenter of St Sernin was being operated by "dames and girls and married women" in the city. A stone from it struck down Simon as he ran to the aid of his brother wounded by an arbalest. It

52. Swordsmen. (Knight ii 125)

hit him, sang the *Chanson de la Croisade*, "exactly where it should," and he died. The crusaders, disheartened, went off in late July, now under Amaury, Simon's son. They had been doing badly elsewhere. The count of Comminges drove the French out of his country, and the younger Raimon was fighting to recover upper Languedoc.

The Pope ordered a new crusade and again put pressure on the French king. The king, now old, was not keen for the war, but he at last agreed that his son Louis should again lead a force south. In May 1219 Louis moved with French troops and some crusaders. French knights were defeated near Bazière, but the invaders took Marmande; and though the nobles were let go, Amaury massacred the townsfolk, some 5,000 of them it is said. The French army now camped all round Toulouse, where new defence-works had been built. The investment began on 16 June 1219, but on 1 August Louis went off. Why he did so is not clear, but it is possible that he wanted Amaury to be defeated and forced to relinquish his claims: after which the French would be able to act solely for their own benefit.

Raimon VII now set about regaining his whole county, and by 1225 was pressing on the viscounties of Albi and Béziers as well. Many French lords had left the lands they seized, and had taken to banditry. Amaury, centred on Carcassone, was in difficulties, unable to pay his hired knights despite the pope's appeal on his behalf. After some fifteen years war, Languedoc was nearly back under its own lords; but neither the pope nor the new French king Louis VIII could accept that situation. In November 1225 Raimon, despite his attempts to conciliate the pope, was again excommunicated, and with him Raimon Trencaval and the count of Foix. Louis, no longer interested in pretences of a crusade, prepared to conquer the south and incorporate it in his kingdom. A large army was collected at Lyon in June 1226. A brave defence at Avignon halted the French advance for a while. Tomier and Palazi composed a *sirventes* which tried to encourage the defenders with a promise of aid that wasn't likely in fact to come:

> God yet will send strong aid, lords, credit me.
> We'll beat the French. For fighters unafraid
> God sends his vengeance swooping suddenly.
> Then, lords, be firm, relying on strong aid.
> They come with their false banners of crusade.
> They'll run without their campfires lit, you'll see.
> Strike hard and even a mighty host will flee.

On 9th September the town surrendered. This time only captured mercenaries were slaughtered. The southern nobles, overawed, submitted in large numbers to Louis, but he made no attack on Toulouse. In October he marched back north and on 8th November he died.

He had however done his best to organise the submitted areas with seneschals and baillis, under Humbert of Beaujeu. Desultory fighting went on through 1227, with atrocities the order of the day. In early 1228 Humbert began systematically to ravage the land round Toulouse; and Raimon, heavily in debt to his own subjects, with his eastern territories in pawn to their towns, had to give in. The Peace of Paris, in twenty-one articles, established the French victory, with Raimon surrendering two-thirds of his lands. The church's will was to be accepted, Jews were to be dismissed from employment by the count, and anyone under excommunication for a year was to have his property confiscated. A large indemnity was to be paid, and four thousand marks were to be made available over ten years as salaries for professors of theology, law, the arts, in a university at Toulouse. The count was to give all aid for the tracking-down of heretics. All his subjects were to take an oath giving a similar pledge, and the count was to pay two marks for each heretic arrested in the next two years, one mark after that.

Bernart de la Barta, otherwise unknown, denounced "this forced peace, the peace of priests or Frenchmen," and opposed to it a peace that would be "sure and firm, a peace of friendship serving both the parties, a peace between honest folk, loyalty concluded and leaving no rancour behind." More evil than good would come out of the existing peace.

> In courts of kings just dealing should be found.
> In the church, mercy, discretion, pardon
> for faults, even mortal ones. Such rules abound
> in Scripture. If a king leaves righteous ways,
> he'll meet with darkening days.

There seem references to the peace also in two pieces by Gavaudan. The poets saw clearly enough what a disaster had come on their homeland.

XIV

Response to the Crusade

A CONSIDERABLE number of poets were carrying on through the years of the crusade and the Inquisition. Some of them seem unmoved by the political events, afraid or unable to encompass them in song. However, as many works have not come down and as it is hard to date many that have, we cannot be sure that there were not more inter-connections of the poets and the violent changes of the century than we can trace. First to glance at those who seem largely unaffected. Gausbert de Puycibot, son of a poor castellan of Limousin, went early into a monastery but soon left and took up a singer's career. Among his works is a *tenson* which compares in coarse lively terms the merits of young women and old ones. Savaric of Mauléon was his protector and he was well known in the first quarter of the century. His song on an Unfaithful Lady has the *tornada*:

> Lady, if foolish things I say,
> yet foolishly to your own cost
> you act, and so you'll soon be lost.
> My every word, your every deed –
> they all to your destruction lead.

Peire Raimon of Toulouse was active in Spain, Languedoc and Italy about the same time. With a light delicate style, he renews the com-monplaces:

> Of love I've learned quite well
> how he can aim his dart;
> but how he cures the heart,
> that's something I can't tell.
> The doctor who can dispel
> my pain, I know. But where
> is aid, if I don't dare
> to show my mortal wound?

Cadenet, son of a poor knight, took his name from the capital of the canton of Vaucluse. This locality was wrecked by men of the count of

53. Baptism of mother of Thomas Becket. (Royal MS 2B vii)

Toulouse and Cadenet was carried off by Guilhem Hunaud de Lantar who adopted him. After a difficult start as a poet, he returned to Provence where he was protected by Blacatz, then he withdrew from the world and died at Orange in the house of the Hospitallers, some time after 1230. In one poem he meets a shepherd who complains of the scandalmongers, *lauzenjadors*, and the harm they have done to his love. Cadenet replies that such jealous creatures honour him by saying daily that he has succeeded in love. "The fear they feel would be the truth if in my power it lay." The shepherds insist that they have cut him off from his love. Cadenet says: "Shepherd, I am not like you at all. I'd like the husband to strike my lady now and then. It's with flowers of that sort the jealous make their wives worse. With the better ones, bad behaviour brings disadvantages and courtesy brings profit."

Aimeric de Péguilhan seems to have been born in Toulouse as the son of a merchant, though Péguilhan is a village in the Haute Garonne. He started at the court of Ramon VI near the end of the twelfth century, then tried Spain for some ten years, then seems to have gone to north Italy and especially frequented the court at Malaspina. He exchanged verses with the young Sordello in the mid 1220s. He was very much a professional poet, always thinking of patrons and trying to produce works well written within the accepted tradition. Such works were welcome at the Italian courts where the new poetry was relatively recent. Troubadour poetry, now in difficulties in its homeland, was finding roots in Italian soil. Aimeric attacks the "new minstrels" flocking in.

> I'm like the gambler who with care begins,
> he makes small bets and masterfully wins,
> then, losing, grows excited, till he calls
> high bids and deeply into folly falls.
> So I went down that road with easy heart,
> quite sure I'd love with mastery, and quit
> the game as soon as I was tired of it.
> Now I'm committed deep and can't depart.

He evaded the problems of his own troubled land, but seized on the chance to lament the conflicts between the kings of France and England, the rival claims to the Empire, while praising the pope and supporting his proposal of a crusade in the east in 1213.

Uc de Saint-Circ was the son of a poor vavassour (a vassal holding of a vassal) of Thégra, canton of Granat (Lot). His father Arman de Saint-Circ had taken his name from the city where he was born, at the foot of Sainte-Marie de Rocamadour – a city destroyed in some war. Arman wanted Uc to be a cleric and sent him to study at Montpellier. But Uc turned to poetry and sang during the first half of the century in Spain, Languedoc, Provence, Italy. He left some forty pieces and the editing of certain *vidas* is attributed to him.

> She's gracious, she is gay,
> she charms with courtesy,
> her face all love to see,
> the lovely girl I sing.
> As rich and lovely a thing
> should be this song of mine,
> melodiously fine,
> which now down there I send
> > to tell my friend
> > how much I pray
> to see her, gracious, gay.

And the tornada declares:

> Dauphin, the song you hear
> in sense is crystal-clear
> so she might realise
> > and rightly prize
> > this heart all hers
> which only true love stirs.

So he attempts to set out an aesthetic of simplicity which reflects the clarity of concentrated emotion; beauty in art reflects beauty in nature.[1]

Now we turn to the poets who sought to express the agony of their country, their culture. Bernart Sicart de Marjevols may have come from the town of that name in Lozère, but we know nothing of him. We have a *sirventes* of his dated round 1230. He feels nothing but despair as he looks around; the world is upside-down with a vengeance.

> Religion's now gone rotten,
> good faith is quite forgotten,
> oaths treated as mere toys.
> In evil now we see no bound;
> vying in mischief each man's found;
> and in destroying all around,
> it is himself that he destroys.

> I'm angry all day,
> in anger deep
> all night I stay,
> awake or asleep.

> Turn any way,
> I want to weep.
> "Sire," the courtly say
> to the French and creep;
> and the Frenchmen bend a merciful brow
> if we fill their greedy hands and bow.
> No other law at all they avow.
> Ah. Toulouse, Provence,
> and the land of Argence,
> Carcassone, Béziers,
> what has been once and what is now!

The knights of the Hospital or of any other order no longer please him:

> They are liars we see
> and blown up with pride;
> by simony
> their lands grow wide
> Great wealth you need, to be
> one of their company,
> with rich estates in fee.

54. Water Tournament. (Knight iii 197)

> They live still at their ease,
> stretcht amid luxuries;
> and in their rules you'll meet
> treachery and deceit.

His only consolation is the fact that

> The vile and evil yet will see
> their heritage of calamity.

Guilhem Montanhagol of Toulouse went through the later struggles. His fourteen pieces (1233–57) show him a fervent patriot, an enemy of the French and of religious oppression. In one poem he says that all the classes complain of one another, clerics and laymen, lords and commoners.

> But out of the East the Tartar hordes will sprawl
> and to a common measure reduce them all.
> Why such rich clothes do clerics want to wear,
> living in splendour for all men to see,
> with stables and fine horses champing there,
> when God was pleased to live in poverty?
> Why with the goods of others are they swollen,
> knowing that what they spend for their display,
> apart from food and clothes, is surely stolen,
> all of it, from the poor, as Scriptures say?
> And the great lords, why do they feel no care,
> doing the people wrong most callously?
> Violence to one's own people, I declare,
> is bad as snatching others' rights away.

He goes on to advocate a balance of service between lords and people.

In *Del tot vey* he deals with the inquisitors. The clergy and preaching friars forbid men "to give for merit's sake and act with generosity."

241

He goes on, "Now they've set themselves up as inquisitors, and judgment they dispense just as it pleases them." But he is afraid to go too far and adds that the Inquisition itself doesn't displease him and he wants to see heretics reclaimed – but with "fair pleasant words, and with no anger," with "sweet mercy." He adds that he would like to see the Inquisitors "conduct their business rightly, without neglecting right and wrong." He complains that they attack ladies for wearing cloth of gold. But if a lady does dress up in a haughty way, she doesn't lose God through her clothes, and as for the friars:

> Not through black cassocks and white robes, it's true,
> will they find God, if nothing more they do.

Elsewhere he expresses the ironic hope that

> our clerks will hold this wicked world as nought
> and only for the next one now have thought.

But he did not neglect the love-song. He insists on the necessary link of the new and true in the Troubadour tradition.

> The early *trobadors* did not sing or say
> of love all things,
> then when the world was gay,
> so that we can't compose a song today
> worthy, new, true, and fine in every way;
> for he who sings
> can find themes yet unsaid and true.
> No *trobador* can play his part
> unless things new and true he brings,
> new things with a new art.

So, difficult as it may be after the way in which the early Troubadours were inspired by love, it is still possible to be original "A song is new when the learned, *li doctor*, say what has been nowhere said in song; it's new when someone says what he had never yet heard; it's new when I say things yet unsaid."

> Love teaches and puts knowledge in the heart.
> Had poets never been, as poet still I'd start.

When a woman sees her lover true and without fault, she should not delay.

> Men wouldn't die, it's my belief,
> so soon as now they do
> if they had joy of love.

Montaghanol was one of the few Troubadours who had a *planh* written on him. Pons Santolh of Toulouse wrote it.[2]

Guilhem Figueira of Toulouse spent much of his career in Italy, perhaps to avoid the Inquisition. He was a fierce enemy of the new order. In one *sirventes* of twenty-three stanzas he pours out his indignant rage. He says that he has a suitable tune, so the words won't take him long, though he's sure that they will bring malice upon him; for he feels that he must attack Rome, "the head of the decline, where everything goes down." He is in fact using the melody of a pious piece, *Flor de paradis*, a prayer to the Virgin, so that his work is a bitter parody of that tribute.

> Rome, the spiritually-frail
> flesh and bone you're corroding.
> Rome, the blind without avail
> towards the pit you're goading.
> At no trespass now you quail.
> A bad end I'm foreboding.
> You sell in greed, you hag,
> remission of sins, and brag
> with chinkling moneybag.
> Rome, your back you're heavily loading
> with evil for your swag.
>
> Rome, your cheats are clear,
> money-mad ways you keep.
> Right to the skin you shear
> the wool from your poor sheep.
> May the Holy Spirit hear
> the angry prayers I weep.
> Once he took flesh. He'll be
> your shattering enemy.
> Rome, now no truce with me,
> your villainous crop you'll reap.

The remark about God taking flesh may have been put in so that he cannot be accused of Catharist heresy. For the Cathars said things about the church which are in the key of his poem. "P. Garcias called the Roman Church Whore, giving poison . . . Others called the true church Mother of Fornications, Great Babylon, Whore and Basilica of the Devil, Synagogue of Satan."

243

Figueira goes on to blame Rome for disasters in the east and the death of king Louis. Rome does little harm to the Saracens, but sends the Greeks and Latins to be slaughtered. "In the fires of hell, Rome, you've chosen to dwell." Rome slams the door of salvation shut and leads men to the inferno. "In derision you make martyrs of Christians now." "Rome, you were too hasty in the hypocritical pilgrimages you proclaimed against Toulouse." If only the brave count lives two more years, "France will endure the penalty of your perjuries." So he goes on and on, accusing cardinals of heavy sins and the papacy of every possible crime."You want to rule the world in such a way that you fear nothing, neither God nor his prohibitions. I see that you do more evils than I can list, at least ten times more." In all these events and practices we see "the miracles wrought by your pope."

The date seems to lie after the death of Louis VIII on 8th November 1226 and before the Treaty of Meaux on 12th April 1229. The announcement of the coming triumph of Raimon VII is probably only hopeful thinking and doesn't mean that Figueira was misinformed. He seems to be writing in Italy, perhaps under the protection of the Emperor and his officers.

Pons de Capdueil in *En onor* calls on the kings of France and England, Frederick II and his rival Otho, to stop fighting among themselves. He attacks the clergy for their readiness to despoil their own people while neglecting the cause of the faith. "Those who know the laws and the lessons of the psalter have no taste for setting out in person" on any eastern crusade. "I know such who much prefer to disinherit Christians than villainous Turks. Those who preach to others should begin by preaching to themselves. But Covetousness has made the clergy lose all sense."

This sort of complaint appears in other songs. In 1265 when things were worsening in the east, Ricaut Bonome, a Templar, wrote bitterly:

Cross and Faith have been no use to us against these scoundrelly Turks, whom God curse! Rather, as far as we can see, God appears to protect them and to will our harm. For a start they've captured Caesareum, then stormed the stronghold of Arsur. Lord God, what a road have they taken, all those knights, all those soldiers, all those townsfolk, who were enclosed within its walls. Alas, the kingdom of Syria has suffered such losses that, to tell the truth, its power will be weakened for ever.

And don't think the Turk will stop there. No, he's sworn, he shouts out, that he won't leave a single follower of Jesus Christ in that land, if he can, and that he'll make a mosque of the Holy Virgin's temple. Well, as that's the will of her Son, we also ought to want it to happen.

A man is then mad to fight the Turks since Jesus Christ himself refuses them nothing. They have conquered and go on conquering French and Tartar, Armenian and Persian. What a misfortune. Each day they defeat us, for God, who was once awake, is now asleep and Mahomet acts in his place . . .

In 1268 the Genoese Calega Panzan wrote on the distresses of the Christians in Syria, attacking the papacy and Charles d'Anjou.

The moment is come for rejoicing. Soon we'll see these villainous clerics lamenting their ruin . . . You treacherous lot, you had Tuscans and Lombards massacred, and little you bother about Syria. Down there you have a truce with the Turks and the Persians, and here you have Germans and French killed off. Beside Charles, Greeks and Latins can find no peace. But the infidel dogs of Lucera carry on at their pleasure and can shout out Mahomet. Soon there'll be no more monasteries consecrated to God and his Mother; for the pope, who is endangering the divine faith, won't allow it.

Europe had been trying to "deliver God" in the East, but God didn't seem to want to be delivered. Austore d'Aurillac reproached him for handing over Louis IX and his army to the infidels.[3]

We saw how several poets wrote songs to hearten the resisters during the war. After the defeat Betran d'Alamanon remained closely attached to Raimon VII, unlike other poets who went over to Charles d'Anjou. He complains sadly of the way things have gone wrong. The count is getting much less out of his salt-tax, and he himself, who used to spend his time in visiting and wooing ladies, has now to consult lawyers and get down to writing his memoirs. Other poets tried hopelessly to draw in the English or the Catalans to attack the French. Boniface de Castallane reproached Henry II (1250–4) for not "reclaiming his heritage" and James I for not avenging his father. Early in 1254, Bernart de Rovenac addressed the kings in sharply ironic terms for failing to take advantage of "this conquered king by which they had let themselves be conquered." They have agreed never to defend their own lands or to do evil to him who does it to them; it was very courtly of them to let the king who is taking over Syria keep hold of their fiefs unchallenged; Jesus won't fail to hold it to their credit. Montanhagol kept hoping for the Catalans to come to their aid. As late as around 1265–6 an unknown Troubadour, who had been subject to Charles d'Anjou, fled to the court of Aragon and exhorted the presumptive

I

heirs of England (the future Edward I) and or Aragon (the child Pedro) to strike an alliance and start off "such play as will break a lot of helmets and undo the meshes of a lot of hauberks." (The poet was perhaps Paulet de Marseille.)

In 1262 came a revolt of the Marseillais. In a *sirventes* written in mid-conflict Boniface attacked once more the scared Provençals, impoverished and scorned by the French, and the traitors who wouldn't be much use to their new masters. He himself was ready to redden his sword with blood if he encountered such creatures. In the amnesty finally given to the Marseillais, Charles d'Orléans refused to include Boniface and the poet Uc de Baux. Boniface went to Aragon. There Paulet wrote a *pastorela* in which he expressed the hope of seeing Charles' Italian venture defeated. Before his exile Boniface had written of the French: "Daily I become more and more the enemy of chicanery. They horrify me, these lawyers whom I see arrive with their bundles of documents. When a man has thoroughly proved his rights, they reply: Nonsense, all that is the count's property in point of fact." Granet wrote a poem in which he bids Charles listen. "My task's to praise the good and blame the bad. This right of mine you must maintain." He tells him that if he wants loyalty from the Provençals, "you must guard them from your officials' violent ways." The latter hold that anything is just that brings them in money.

We see then that there was no lack of poets to speak up for their people and to defend their cause.[4]

XV

The Inquisition and the
French Conquest

AFTER the Peace of 1228 the area continued to develop economically, but under the new system, with the church dominant and with royal officials in many regions. The work of detecting and arresting heretics went on busily under the Dominican friars despite some pockets of resistance. There were no wholesale denunciations, but heretics and their sympathisers found life increasingly difficult. In 1230 the pope decided to initiate a new drive against dissidence, with a special tribunal "to make inquisition of heretical depravity." Everyone had to take an oath, renewable every two years, to remain a good Catholic and to denounce heretics. Boys took it at the age of fourteen, girls at twelve. Failure to swear, to confess, or to take communion at least three times a year made a person suspect. To own either of the Testaments, breviaries, psalters, or books of hours in the vernacular was forbidden. Anyone accused or reputed to be a heretic was brought before an episcopal court, and legal aid was hard or impossible to get; appeal from sentence was not allowed.

The Dominicans were in effect a new order. St Dominic had been at times with the crusading army, at other times preaching in Toulouse, Carcassone, lower Languedoc. As there was a ban on new orders, he was told by the pope to make use of an existing one, and he chose that of St Augustine. What he produced was a new militant missionary order, called the Friars Preachers. Personal poverty was stressed, but as with other orders it was not long before ways were found of getting round the rule. Dominic died in 1221. By 1234 there were already nearly a hundred houses, and in April 1233 communities of nuns had also been set up. Pope Gregory (1227–41) issued bulls establishing the Inquisition in Languedoc.

The usual procedure was to start with a public sermon and a call for confessions, then a period of grace when voluntary confessions would gain more lenient treatment. Soon we hear of Inquisitions compiling books of confessions and the tribunal built up its own staff of notaries. Despite strong popular protests, corpses were exhumed and burnt at Albi, but at first there were not many burnings of live persons. Suspects were questioned at Toulouse, but only two burned. The bishop here sent to the fire an old woman he had trapped into confession on her deathbed. At Narbonne Dominican activities caused an uprising. Clearly the Inquisition was disliked by even many of the orthodox. All its acts were felt to impair or attack the freedoms and customs of the towns. Raimon VII tried to protest in 1234 that the friars heard testimonies in secret, encouraged accusations of men of good repute, accepted the words of personal enemies against innocent people, harassed anyone who dared to appeal, and allowed no defence-advocates, acting as if they aimed at driving the faithful into error.

At Narbonne troubles went on. The archbishop tried to excommunicate a confraternity of artisans and merchants, who seem to have sought the support of the consuls in defence of the bourg's rights. In 1235 there was more bloodshed; a crowd sacked the Dominican convent. A truce was patched up, but armed clashes occurred and a new truce was arranged in 1238. Only eleven men were punished and nothing was said of heresy. In November 1235 the Dominican convent at Toulouse was invaded by the consuls and the friars were expelled. Count and consuls were excommunicated. The count agreed to the return of the friars, which came about in 1236. In April that year Raimon Gros, after twenty-two years as a Good Man, went to the friars, asked to be reconciled, and named a large number of persons as heretics. Bodies were dug up and living persons convicted, on into early 1238. Then the pope, wanting to negotiate with Raimon VII, in May suspended the Inquisition in the town till the arrival of a new legate for Languedoc. Elsewhere, however, the friars went on with their activities.

In 1240 and 1241 came the last two military attempts to break French power in the Midi. The Trencavel heir invaded from Spain but was beaten. Then came a weak and ill-prepared war against the French in which Raimon VII was involved. He was now in no position to resist the friars and the disastrous effects on the small rural nobles deprived Cathars and Waldensians of their protectors. In June 1243, after an interregnum at Rome, a new pope, Innocent IV, was elected, and Raimon VII tried to act as negotiator between him and the German emperor, to no effect. He was however praised by both sides for his

55. Graffito from one of the dungeons at Carcassone. (Coulton 2)

efforts. Absolved from his excommunication, he held at long last a gala court at Toulouse for Christmas 1244, when he created two hundred new knights. Louis IX wanted to go on an eastern crusade, but feared to leave Raimon in Languedoc, so with the pope's aid he drew him into taking the cross. Yet Raimon still failed to get permission to bury his father's body. He had now lost, and he co-operated with the Inquisition, dying in September 1249, aged fifty-two. He was succeeded by the count of Poitiers who had married his daughter Jeanne. On 1270 Louis again went east, and the count and his wife followed him. All three soon died. The new French king, Philippe III, took possession of the count's lands and ruled them himself as count of Toulouse. In effect all Languedoc was politically now part of Capetian France.

Thus was finally ended all Catalan hope of expanding into the Midi, which had stronger cultural and linguistic connections with Barcelona than with Capetian France. From 1112 the counts of Barcelona had been counts of Provence; of Milhau and Carlat from 1130; suzerains of a host of southern lords. Viscounts of Béziers (vassals of the count of Toulouse) held from them the Razès (Limousin) and the Carcassès. The counts of Foix and Comminges held from them all their possessions in Spain; in 1170 a viscountess of Gascony and of Béarn gave them homage; in 1174 they acquired the Roussillon and the Cerdagne. When Pedro II in 1213 decided to aid Raimon II, it was not with the aim of establishing his rival's shaken fortune but to secure his own

249

supremacy in the Midi. The Treaty of Corbeil, 1259, ended Catalan pretensions, and Philippe's action was the logical consequence.

All this while the Inquisition had been carrying on, with the final defeat of Catharism dramatically expressed by the siege of the stronghold of Montségur in the mountains south-east of Foix. Here the castle and cliff-huts had become a refuge for Perfected Cathars. Raimon of Alfaro acted as contact between the garrison and men outside who hated the French and the Inquisition; he joined with Peire Roger of Mirepoix in murdering a party of eleven, Inquisitors with their officials and the local prior, at Avignonet. This act of 1242 brought opprobrium on Raimon as he was making his last effort against the French, and he was reported to have encouraged the deed. In midsummer 1243 the royal seneschal of Carcassone led an attack on Montségur and the place was finally taken in March 1244.

The Inquisition now had two centres. A friar at Carcassone had charge of most of the ecclesiastical province of Narbonne, while two other friars looked after the dioceses of Cahors and Agen with part of that of Toulouse. The judges of the cases of heresy had aids, regularly or casually employed. In the latter group there might be a Dominican who acted as one of the judges for a day, was delegated to try a particular case, or was sent into some remote area. Two witnesses were required at interrogations, and many persons attended when sentence was given. Procedures were built up out of a long experience of tackling the problem of ensnaring the heretic. Bishops, who had at first acted on their own initiative, fell into an advisory role. Church councils provided a firm basis by legislating on heresy and on Inquisitorial methods, by giving definitions of the various degrees of guilt and setting down the lines of action for dealing with persons who confessed during a period of grace or held out till they were uncovered by investigations. They also laid down the kinds of penance to be imposed. Special problems were referred to bishops in council or to individual prelates. About 1248–9 a small manual was compiled; during the next century came many more.

Each step in a process was recorded with care. Copies of records were made, since at times originals might be burned, as at Avignonet in 1241 or at Caunes where messengers were ambushed in 1247. First of all the people of a district were summoned to a General Preaching. In 1242 the baillis of the count of Toulouse were told to enforce attendance even on workdays. Oaths were taken, and even children were brought in if they were thought to know anything of heretics. If there had not already been a period of grace, one was now announced of six to twelve days; but by 1248 most districts of the county of Toulouse had already been visited and no further periods of grace were given. A technique of thorough probing and questioning had been worked out for detecting persons touched with heresy and for uncovering persons who had evaded suspicion. The Inquisitions searched back for evidence as far as forty years and insisted that husbands must inform on wives, children on parents. They grew expert in using one person to betray another and in finding out when a group had agreed to say nothing about a neighbour or to put them off by laying false trails. An accused person was given a summary of charges, but not the names of informants. As he was allowed no lawyer, the best he could do was to name enemies whom he thought might have tried to get him into trouble, or to call in friends who would support his words. No other witnesses were permitted. Two witnesses to guilty acts were required; but in practice often suspicions, chance meetings and the like, were taken as proofs. The judges did their utmost to force the accused into admitting his guilt, on the grounds that thus a sinner might be brought to repentance. In 1252 Innocent IV authorised the use of torture by secular officials for the gaining of confessions; the church could claim formally that it had nothing to do with such methods, while in fact using them. Suspects might be held indefinitely and questioned again and again till they gave up and confessed. Proof of confession lay in the providing of information that led to the arrest of further heretics.

When the case was concluded, sentence was passed. Penance could be imposed only on those ready to accept it; but to refuse acceptance was taken as evidence of contumacy. From early days sentences refer to consultation with local bishops; after 1270 summaries of questions were shown to groups of lawyers and theologians. Up to this point all the proceedings had been secret. But sentences were given out with a General Sermon, so as to affect, impress, and overawe others. The penalty of death at the stake for the contumacious heretic was laid down by both civil and canon law, but in theory such a penalty was the work of the secular officials, usually comitial or royal. We have no accounts of the early burnings, but they were doubtless like the later ones. The victim was bound to a stake with chains round torso and legs and with faggots piled below. We do not hear of the condemned being first strangled; they were presumably burned alive.

Imprisonment was more common than the stake, and was considered an act of penance. There was lack of prison space; prisoners were expected to feed themselves, and if they were too poor for that, the bishop supplied bread and water. Pope Gregory IX in 1231 ordered confinement to be solitary, as did the Council of Béziers; but lack of space prevented the order from being strictly carried out. Later a distinction was made between confinement in chains and confinement with a little more freedom and the right to visitors. With a sentence of death or prison went the confiscation of property by the civil power, though at times prelates were granted the right of seizure. Legal problems often resulted, for instance over the dower of an innocent wife or feudal obligations imbedded in land. The officials with powers of confiscation were rarely concerned with questions of justice in taking over all they could.

The less severe penalties included pilgrimages. Penitents might have to wear crosses on their clothes and get letters from clerics to prove that they had indeed gone to the prescribed holy places. They might have to carry cloth crosses on their garments for so many years or for life. A man with such crosses might be badly treated and refused work or shelter. Houses that a heretic had frequented were condemned to be destroyed, though this action was not always carried out. Heirs had to pay fines for a heretic who died before completing his penance. Exile was seldom used as a penalty, but a suspected man might flee, particularly to Lombardy. A rich man with influence might ward off imprisonment for a long while. Estimates of the sufferers are hard to work out. Thus, the diocese of Toulouse in its records for 1249–57 shows twenty-one persons given the death sentence, five relapsed heretics, thirty fugitives, eleven condemned after death, and two hundred and thirty-nine imprisoned. But we have to recall that in 1249 Raimon VII on his own initiative burned some eighty persons and that in the 1250s officers of the count burned a number of men who had been sentenced only to prison.

In the later 1240s the pope allowed many persons to take off their crosses and undergo lighter penalties. The Inquisitors strongly objected, as did some bishops and abbots. The Dominicans withdrew and for a time the bishops had charge of the Inquisitorial process, but soon wanted to get rid of work that was onerous and unpopular. The new count of Toulouse, however, did not want to see a slackening of the revenue coming in from confiscations. The pope appealed to the friars in Languedoc and then to the prior in Paris for new judges, but got no

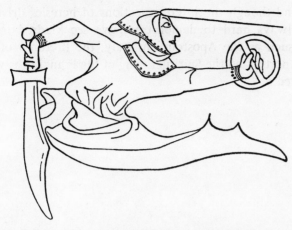

56. Grotesque fighter with curved falchion and fist-shield. (Louterell Psalter)

response. He then asked the Franciscans to take over, but soon afterwards died. The new pope, Alexander IV, gave in to the Dominican
terms. Now they could work without interference from bishops, their
own superiors, even papal legates. In 1256 they were granted power
to absolve one another for any canonical irregularities perpetrated
during their duties. They were almost wholly independent, and, being
able to pardon one another for any incorrect act, were able to send a
prisoner to be tortured or to be themselves present at his interrogation.

We need not follow things further. The independence of Languedoc,
its counts, its lesser nobility, its towns, was ended. The area was in-
corporated in the kingdom of France. Under the new political controls
and the dominating Inquisition its spirit was broken. The Midi henceforth played its part in providing agricultural and other products, much
strengthening the French kingdom, but its independent role was over.
The Troubadour tradition petered out, with its powerful influences
spreading out all around, into north France and England, into Germany
with its *minnesingers*, into north Italy where its direct impact culmi-
nated in Dante. Again we cannot follow out this rich fertilisation
which it gave to all the surrounding areas; but we must note its
primary importance in building the bases of later medieval and modern
European culture. The heretics of Languedoc were largely stamped
out, partly through the direct attack of the Inquisition, partly through
the breakdown of the tolerant society in which they had flourished.
Here too there was a legacy. The need to stand up against the heretics
with their appeal to an apostolic way of poverty led to the growth of

the friars; and though the interconnections of heresies driven underground is always hard to demonstrate, we see kindred movements developing such as the Apostolics in Italy, the Brethren of the Free Spirit in the north, and the Spiritual wing of the Franciscans which had to be outlawed.

XVI

Peire Cardenal

THE Troubadour movement carried on with weakening energies until the end of the thirteenth century. Some Troubadours tried to evade trouble, as we saw, by going to Spain or Italy. Cerveri de Gironi, who seems of the lesser nobility, was a Catalan who shows the system taking root in Spain; he left about a hundred pieces and was protected by Pedro III of Aragon and count Henri II of Rodez. In a poem on the dangers of a bad woman he writes:

> It's hard to mark a track across the sea
> although you watch the boats and ships go by,
> although the waters smooth and tranquil lie;
> it's hard to measure them with certainty.
> Still less you'll grasp or plumb or understand
> the tricks a treacherous woman has at hand.

But he only goes on with a string of banal comparisons. As hard to count the stars of the sky, the leaves of one pine or two beeches; to imprison the four winds in one's house; to bridle a savage lion, and so on. Bertran d'Alamanon was one of those who went over to the French. He had held high office at the court of the count of Provence, Raimon Bérengar, but he then became one of the favourites of Charles d'Anjou, with whom he was closely tied politically. He probably held fiefs from him. His death is recorded in 1295.

With Sordello we come to the birth of the Troubadour tradition in north Italy. He "was born in the land of Mantua, in a castle named Goito. He was a noble captain, a handsome man, a fine singer, a good Troubadour, and a great lover. But he behaved with much scurrility and trickery to the lady Cunizza, sister of Messire Ezzelin and Messire Alberic de Romano, and wife of the count of San Bonifazio, near whom he lived at the time. And by the will of Messire Ezzelin he carried Cunizza off." The count's friend wanted to kill him. "So Sordello kept himself under arms in the house of Messire Ezzelin. When he went about the country it was on good chargers with a large company of

57. Horse Baiting. (Knight iii 197)

knights." But through fear of those wanting to kill him, "he went off to Provence where he stayed with the count Raimon Bérengar. He loved a lady of the country whom he called in his songs Sweet-Enemy." Another *vida* says that the count and countess of Provence gave him a good castle.

He was the son of a poor knight, who began frequenting the courts of Lombardy in the mid-1220s. He kidnapped and apparently seduced the countess in Verona. From the early 1230s he was in Provence. Raimon Bérengar died in 1245, and was succeeded by Charles d'Anjou. A series of documents, 1241–69, attest Sordello's growing importance as a court functionary. In 1265 Charles carried out extensive campaigns in Italy; Sordello, now a knight, accompanied him and was called by the count *dilectus familiaris et fidelis*. In 1268–9 he got several feudal holdings in the conquered kingdom of Naples, but in August 1269 they were made over to another knight in Charles's service – why, we do not know. There are no more references to him and he may have died. His twelve *canzos* are rather conventional, with stress on honour. He represents the transition from the complexity of the true Troubadour love-tradition to the spirituality of the *dolce stil nuovo*. He wrote a long didactic poem, *Ensenhamen d'Onor*, cataloguing the courtly virtues of which honour is composed. In general he deplores the moral state of the world.

> Those who recall the century that's past
> so rich in deeds, so full of charms, and then
> compare it with our age so poor in men,
> our sad, bad age which promises at last,
> to comfort us, an age still worse by far ...

Dante in his *Purgatory* makes him the critic of kings and princes: a bad judgment probably prompted by memory of his *planh* written in 1237 on Blacatz, a Provençal noble.

> I mourn Blacatz, with simple words I bleed,
> with vain regrets, and rightly. People, heed.
> I sing my friend, a lord with power to lead :
> and manhood died with him and ceased to breed.
> We'll never see again a worthy deed
> unless upon his heart the barons feed :
> it holds the greatness that they sorely need,
> and if they're wise, they'll wolf it up with speed.
>
> First let Rome's Emperor have a proper bite.
> If with the Milanese he means to fight,
> he'll want it. He's the man who in despite
> of German levies lies in wretched plight.
> And France's king must next recruit his might
> to gain Castile : a loss that I indict.
> But if his Mother frowns, he'll take to flight,
> unfed. He does what she decides is right.

And so on, with increasing sarcasm, for three more stanzas, mocking at the kings of England, Aragon, Navarre, and ending :

> Toulouse's count should gnaw it for his pains,
> thinking how once he reigned, how now he reigns.
> He needs a new heart that can meet such strains;
> the one he has won't help him to more gains.
> Provence's count should gulp. His fortune wanes;
> to lose one's heritage is the worst of stains.
> Though, fighting hard, himself he still maintains,
> he needs a bite, such burdens he sustains.

Folquet of Marseille is the one Troubadour whom one can call a complete traitor to the tradition. He was the son of a merchant from Genoa. The family name was Amfos. In Genoa of the thirteenth and fourteenth centuries a family of bakers with this name had a quarter of the city called after them; and at Marseille in 1178 and 1183 we find a townsman named Amfos. Folquet inherited a large fortune, the *vida* says. "The young man was smitten with honour and valiancy, and set himself to serve the valiant barons." He was received by king Richard, count Raimon of Toulouse, and Barral his lord of Marseille. "He was a good poet and very well made in his person. And he loved the wife of his lord Barral and wooed her and made songs on her. But never by prayer or by song did he move her to pity or obtain from her any benefit of love. That is why he always complains about love." Then she and her husband died, "and also the good king Richard and king Alfonso of Aragon." In grief Folquet "abandoned the world and withdrew to the order of Citeaux with his wife and the two sons he had. And he became abbot of a rich abbey in Provence called Le Toronet" (Thoronet, Var). "Finally he became bishop of Toulouse, where he died." He was bishop in 1205 and died on 25 December 1231.

He played a particularly cruel and violent part in the persecutions. *The Song of the Albigensian Crusade* declares:

> And when at Toulouse as bishop he was named,
> the fire he stoked across the whole land flamed.
> No water on earth could have quenched it then.
> Small folk and great, in all ten thousand men
> lost their lives, lost bodies and spirits too.
> My faith! By his deeds, his words, you'd think it true,
> and by his way of acting, that he had come
> as Antichrist, not as messenger from Rome.

The Count of Foix at a Lateran Council accused him of being responsible for the deaths of more than five hundred persons, of every age. In praise for his ruthless piety Dante put him in the Heaven of Venus. Among his fifteen poems are two crusading songs and a religious *alba*.

> True God, your name and Mary's I shall say
> henceforth on waking, for the star of day,
> risen on Jerusalem's side, bids me to pray . . .[1]

But there is one magnificently vigorous poet of the thirteenth century to redeem the name of Troubadour. He has the force of Marcabru and the joy-in-life of the Monk, and a wider grasp of what was happening in his world. A *vida* says that he was born at Veillac, in the country of the Puy Notre-Dame. "He was the son of a knight and a noble-woman. His father, who meant him to become a canon, put him at an early age in the canonry of the Puy. So it was that Peire Cardenal learned his letters and was able to read and sing well. And when he'd reached manhood, feeling himself handsome, young, and frisky, he found pleasure in the world's vanities. And he composed many fine poems with fine themes. He made songs and many *sirventes*, in which he sharply blamed the world's folly and rebuked the bad clerics." He went round the courts with a jongleur who sang his *sirventes*. "The good king James of Aragon and the noble barons made him a thousand marks of honour and friendship. And I, Michel de la Tour, who write this, tell you that Messire Peire Cardenal, when he passed from this life, was nearly a hundred years old."

He had studied in the cathedral college of Le Puy. Documents show an important Cardenal family there. (A Petrus Cardinalis appears as scribe of the court of Toulouse in 1204.) The earliest poem of Peire that can be dated seems of 1216, the latest about 1271. Some ninety-six works are attributed to him, though fifteen of them are dubious. He wrote many *coblas* of one or two stanzas which usually summarise themes treated at more length elsewhere; of his three love-songs at least two are satirical. Unusual forms that he uses are the *estribot*, the *descort*, two sermons. In his *sirventes*, of which there are nearly sixty, he fuses moral and courtly positions. At times in mocking terms, often in fierce invective he deals with the crusades, the Inquisition, and the French occupation.

A fable of his shows how he feels that the poet, the man with a deep sense of human values, becomes the one sane man in a mad world.

One day there fell on a certain town a rain with the property of making those whom it touched lose their reason. All the folk, save one man, were out in the open and were wetted. They began to do a thousand extravagant things, which surprised nobody. But when the one uninfected man came out, he was the one considered a madman. All the others began to hoot and maul him, and he had to run into his house in a hurry.

This town is the image of the world. The greatest wisdom that can be practised is to love God, fear him, follow his commandments. But this wisdom is lost. In effect a rain has fallen, a rain of greed and pride corrupting everything, so that if there is still a man honouring God they hold him for a lunatic and maltreat him.

He never loses a chance to attack and expose the clergy:

> Yelling, about the world they stray.
> "God has forbidden theft," they say
> and bear their swag of loot away.
> We see them, rank with brothel-scents,
> administer the sacraments.

The crusades are a means by which the clergy exploit and use the knights:

> While clerics are there to give commands,
> the knights will rush to sack Tudelle,
> Le Puy, Montferrand, or other lands.
> In fact the clerics at their will

send them to be killed or kill.
They give them first some cheese and bread,
then send them with a battle-yell
where arrow-pierced they'll soon be dead.

He denounces them continually for their merciless greed:

Shepherds the clergy go.
They're murderers, we know,
though cloaks of saints they show.
When they come darkly near
I seem to see appear
that Ysengrin of old
who wanted to get in
a park and yet not fear
the dogs. He took a skin,
a sheep's, and entered bold,
fooled them, and at his will
of sheep he ate his fill.

They're emperor, they're king,
they're duke, count, anything
that's lordly swaggering
to rule this world of ours.
They've cornered all the powers,
these priests, and here's the reason:
they've practised at all hours
hypocrisy and treason.
They've plundered, smashed, and lied,
violent in their pride,
coveting all, they ride
and break him who's defied.

The more they strut their way,
less worth can they display;
more folly every day,
but honesty they lack.
Of lies they've a great pack;
of learning they're quite bare.
More sins upon their back,
but less of love to share.
Those wicked clerks I mean,
God's enemies unclean,
the worst that yet have been
in all the ages seen.

Buzzard and vulture smell
a rotting corpse afar;
clergy and priests can tell
where the rich people dwell.
Soon their best friends they are;
when death brings up his threat,
nothing the kinsfolk get.

Frenchmen and clerics are notorious for evil; usurers and traitors likewise own the world.

With cheating and lying turns
they muddle folk these days;
each religious order learns
from them its devious ways.

But the great robber Death will take away in time all the ill-gotten
gains. Of the friars he writes:

With expert angel-voice, no lisp or stutter,
smoother than English cloth, they speak their part.
No repetitions, shrewd the words they utter,
heard with no cough, not taken to the heart.
With moans and sobs their role is subtly wept,
telling us of the ways that Christ once kept,
the ways that should be kept by you and me;
they preach to us how God we yet may see.

And if we don't, like them let's try good fare:
purée so pulped that you can drink it down,
thick soups in which farm-chickens richly drown,
young verjuice served with shards. All these we'll share.
And wine, the best wine cherished by the sun,
such as would quickly make a Frenchman drunk.
If by luxurious living God is won,
then God is in the reach of every monk.

Whoever hopes in God should drop the thin fare he is used to, and
should feed on these dishes – if he can get them.

There was an Order founded long ago
by men who banished babble and vain noise.
But Jacobins aren't dumb when eating cloys;
they argue what's the best wine that they know.

261

58. Wrestling. (Royal MS 2B vii)

Courts of inquiry they've set up, and cry
"You're a Waldensian," if to frown you dare.
In each man's secrets they attempt to pry,
hoping to spread their terror everywhere.

They dress in soft tunics of English wool, not sackcloth. "And as for alms, once used to help the poor, they want the lot themselves and ask for more."

Were I a husband I should find it scaring
that by my wife will sit a breechless man.
Their skirts and hers have just as full a span,
and fat with fire will suddenly go flaring.
Of Béguine nuns I've not a thing to tell;
yet fruit a barren woman somehow bears.
Such miracles they work; I know it well.
The saintly fathers get more saints as heirs.

In his *estribot* of thirty-eight lines all rhyming *-atz*, he sets out an orthodox belief in twelve lines, then slides off into his attack on the clergy. They seduce all the women. "And when they're mounted on top and the cunt is sealed up with the well-rounded balls that dangle from the prick, as a letter is closed and the opening is shut, out of that enclosure the heretics emerge, and Waldensians too, who curse and renounce and juggle with three dice. That's what the Black Monks do instead of practising charity."

As we saw, he does not treat the clergy in isolation, but links them with the rich man and the usurers among the laity.

Lonely the rich need never be,
they have such constant company.
For Wickedness in front we see,
behind, all round, and far and wide.
The giant called Cupidity
is always hulking at their side.
Injustice waves the flag, and he
is led along by Pride . . .

If a poor man has snitched a bit of rag,
he goes with downcast head and frightened eye.
But when the rich thief fills his greedy bag,
he marches on with head still held as high.
The poor man's hanged, he stole a rotten bridle.
The man who hanged him stole the horse, O fie.
To hang poor thieves the rich thieves still aren't idle.
That kind of justice arrow-swift will fly . . .

The rich are charitable? Yes,
as Cain who slew his brother Abel.
They're thieves, no wolves as merciless.
They're liars, like a whoreshop-babel.

O stick their ribs, O stick their souls!
No truth comes bubbling from the holes,
but lies. Their greedy hearts, abhorrent,
are rabid as a mountain-torrent . . .

With loving-kindness how they quicken,
what hoards of charity they spread.
If all the stones were loaves of bread,
if all the streams with wine should thicken,
the hills turn bacon or boiled chicken,
they'd give no extra crumb. That's flat.
      Some people are like that.

In love he demands equality and fair treatment.

      No mistress will possess me
      unless I possess her too.
      If with joy she should bless me,
      I'd bless her with joy and be true.
      My decision's a good one and complete :
      as she treats me, so her I'll treat.

He is sceptical of the old commonplaces: "He's a fool and wastes his time, I think, who links himself with love – who trusts and gets the worst in love. He means to warm himself before the fire and burns himself." "Losing her, I won back myself." "He who gives more than he keeps and loves another more than himself, takes on a bad bargain." He draws up a list of clichés, and felicitates himself for not being in love, so that he escapes the need of working out these banalities. Love "doesn't take away my appetite, my sleep. I don't shake with fever. I don't yawn or sigh, nor am I, all the bitter night, the prey of nightmares. I am not sad or moaning, betrayed or deceived. I don't fear any traitress or traitor of jealous wildman whose anger menaces me." And so on.

Un sirventes novel is a joke about Judgment Day, which shows how far we have travelled from the tenth century. If God proposes to send him to the devil, he answers, "Lord, in mercy don't do it. In the wicked world I was tormented all my days, so save me now, please, from the tormentors."

> I'll set the whole court marvelling at my pleas.
> He fails his own (I'll tell him to his face)
> if he will simply sink them with no trace
> and send them down to hellish penalties.
> Who throws away what he might gain instead
> finds dearth where could be plenty. Rightly so.
> Gently solicitous God himself should show –
> take to himself the souls of all the dead.

If God dispossessed the devils, he'd have more souls for himself.

> Happy I'd be if he destroyed the lot.
> We know you could absolve yourself for it,
> dear God. Then make the ruthless devils quit.
> Yes, dispossess them all. I ask : Why not?

> You shouldn't close the gate. Lord, I declare,
> St Peter, keeping it, feels quite disgraced.
> Unbar and let the souls in merryfaced,
> Yes, every soul that wants to enter there.
> No court would be complete in any way
> if some laughed loud while others wept inside.
> Though you're my sovereign, I won't be denied.
> Open for me, or a complaint I'll lay.

264

59. Corn hand-mill. (Knight iii 200)

Dear lord, I don't want to despair of you.
Don't let my trust in your intentions fail.
At the death-moment let my hope prevail,
then save me soul and body. It's my due.
Here's a fair offer. Let me now return
there whence I sprang on my first earthly day,
or all my wrongful actions wipe away.
I'd not have done them if I'd not been born.
If, moaning here, in hell I moaned again,
it's wrong, and it's a sin. For I, indeed,
against you, lord, this charge can truly plead :
One good thing brought me thousand times the pain.

He ends with a prayer to Mary to be his guarantee (*garentia*) with her Son. The humanisation of God has reached its climax. Cardenal in fact dares God to be as human and loving and decent as himself, against all the priestly interpretations. As a final expression of his character we may take the following passage :

Others weep for a son, a father, a friend snatched by death. I weep for those remaining in the world, treacherous and disloyal, felons and liars, whom the devil teaches as if they were little children. I weep for the rapacious man, the ravisher, that great man there, since he stays unhanged. I don't lament that these must die. I weep because they aren't yet dead and are sure to leave worse than themselves.

Thus in Cardenal the humanism of the Troubadours reaches its height : a fitting retort to the terrible cruelties that the church and the French were inflicting on Languedoc.[2]

Giraut Riquier could however claim to be the last of the Troubadours, and we may end here with him. Born at Narbonne, he was at first protected by small nobles and leading townsmen there. He then went to the court of Alfonso X of Castile for some nine years, but does not seem to have found the life he wanted, despite aid from such lords as the count de Rodez. His earliest poem is dated 1254, the latest 1292. His main theme was the failure of noble society to keep up courtly values or to value truly its poets. He himself struggled to keep the tradition alive despite an increasing lack of support. He left over a hundred poems. He tried all sorts of genres but had no underlying originality.

> From singing now should I refrain;
> for song needs gaiety, and care
> has hemmed my life in everywhere,
> and what have I to tell but pain?
> when I recall the hard times past
> and on the present stare aghast
> or turn my eyes to future years,
> I've cause enough for ceaseless tears.
>
> From song no pleasure should I gain;
> no gaiety stirs it. Yet I share
> such art from God that I declare
> in song my folly yet again,
> losses and gains, delight, despair,
> and tell the truth of all I bear.
> How else may words of mine stand fast?
> I come too late, amid the last.

One of his poems is a sort of inverted *alba*. Instead of cursing the dawn for coming too soon, he curses the dusk for taking too long to come.

> At last his lady of her grace
> pitied her faithful lover's plight.
> She named the time and meeting-place.
> That day, when she'd be his by night,
> he wandered aimless to and fro
> > *and cried with grievous breath*
> > *"Day, you will be my death.*
> > *Your light I hate*
> > *as still you grow and here I wait."*

> What hours of anguish did he trace,
> in misery waiting for delight.
> All day unsolaced did he pace,
> cursing at fate and endless light.
> Still torn, he watched the moments go
> *and cried with grievous breath* . . .

Riquier had only such small novelties to offer; he quite lacked the broad and deep vision of Cardenal as to what had gone wrong. We saw how he appealed to the Aragonese king about the use of the terms *trobador* and *joglar*. It seems that as he aged he gave more and more a religious coloration to his work, sure that there was no hope for poetry.

> No one earns thanks in this our world today
> for pleasant airs and fine words well-devised,
> for holding that good fame should still be prized –
> so much the world is falling in decay.

This late period saw various attempts at textbooks. *Doctrina d'Acort*, aiming at a versified grammar based on Vidal, was written by a Pisan in Sardinia where he seemed connected with the Pisan administrative circle. The living tradition is lost. For the author the language of the Troubadours is something dead, to be studied by the aid of documents. *Regles de Trobar* was written by Jofre de Foixà in Sicily. He seems to be writing for a circle of aristocratic amateurs who want to compose Provençal verse correctly; he has to give advice on elementary aspects of versification, and explain the nature of rhyme and the role played by the position of stress. *Doctrina de compondre dictats* was written by a Catalan. He has no idea of the way in which in certain genres the musical and metrical structures were related, but he does grasp that the poems were composed for performance and he makes some observations on the music of each genre. He shows the mania for classification of new genres that is found in the works of Riquier and Cerveri di Girona and in the *Leys d'Amors*. These and other treatises bring out the way in which the living Troubadour tradition was at an end. European poetry was now entering the phase in which the impacts and influences of the Troubadours in western Europe were to bring about extensive and varied effects in new directions.[3]

XVII

Last Words

DURING the two centuries of its existence Troubadour poetry had radiated influences throughout western Europe; but now it died out in its own native areas. Because the united efforts of the papacy and the French kings broke down Languedoc culture, Troubadour poetry cannot be claimed as lying at the roots of any national culture in Europe. Even though its remarkable achievements and the enduring range of its effects have been in general admitted, the fact of its not strictly belonging to any national group – French, Catalan, or north Italian – has somehow seemed to leave it high and dry, a sort of strange and temporary phenomenon belonging to no national inheritance. Yet unless we understand it and see it in its full perspective we cannot understand European literature.

First we may reconsider the extraordinary way in which it suddenly arises, a highly developed vernacular literature which does so much to stimulate vernacular developments in the surrounding countries. Before it we find only forms in prose or verse that are relatively primitive in form and content. Then in a few years a highly complex poetry, precise in form and expressing a powerfully unified view of life, is born. It is natural and right that we should seek for origins and preconditions to explain as much as possible the outburst; but none of the spheres which can be shown to have contributed to the Troubadour system and tradition can be even remotely equated with it. Latin poetry, medieval and to a lesser degree classical, was one factor making the new poetry possible; church songs and church music again played their part, as well as elements from an immemorial minstrel tradition. Folksongs of the romance-dialects at one level, and the philosophical and theological ideas and systems maturing in the twelfth century at another level, met and merged; and strong influences from the Arabic world, philosophical, metrical, musical, flowed in to strengthen and deepen the other elements. No single one of these factors can be used to explain what happened, though all were necessary. We need to understand their roles and at the same time to grasp fully the completely new and unprecedented element that lies at the heart of the Troubadour inspiration. All the contributing factors are transformed inside the new unifying impulse.

As far as we can judge from the evidences that have come down, the two most important immediate influences bringing about the crystallisation of Troubadour form were the church *conductus* and the Arabic *zéjel* or Mozarabic equivalents. In the eleventh century Arabic poetry was incomparably more highly organised in form and content than anything in the romance-dialects or the Germanic tongues. But it cannot be equated with the poetry of Guilhem IX and his successors. What the latter has which distinguishes it from all previous lyric poetry (including that of the ancient world) is a basis which in form is both precise and limited, and yet capable of infinite elaboration without the loss of the original basis; and which has a thematic character, a kind of content, which is both specific and yet again capable of infinite elaboration and reapplication without loss of its essential qualities.

In reading, say, Abelard, we need to bring our historical sense to bear if we are to enter at all fully into his expression, his situation, his significance. But when we read Guilhem's Enigma or one of Bernart de Ventadour's lyrics, one of Marcabru's or Cardenal's satires, we can appreciate them at once in something like their fullness, with an immediacy of reaction and comprehension. The reason lies in the fact of the new dimension or level of consciousness which these works achieve, a dimension that we still inhabit. The key-thing is not that we find in these works merely an outpouring of emotion with certain elements of universality that overleap the barriers of time. It is rather that the outpouring is in terms of a complex dialectic of experience and growth, out of which all that is deeply significant in European literature has come. We can perhaps catch glimpses of this new kind of apprehension in, say, a poet like Catullus; but with the Troubadours it reaches a stable level, providing a new kind of creative technique, which is also the objectification of a new kind of consciousness of the unity and conflict of opposites in the movement of thought and emotion, in the movement of society itself. The themes around which the new consciousness mainly plays in the Troubadour is that of loss in possession, possession in loss, with all the complex psychology that results. But in working out these themes the Troubadours provide the system that can tackle life in all its forms and at all its levels, though they only hint at these wider applications or tentatively move towards them. We feel in their expression the ceaseless conflict between the passing facets of experience and the totality of desire (purpose, ultimate personal and social aims): the facets embodying the totality and losing it, the totality subsuming the facets and then blurring them out. The dialectic thus in the last resort becomes the revelation of the conflict between the potentialities being opened up by society (mainly through concrete labour and production) and the continual frustrations forced on these potentialities by the limiting factors of power and exploitation which seem inextricably bound up with the positive or liberating forces.

Not that all the Troubadour poems are on the same high level, as we have abundantly seen. Not even the best poets can live at their full intensity; and many of the poets repeat in diluted form the themes of the more important poets, losing their vital tensions and inner conflicts. But even these lesser singers have their interest in showing the working-out of the tradition, which, at moments when it seems to be growing exhausted and repetitive, regains its force by the rediscovery of the impulse in terms of the new situation, widening the angle of applications.

Guilhem IX broadly sets the stage, unfolds the main issues, defines the system through which a new grasp of the unity of the life-process is to be achieved without blinking the enormity of the contradictions and opposites involved. Rudel and Bernart de Ventadour work out the results of utter devotion to a love, a cause, an ideal of self-fulfilment, in a situation where objectively the desired resolution is impossible. Marcabru widens the issues, turning outwards to judge the world which distorts or betrays the ideal. Poets like Cercamon, Peire d'Auvergne, Bernart Marti, Peire Rogier, expand and extend the application of the ideas and images, the symbols and definitions, without anything vitally new in their poems. But in the process *trobar clus* comes up. The struggle for the truth of things is found to be far more complicated than it had seemed to Rudel and Bernart with their extreme and simplified tension between actuality and potentiality. The difficult form of Raimbaut d'Orange is linked with a sense of inner conflicts and entangled problems that can be grasped in momentary intuition but cannot yet be brought out into clear statement: a sense of the vast and deep distortions and alienations that have to be somehow realised and overcome.

Bertran de Born, speaking as a champion of feudalism, represents a use of the evolved techniques for a purpose opposite to that of the creative dialectic; for he thus breaks down the delicate balance between feudal systems, terms, and ceremonies on the one hand and anti-feudal emotions and aims on the other – between hierarchy and the rejection of all divisive relationships. But such a deviation can only be temporary if the movement and its possibilities are not to be halted. What is positive in his work is the joy in life as it is, in all forms of energy that can be contained within the feudal limits. Bringing to a head elements present in Marcabru, he develops the *sirventes*, the poem of action impinging directly on the feudal world and its values. His contribution, then, when brought back within the sphere of the dialectic, helps to enlarge the range of Troubadour expression. As well as Raimbaut d'Orange, G. de Borneil, Arnaut Daniel, Vidal and others continue to explore some of the new areas opened up by *trobar clus*. Women, *trobairitz*, introduce a new direct note, stressing the theme of equality in love. As the poetry tends to grow inbred, lost in its own systems, its enjoyments of subtleties for their own sake, the Monk brings things down boisterously to earth again. Lesser poets further extend the techniques and the questionings. Conflict is socially and politically maturing in Languedoc, where feudalism may be said to be insecure, breaking down into forms that look too far ahead without having the bases on which the new forces can stabilise themselves. Poets like Montanhagol, Sicart, Figueira attack the enemy of the good life: the life of which courtly love, as understood and developed by the poets, was the summation and symbol. The defeat of Languedoc produced a scattering of forces. The poets turn to Spain and Italy as an escape. They weaken, and the Troubadour system, which began as a secularisation of religious imagery and ideas, reverts to religious positions. One splendid poet, Cardenal, however, left his testimony of denunciation, boldly tackling the enemy: the papacy and the Inquisition, with French feudalism on the one hand, and the rich burgesses, traders and usurers on the other. His attack on the latter is quite different from Bertran de Born's attack on townsmen, for Bertran hated them as sapping feudal hierarchy, while Cardenal is concerned with the urges of greed and power which are shared by priest, French lord or official, and money-making burgess alike, whatever conflicting elements there may be in their ways of life. Cardenal is thus validly extending the concept of equal rights in fellowship or love to the social system itself – though of course he had no political programme in his criticism any more than had the heretics who saw the contradictions, falsities, and discrepancies in all existing social forms, using the ultimate criterion of apostolic equality and community.

The Troubadour dialectics and concept of unity had had their severe limitations, being applied only directly to the experience of a man and a woman alone in love. From one aspect, as we saw, they translated the mystical experience of the soul alone with God into the ecstatic experience of lover alone with lover. But by substituting for a cosmic and social abstraction a real person they had taken the decisive step of breaking from metaphysics and making the life-process itself the source of all knowledge and self-realisation. They drew back into life the energies that had alienated into God. In the process the lady tended to become God, or the Virgin Mary, but at the same time God was humanised, seen as an abstraction of the human essences. The systems and symbols of quest, of ascent, of growth, which had been projected on to a goal off the earth, were now brought back to origins and re-embodied in daily experience; and at the same time they bring about a new consciousness of that experience, a deeply enriched consciousness which was capable of expansion and application in every sphere of living and thinking. The goal of joy, seen as the motive force of love, was interpreted in terms of the lover's experiences as he maintains devotion in the face of setback and disappointment. But the system, its structure and its symbols, reacted back on experience at all levels. The lady in the last resort represented Otherness, in all its variety with which the self must unite, and which it must yet control in objectification. The lonely lover becomes the personification of all men who rise above the animal and egoist level of blind satisfactions. But one carry-over from the idealistic systems that are being inverted and made concrete is the fact that the goal remains rapturously vague. The obvious goal of the love-quest is the moment of complete physical and spiritual union; but if this point were crudely stated, then the quest would come to a halt as soon as copulation had occurred. Hence the way in which Troubadour imagery has much to say of sight and touch, but sheers off any description of copulation. As a result it is possible to argue that the Troubadours wanted "pure love" in the Avicennan sense, not "mixed love." But to try to make a system thus out of a difficulty in formulation is to reduce the Troubadour experience to a mysticism which it is seeking to eliminate. There is no dogmatic position in this matter, only a problem in definition of goals. By removing the lovers from the complex entanglements of life (apart from the attacks by the jealous and the scandalmongering), copulation becomes the goal but cannot be mentioned as such. For the same set of reasons it becomes impossible for the Troubadour to criticise society except for a failure to live up to some lost standard of honour and courtesy: that is, in terms of an idealised feudalism. Cardenal is the one poet who fully breaks through this impasse; but he is able to do so because the extreme pressure of historical circumstance draws him away from the love-theme, so that he makes no direct effort to relate his political position to that of his love-ethic, his experience as lover. However, Marcabru in his extended application of *Amors falsa* had prepared the way for Cardenal's positions.

With the breakdown of the direct Troubadour tradition, in the fourteenth century, we find the elaboration of systems of Courtly Love as a sort of game, idealising feudalism without the awareness of sharp inner conflicts which gives the creative depth to the work of the Troubadours. To analyse the new problems that now arise, the new achievements and confusions, would carry us on to Dante and Chaucer. There are gains and there are losses, but the compactness of the Troubadour tradition is gone. There is a broader front, with greater possibilities of comprehension and increasing chances of losing oneself. But we cannot enter into that here.

The plea that I have made is against any attempt to schematise the Troubadour concept of love and experience in general. If we make that attempt, we deny the creative essence and tend to reduce the concept more and more to the very thing that the Troubadours were rejecting and transforming. As we have seen, in a period of deep-going liberation of the human spirit – a liberation linked at all points with the great productive advances and the relationships they involved – the Troubadours sought to take over various symbols, images and intellectual systems in which they could express the ways in which the liberation affected them. They sought to define, strengthen, and direct the new forces. Their dialectic of union and loss, of joy and despair, expressed the conflict between potentiality and actuality, between the existing structures of power and of submission, of productive activity and of the exploitations of labour-power – all canalised in terms of personal love. The terms in which this dialectic is framed have their historical limitations and colorations; the essential thing that is being said is free of such limitations and finds its echo in all periods, in all movements of experience with their mixture of achievement and failure.

The concept of life or experience as a conflict between actuality and potentiality, between things as they are and things as "desire" could have them be, does not involve arbitrary factors. For desire is true and real insofar as it arises out of the concrete potentialities and effectively expresses them. A new concept of the inner life is present. Outer and inner, body and spirit, are realised in a new dynamic inter-relation; and this interrelation, involving conflict and the resolution of conflict, in turn involves a realisation of life as something in ceaseless movement and change. Not merely change in the abstract, as a cease-less combination of varying factors, but change in the concrete, change proceeding out of conflicts and contradictions inside the given moment and therefore moving in a definite direction, towards a "goal." Not any random conflicts and divisions, but those that emerge most deeply from the unity of the moment, the moment grasped in its fullness.

> In place of joy, let sorrow be my fate.
> But steadfast hope gives patience, so I wait.
> Rather I'd chase and lose, my soul still fired,
> than catch what doesn't satisfy. I rate
> more than a thousand others one good thing desired. (Aimeric)

Such ideas can be found present in ancient culture in a general way: a philosophic sense of dialectical movement, a profound artistic ex-pression of the nature of conflict and rebirth in tragedy, and so on. But they did not beget an art tradition in which the urgent pressures of growth were pervasive, coherently driving in a direction determined by the continual new potentialities opening up before man. Slave-society had too strongly a closed aspect. The potentialities opening up in the twelfth century are already those that reach forward to our own day and beyond; and a radically new kind of artform is needed if this new situation is to be truly expressed. That artform is Troubadour poetry.

One small point. It has been noted that the longer biographies of the poets anticipate, in simple but definite form, the novel. They have dialogue, dramatic presentation, psychological analysis, a clear narra-tive moving to its natural culmination. Examples are those of Vidal, Bertran de Born, G. de Balaruc, Raimon de Miraval. We cannot claim that they directly affected the birth of the novel, but the extent to which they reveal a new form with the embryonic elements of the novel is one of the testimonies to the deep stirring of the spirit at this time, the way in which artistic thinking is turning in new fundamental directions.

The points here made about the Troubadours and their work might be greatly elaborated; but enough has been said to support the claim that these poets represent something radically new in the artistic con-sciousness and that we still live substantially in their tradition.

Notes

I should like to express a special debt to Jeanroy (J.), Dronke, Denomy (D.) – though I disagree with findings of the latter two, I am grateful for their many effective contributions; Dronke with his reading in all forms of medieval poetry provides a wide perspective.

Foreword: Lewis 2–4; Davenson 10; Curtius's lecture on 'The Medieval Bases of Western Thought'; Bezzola ii 242, 249; Dronke (1) 2f. Dronke goes on to exemplify his point, starting with songs of ancient Egypt (c. 1160 B.C.)

I. Guilhem of Poitou

1. Link of Roland and late romanesque cathedral: Farnham; Uitti 126f. Roland in art: Lejeune. General: Siciliano; Pidal (2).
2. Dronke (1) and (2). About time of First Crusade, the French marched to a song with refrain *Oltraie*, Forward! which spread over Europe. *Eulalie*: Winterfeld.
3. Greek poets: they lack the close integral relation to the following stages of Greek literature that the Troubadours have to modern literature.
4. Ordericus iv 132. Barbastro: Ibn Khaldum, see Pidal (1) i 165f; Briffault 44f. Time in Spain: A. Richard i 404ff. There seems confusion of dates of the two expeditions but chronicles date victory near Cordova 17 June 1115.
5. Goldin (1) 5. J. i 109, 114, 85; *Hist. des Gaules* xii 445 and 444, cf. *Hist. de Languedoc* vi 60; J. (1) ii ch. 1. Also J. (2); Press 9.
6. *Conductus*: Dronke (2) 44, citing Spanke, Chailly etc. Two lines of eleven syllables, a third of fourteen, cesura in each line after seventh syllable. Horses: J. (3) 53 nn 1 & 519, on the same play on words in Lucilius and Artemidorus. But Guilhem was quite capable of inventing it.

Conductus was developed at St Martial as accompaniment to the liturgy shortly before Guilhem's birth; the term was used for a song of any structure, for one or more voices, sung along with a procession during service, or the song filled in time during preparations for a part of the mass. Used in liturgy, it was not part of it, see Dronke (1) 288–94. Guilhem seems to have known Latin very little; Richard i 444; Nykl (2) p. cix n16.

7. Names: Limoges, Garin, Bernard, Leonard. High class chatter is: *en son latin.* For tale, cf *Decameron* III i. For attempt to find Arabic under the babble: Nykl (2) p. cxiii, Briffault 191, who points out many borrowings from Arabic: *douane* (*diwan*), admiral, nautical terms (cable, *goudron, caravel*; wares (café, sugar, candy, candle, cotton, jar); clothes (chemise (*kamis*), *jupe, jupon, savate*); flowers (lily, jasmine). Note also *galaubia* (magnificence, generosity) from *galib*, a chivalric term (like-Ali). Further on the babble: Heger 197f; Lévi-Provençal; Dronke (1) 50–1. Topsfield; Goldin (1), J. (1) ii 7.

8. Peire Gauceran gives a solution to a riddle set by Guillem de Berguédan.

9. The oath is "by the Head of St Gregory." Note the third and fourth line of each stanza is built on the 15-syllable trochaic line (which had cesura after eighth), the marching song of the legions early taken over by the church: it was still used in hymns: Goldin (1) 13. It is also the basis of the long line in the triplets. Fourth Stanza: reminds of *Matt.* xvi 25. The fourth line of each stanza ends with the verb love: *am* or *amam*, preceded by word for lady, *dompna*, or a pronoun referring to her.

10. Echo from *Ecclesiastes*: Goldin (1) 11. Last stanza: Goldin takes worth to refer to the man who understands, not the poem: he who understands the love-ethic is ennobled and cut off from the vulgar, the silent serf. For importance of Joy, *Jois*, in Troubadour system: D. (5) and J. (13) 31, 54; Dronke (1) 36f. Among minnesingers; Arnold 9. Also Fauriel; 499.

11. Translation in JL (1) 76–8; Raby; Dronke (2) 34–6, 27, music 230.

12. He blesses the man who brought him up for making him a *maestre certa*, Dronke (4) for folksong and vernacular background.

13. Weston (1) i 288 and (2); Brugger, ZfFSL xlvii 1924 162ff; J. Van Dam, Neophilologus xv 1929 30–4; Loomis (1) and (2) 193–5. Breri: Legge 51f, Weston (2) 338, (1) i 241; *Tristan*, Thomas, ed. J. Bedier i 337, ii 95–9. Pygmies: Loomis (2) 66ff. Also JL (3) 402. For Bleheris and the Petit Chevalier, Weston (2) 100(3). Tristan and Troubadours: ZfRP xli 1926 223ff; MP xix 1922 287ff.

14. J. (1), 151–5; Zingarelli 41–53; Paris, *Rom.* xii 525; Keissman. Anglo-Norman literature started by Life of Celtic saint Brendan by Benedict writing for queen Adeliza.

II. The Twelfth Century

1. Allods: Hodgett 22. Watermills: Bloch (2) 136–8.

2. Duby 193; Anderson 190. Gilds: Fourquier 240f.

3. Bloch (1) 354; Marx *Sel. Corr.* 89; Lopez (1) 234; Anderson 194; Waley 12–21, 56–92. N. France: Petit-Dutaillis (2) 81.

4. Monks: JL (3). Saved: Wolff 55; Christ, Hallinger 41f; *occupatio* (meditation), Morghen 21f: vii 579–84, 649–51.

5. Odo: Hallinger. Pilgrimages: N. Hunt 5–8; Topfer. Relics: Brooke (3) 258; Hunt 8f. Attacks: Leclercq (2), Hunt 9. Monasticism now helping to inaugurate a new phase of feudalism: E. Werner. Towns: Agus.

6. Davis 197; Lerlercq 232.

7. H. Waddell 132; Sylvester 8.

8. Southern (2) 38, 47, for poem on *fallacem pacem* that *sophismata* gave him.

9. Thorndyke (1) 3–6; Waddell 131f; Peter Ven., Migne *PL* clxxxix 347.

10. Norton 19–21. More attacks: Haskins (1) 99, Lloyd 87.

11. S. Pegge; Sylvester 15f. Churches: St Paul's, St Mary-le-Bow, St Martin-le-Grand.

12. Roddy 168. Peter; *Sent.* iii dist. 19a. Leviathan: *Hortus Deliciarum*; Mâle (2) 480; Martin and Cahier, *Vitraux de Bourges* 19.

13. Leigh 76.

14. Cluny: Morall 103. Theophilus ed. C. R. Dodwell: Theophilus may have been Roger of Helmershausen, early 12th c., Brooke 114f. The artist gains confidence, sustained by the seven gifts of the spirit. First, spirit of wisdom and understanding teach him how all created things proceed from God, and provide the necessary skill, order, variety, and measure, with which he proceeds, on to spirit of godliness and fear of the Lord by which is regulated the nature of the work (including the amount of the reward, "lest the vice of avarice or cupidity steal in"). Note the paradisiac church of the Grail in Albrecht von Scharffinberg's continuation of *Parsifal* (c. 1270): Coulton (3), app. 31; Röthlisberger.

15. Southern 258; W. F. Wilson; JL (3). Church: Morall pl. 8c (12th c. capital of St Nectaire, Puy de Dôme).

16. Woolf 237, Brooke 37. Anselm of Laon tried to systematise theology, early 12th c. In 1215 priests were forbidden to help in administering ordeals.

17. Universal history too gains a new impetus. Otto of Freising, after studying at Paris, introduced the new logic into Germany and wrote a chronicle ending in advent of Antichrist and world-end. Sceptics: JL (3).

18. Unity of culture shown in script: Woolf 216. Scholars: Waddell 51f. Also, Lloyd 34, Southern 22. Bernard: Parabola I, *Opera* Paris 1839 iii 446; Schell 282. Contacts: Bréhier 89–100; Jews as slave-dealers, Nykl (2) p. xxxv. John: Anastos 149–63. *Almagest*: Haskins (2) 157–65.

19. Ripoll: Beer; Southern 69; Crombie 91. P.A.'s stories: Rickard 32; H. Schwarzbaum, *Sefarad* xxi 1961 267–99, xxii 1962 17–59, 321–44, xxiii 1963 54–73 (Folklore motifs); ed. A. G. Palencia (Madrid) 1948. Gerbert: Picavet 30–7; Thorndyke 697f; Nykl (2) p. lxxxiv. Crombie 198f on mills, paper and books, 202, medicine 224f, music 185, theory 178f.

20. In episcopate of Raimon I (1126–51) John of Spain and Gundisalvo

at Toledo translated into Latin works of Ibn Sina (Avicenna). Ibn Gabriol, Al-Ghazzali etc. Willehalm: Brooke 156–8. Peter: Southern 40f.

21. Gothic: J. Harvey; Brooke 102. Narbonne: Southern 124ff.

Note that in this chapter the term *dialectic* is used in its medieval sense as a synonym of Logic as applied to formal rhetorical reasoning; as logical disputation. Elsewhere, speaking of the *dialectics* or *dialectical* attitudes of the Troubadours in their poems, I use the term in its modern post-Kantian sense, as developed by Hegel and Marx, where it defines the processes of life and thought as a unity of opposites, in which conflict and resolution are the form whereby contradictions are worked out and overcome, and new levels of organisation are achieved.

III. Cercamon, Marcabru, Rudel

1. Dejeanne; J. (1) ii 21–3, and (2); Rajna; D. (2) 151–3. Doubtful poem of uncertainty in love: 'If only I might see her the hour when I might lie at her side."

2. Goldstein 81–3.

3. Dejeanne (2); Spanke (2); Press 41–61; J. (1) ii 23–36; F. Pirot, *Le Moyen Age* lxxiii 1967 87–126; Goldin (1) 51–93; Berry 73–109; Audiau 265–72. For tale of M. in London: *Roman de Joufroy* (Hofmann) 3599ff. Misogyny: J. (1) 11 192f.

Catrola, unknown apart from dubious attribution of a dialogue-stanza.

Per savi: I can't accept idea of Lewent and Goldin that first stanza runs on into second, so that "obscurity" is of the others.

4. *Pax*: he attacks the lechers, tipplers, gobblers, fire-squatters, stick-in-muds who "stay behind in their squalor" while the brave and the humble go to be washed. *A la fontana*: scheme AAABAAC, B and C recurring in each stanza.

5. J. (11); Press 27–39; D. (2) 16f; Dronke (2) 119–21 and (1) 166 (Ovid); Bezzola (2) 217n and Frings (2). Dronke (1) 212. Spitzer (1); Appel (7); Lot-Borodine (1) 225 and (2); Bezzola (1) i 74; Casella.

Brother and sister: taken literally by Nykl, see also J. (1) ii 20 n2.

6. She is Eleanor: Monaci. Virgin: Appel (7). Helen: Vossler (2). Human, divine: J. (11) p. iv. Holy Land: Frank (1). See D. (2) 158. Casella and Spitzer (1), no objective reality, poem reveals inner life of poet in midst of conditioning historical circumstances. *Naturalis dilectio*. D. (2) 158; Casella 190; mysticism, D. (2) 159f.

7. Chenu 34f, St. B. *Cant. Cant.* ser. i 83 (transl. E. Gilson).

8. Spitzer (2) 5.

IV. The South: Languedoc

1. Fontanals 28; Villemain i 14, ii 45–84; Strayer 10 (Occitania). Counts of Toulouse did homage to French and English kings and to German emperors for certain holdings. In general, Wakefield, with bibliography.

2. Magnou-Mortier 133. Poitou: Higounet (5) 223, 229. Communes lost all concern for the oath, they wanted only written law. The villeins before engaging themselves by oath, says Cardenal, "call for a contract first."

3. *Beneficium*: Richardot; Nelli (1) 108, usury-rates 109–11. A. de Mareuil says the townsmen "know the *domney*," the art of courting ladies by the rules. Alphonse of Poitou did his best to change allodial land to fiefs or increased fiefs by attributing such land to them; in 13th c. much allodial land was confiscated on charges of heresy against the holders, enriching the lords.

4. Statute-free villages: Calmette 93f. Partners: Hodgett 63, Provençal trade 13th c., 8. It has been suggested the Albigensian crusaders wanted to seize the trade-routes; no, they wanted the rich land. Merchants were continually on the move, burgesses left town only at certain times of year to visit commercial centres or markets like Barcelona, Beaucaire, Saint-Gilles, and there met foreign traders. Big fortunes were made at the ports, and here the consulates had most power: Narbonne: Lopez (2) 131–5, Nelli 112f.

5. Feudal forces counter-drive after 1250. Toulouse: City the original settlement, Bourg the walled area to north that grew up round monastery of St Sernin, with mills along river etc., Wakefield 61; Coppolani, P. Vidal at court: J. (1) i 160 n2. Poor etc.: Saye, Delaruelle.

6. In general: Ourlic, Dossat (2), Higounet (2), Wolff (2), Mulholland, Wakefield, Léonard, Limouzin-Lamothe. Mousket: Smythe p. xviii.

7. Wives: Nelli 98, 102; B. de V. D. (2) 170f, Appel 236 etc. Man abed, Nelli 82; R. de V., *razo*, Berry 464.

8. Nelli 85, 79 (also for contraceptives). J. (1) i 83; *Hist de Gaules* xii 415; J. (1) i 84; JL (3) on Normans and long hair.

9. Craicel: J. (1) i 97f. Ermengarde, *ib.* 165–7, Appel (5); Dom Vaissete, *Hist. de Languedoc* vi 151, vii 18; Monk of M. ed. Klein 27; P. d'Auvergne ed. Zenker IV 50; G. de B. ed. Kolsen xxvi 98ff. Nîmes: J. (1) i 167 n4; in 1204 Montpellier was fief of Aragon-Barcelona.

10. Grazida: Nelli 89f; women in general, Koch. Hildebert: JL (1); Lewis, ch. i. Andreas: D. (4) 108–110, Parry 122, Pagès 705f and 90–127, Parry 91–107, 110f, 123. Lady in castle: Vernon Lee, 350.

11. Wakefield, Thouzellier, Turberville, Coulton (2), Wolff, Mundy (1), Nelli (1), (3), (4), (5), (7), Niel, Manteuffel, etc. Raimon V: Luchaire 7f, Guiraud 261–300.

V. Bernart de Ventadour

1. Appel (1); Press 63–85; Dronke (2) 121–4; Gennrich (1) 16–34, 291 etc.
2. Henry: Paris (1) 520; the three sons, O. H. Moore 86–9; J. (1) i 153 n1 (another *planh*). Faidot, a *planh* on the three; A. Daniel was at this court. Eleanor: Parry 163–9.
3. Parry 35, 57; D. (4) 116–18. Nature, 130f, plebeian woman, 145; definition of chastity 145.
4. Cf. Clarembald of Arras, disciple of Thierry. Union of opposites: John. Scot. *de div. nat.* (PL cxxix 893bc, 760a, 912c). In general: Economou 45, 60–2, 64, 67, 72.
5. Venus: Economou 72f, 83, 85–7, 92. In lower world: *in mundiali suburbio*. Nature attacks sodomites: their breach of law is shown as the committing of monstrous perversions of the rules of the grammatical arts – grammar seen as a major discipline thought to imitate nature: Chenu (3) 90–107. Quotation: *Commentum super sex libros Eneidos* 9; Economou 85, 194; Green (1) (2). *Anticlaudianus*: Economou 95–101, 197; Wetherbee (1) 121f; Chenu (3) 295; Vasoli; Alan (1) Bossuet 35 n6.
6. Dronke (3) 167; B. Stock; Curtius (2) 204, common in Latin verse from c. 1070.
7. Lewis, 38–9, 74f; W. Neilson, *Rom.* xxix for parallels.
8. Del Monte; Press 86–101; Audiau 131; Dronke (2) 123; J. (1) ii 36–40. "With noble joy" uses rhyme-*am* for each last line, reminding of G. IX's poem on making a New Song.
Alegret: J. (1) ii 33; B. de Vensac, 34; B. Marti, 31; D. (2) 153–7. P. Rogier: Appel (5).

VI. Troubadours and Jongleurs

1. Faral (1) 30; Chambers ii app.; Chaytor (2); A. Brandl; M. P. Jones.
2. Adalbert: Dronke (2) 27f. *Willame*: ed. E. S. Tyler v 126off. Paris tried to refer trobador to musical term *tropus*, melody. Joglar: Faral (1) 3.
3. J. (1) i 141, 87, 137. Miraval: J. in *Rom.* xix 397. R. d'O., J. (1) ii 15.
4. Eblo II: D. (2) 139–43; J. (1) ii 16. Novel: *Novellini* ed. Gualteruzzi no 64. Velay: P. Meyer ii 399, Chaytor 27–31. Uc: J. (1) i 139.
5. *Sirventes*: P. Meyer, *Rom.* x 265; Keller 13 n2; J. (1) ii 181. Ermengau: *Breviari d'Amor* v 1842 1ff; J. (1) i 139. Treatise: Faral app. iii no 267. Note in Wales the contempt of poets for conteurs: Loomis (2) 193 n77. Church: Briffault n70. Satan: W. Hetz, *Spielmanns-Buch* 317; E. Gautier, *Epopée* fr. ii 11; Faral (1) 67. Folkdances were linked by clergy with the devil, especially as they crept into church festivals and vigils: Greene pp. xciff. Masks also horrified the clergy: Ogilvy 614, Marshall 13, Bigongiari etc.

6. Tale: Rickard 19–25. Faidit: J. (1) i 139f; ii 251f. Rovenac, ii 183. Political use of minstrels: Roger de Hovendon *Chron.* (RBS iii 143) on Bishop Longchamp; Henry I and Luc de la Barre, Ord. HE ii 19. T. de Cobham; Coulton (1) 403f, Chambers ii 262.

7. J. (1) i 141, ii 183, i 251 and Appel (6).

8. AM xxvi–viii 181ff; J. (1) i 144–7 and 149 n1, 148 n3.

VII. Raimbaut d'Orange and Bertran de Born

1. Pattison; Press 103–21; J. (1) ii 42–7; Dronke (2) 121, 124f; Gennrich (1) 37. God and Raimbaut: Dronke (1) 98–112 discusses these poems, but sees a union of divine and human love, which is the last thing I see. Exponents of Christian origin of courtly love. Lot-Borodine, Casella, G. Errante.

2. Kolsen; Press 125–51; Goldin (1) 189–207; J. (1) ii 51–4, *tenson* 52n.

3. Appel (2); J. (1) 110, 128, ii 194–8; Press 153–71; Smythe 57–103; Chaytor. Errors in *razos*: J. (1) i 110.

4. Chaytor 63; Stimmung 42, his ed., says Arthur hid in the hills; Ramsay, *Angevin Empire* 352. *Planhs* on Richard, Chaytor 63–6. It is probably not true that *sirventes* were made to existing tunes to ensure a quick spreading. Personal invectives: J. (1) ii 182–4. *Planh* to the young king attributed to Bertran de Born only in one MS of three.

VIII. Arabic Influences

1. Sancho IV: Pidal (6). Miniature: Briffault fig. 24. Pidal 31. Instruments, Briffault 174, Pidal 55ff, Anglès. But see refs, D. (1) 229 n6. Ibn Khaldun: R. Basset, *Bull. Corr. Africaine* 1885 136, 142, 146. Term *segrer*: Pidal 23f (Ribera). Wolfram: Brooke 11, of Dante, *de vulg. eloq.*, ii 12; G. Barbieri, *Dell'origine della poesia rimata*, 1571 etc.

2. *Zéjel*: Ginzburg; Nykl (1) no cxli etc., B. Lewis 220f; Dronke (1) 53f (2) 87, 191 (1) 52ff, 36; Kritzeck 152; Stern (2); Nykl (6); Pidal (5). For works trying to show borrowings from Arabic, see Bezzola ii 153–203. *Zéjel* forms in G. IX; Marcabru (twice), Cardenal: Dronke (1) 53f.

3. B. Lewis 233, 236, 242; Kritzeck 148, 142 (also on tests of love), 149. Arberry (2).

4. *Diwan*, lxxxix, cxli, cxxiii, cxvii, xlvii. Note how Sufi tradition leads in the Persian Hafiz in the 14th c. to positions close to those of G.'s Enigma: "Far through the world I've roamed and found a thing that I can claim/to be most sweet and ravishing, but please don't ask the name./Her footsteps everywhere are wet with tears of my desire/but as to how this came about I beg you'll not inquire./Sad in my cottage left alone, with you gone off afar/I suffer endless agonies, but don't ask what they are." JL

(4) 349. For Arab arts of love: H. Ritter, cf. with those of west, Gorra (2) 201ff; Dronke (1) 54.

5. D. (1) 231f; Hell (2) 298–301.

6. Prose-and-Verse: Eos 237. Submission; Morall 108. Sufis: Kritzeck 122, 124; D. (1) 235; Béroukhim 174; Arberry (3). Cruelty of beloved: Gibb, Hist. of Ottoman Poetry i 22. Bayazid: Nicholson 324.

7. Fachenham 221f, 219 etc. Love-union in Avicenna: Corbin (1) ii 309, Afnan.

8. Spitzer (2); Dronke (2) 89–91 and (1) 26ff, 274ff; Alonso; Garcia Gomez; Frings (2); Roncaglia (2); Heger; Pidal (6); Stern (3).

"Tradition says that at the epoch of Harun a young slavewoman began the fashion of making verse in the vernacular, pedants refusing to consider it poetry." A. S. Tritton, "Shi'r" in Encyc. de l'Islam; Briffault n54. On planh for battle of Calatanazor (998 or 1002), alternating Arabic and romance vernacular: Mariana, Historia de España viii ch. 9.

9. Stern (1) 301. Justus: von Grunebaum 405; Dronke (1) 27, 34; Gennrich (5). Assimilation in general: Asin 304f; Simonet 216–19, 252; Nykl (2) p. xxxv.

IX. Arnaut Daniel and Other Troubadours Including Women

1. G. Toja; J. (1) ii 47–51; Press 173–91; Goldin (1) 209–23; Canello; Lavaud (4).

Moncli: is short for "he of Moncli's love for lady Audierna."

2. Avalle; J. (1) ii 151–5, i 112f; Press 193–215; Smythe 49; Goldin (1) 248–65; Berry, 326, 468.

Mixture of canso and sirventes: E. Hoepffner.

3. Linskill; Berry 281, 462; Eos 365f. Montfort gave him land with good rent in kingdom of Salonica. For Perceval cf. Chrétien's Perceval le Gaulois. C. de Pisan: see 15th c. miniature, J. Dupont and C. Gnudi, Gothic Painting (Skira) 158, for City.

4. Langfors; J. (1) ii 145, i 118; Audiau 66.

5. Andraud (2); J. (1) ii 155–62, i 121.

6. Chabaneau (3); Berry 221.

7. Chabeaneau (4); Tobler; R. Meyer (2); Stronski (3); J. (1) i 370; J. Mouzat ed. 1965. Eos 362 also attributed to Bertran d'Alamanon), 384; Appel (8) 91; Gennrich (1) 103–16.

8. J. (1) i 361; Audiau (3). Gui was a canon, patronised by Marie de Ventadour. See Meg Bogin for Women Troubadours, 1976.

9. J. (1) i 311–17, Berry 265–77, 460; Dronke (2) 105f; Küssler-Ratyé. Patronesses: J. (1) i 162, 167 n4, 196 (Italy) 251.

10. Cour 22, 50, 70; Pérès 412, 427; D. (1) 232; Dronke (1) 21f.

X. *Folk-Songs and Popular Bases*

1. Spitzer (2) 17; Dronke (2) 91; Frings (1) and (2); Gennrich (5); Voretzsch, *Einführugen die altfranz.*

Lit. 62f; J. (1) ii 300 n2 (liturgic dance). Two lines in the *Jeu de Sainte Agnes*. Brawl: *Ann. de St Martial de Limoges*, ed. Duplès-Agier 161.

2. Bédier (4); Chambers ii 153; Rosenfeld; Greene p. cxix.

Interludum: Axton 16, Chambers ii 324–6. Wechssler (1) i 322–5, 332 on Maysongs as source of sensual elements in Troubadours; kiss as feudal rite. Carols: Stemmler 161; Dronke (1) 53.

Note folk-element in Marcabru's starling-songs with rapid rhythm: "The starling needs no speeding/he gives no thought to feeding/but still the message heeding/straight on his way he's winging/he never stays/or careless plays/so well obeys/seeks the best ways/to where he stays/at once to raise/his voice in urgent singing..."

3. Paris (3) 609ff; J. (1) ii 282–304, 337; Dronke (1) 8, 155, 214, 243, 277, (2) ch. 5; Audiau (2).

4. See *Eos* in general, esp, 30–2, 344–89; J. (1) ii 292–7. "When Phoebus": Dronke (2) 170. Modena: Roncaglia shows mixture of classical, Christian, military elements likely in 9th c. Modena. MS at Sankt-Florian (11th c.) with four Latin lines. Dronke 173.

En un vergier: Dronke 174f, *Eos* 358f.

Gaita: Benton 140; horn mentioned, *Eos* 368f, 386.

Parody of dawn-motive in Arabic: *Eos* 220f.

5. Kolsen 342; *Eos* 359; Dronke (2) 176, and German example 177; J. (1) ii 296f; *Eos* 381–3.

Cadenet: *Eos* 383; Dronke (2) 176f.

The 13th c. *De Doctrina* suggests that the writer was much astray or that there are types we have lost: "If you want to write an *alba*, speak pleasantly of love and also praise the lady of whom you write, and bless the dawn if you have had the pleasure for which you went to your lady. And if you haven't had it, write the *alba* blaming the lady and the dawn. And you can write as many stanzas as you like, and you must compose a new tune for the poem. If you want to write a *gayta*, you must speak of love or of your lady, feigning that the watchman can harm you or help you towards your lady when daylight comes. And you must write the poem as well as you can, begging the watchman to help you to your lady. And you can write as many stanzas as you like and the poem must have a new tune. An *alba* is so called because the song takes its name from the hour when it's sung and the *alba* is better sung at dawn than during the day. A *gayta* is so called because it's more suited to be sung at night than day, so it takes its name from the hour when it's sung." P. Meyer (2) and *Eos* 379.

XI. The Monk of Montaudon

1. J. H. Marshall.
2. Philippson, Klein, Lavaud (3); Fabre AM xx 351; J. (1) ii 186.
3. In love, he has the image: "Lady, at all times I shall follow you, like the sunflower always following the sun." Dronke (1) 120, citing Proclus.
4. Gavaudan: J. in *Rom.* xxxiv 497–539. Also Kjellmann.
5. R. de Barbezieux: Chabaneau-Anglade, see J. (1) i 426.

Uc de la Bachélerie, dawnsong, *Eos* 222: in Arabic poetry we meet the longing for the dawn by an unhappy lover.

XII. Symbolism

1. J. (1) 91; Fauriel, *Hist.* i 503; Wechssler (2); J. (1) ii 131–4; Kluckholm.
2. Southern 110; Cluny, D. Knowles. Abelard: *Hist. Cal.*, Morall 105. (Philosophy is female in Boethius.)
3. Taylor 179; E. Lucka, Evolution of Love. Marian cult: Ahsmann, Arnold. Troubs. and Virgin: J. (1) ii 310f. *Lai*: Pauphilet 501; Dronke (1) 5 for different interpretation. *Alba*: J. (1) ii 313f.
4. Marriage: Fauriel i 497ff., cf. wooing scene in Chrétien's *Eric*; Lewis 25f. Schlosser 172. Andreas: D. (1) 185–7.

Scheludko claims there is nowhere in the romances a poet in love with his married patroness, yet "the romances reflect every aspect of the life of their times." But then they should show the poet in his love-pretences! Also it is pointed out in Chrétien's romances only Lancelot and Tristan are adulterous: in the five others adultery appears only in the second part of *Cligès*. (We may note how in *Chevalier de la Charette* the fear of Lancelot to get into the cart is a sin against love; he thinks of his class-position not of his devotion. A true Troubadour conception.) The attempt to make Andreas's passage on Marie de Champagne a mere clerical *jeu d'esprit* is a feeble riposte: Dronke (1) 47, 83, and (5).

See discussion on Adultery, Dronke (1) 46. To woo in Troubadour fashion an unmarried noble girl would be an impossible intrusion on property-rights. See sensible comments on impossibility of proclaiming consummation of love: Sutherland 212.

5. Ladder: Southern 231–7; Chenu 34f; Gilson (3) app. iv; Lot-Borodine; D. (1) 160, 177. Casella one-sidedly sees only the Platonic Augustinian positions. J. Wilcox treats the system only in late phases. Tower: G. Reusch, *Margarita Philosophica* 1508: K. Charlton, *Education in Renaissance Eng.* fig 1. Imagery used widely: Godric, merchant turned monk after journeys where he bought cheap and sold dear: "thus aspiring higher and higher, and yearning upward with his whole heart, at last his great labours and cares

bore much fruit of worldly gain," Morall 123. Life by Reginald of Durham (transl. Coulton). Trade-travels linked with pilgrimages.

See Notker's sequence (9th c.) "A ladder stretching up to heaven, circled by torments," dragon sleepless at foot, then Ethiop with sword, with radiant young man, "a golden apple in his hand" at top rung. "This is the ladder the love of Christ made so free for women", seen in vision by Perpetua at Carthage, A.D. 203 : Dronke (2) 41f.

6. Will : Southern 113. B. de V. : D. (1) 189.

7. J. (1) ii 305f; Carducci *Opere* viii 57; Lowinsky 1–3; D. (2) 181f. Daude : Kjellman 113f. Daniel : Lavaud 60. P. d'A. : Zenkel 122. Gavaudan : J. (12).

8. Tristan : Brooke 21. J. (1) ii 98 : Chrétien de Troyes uses religious vocabulary boldly for sensual purposes, e.g. *Cligès* 1191, 1615, 6091. See further Wechssler; Faral *Ann. Midi* xxii 218; Vossler, *Literaturblait* 1911 87; P. Savj-Lopez, ZfRP xxxiv 480. Death : J. (1) ii 307, Folquet 308f.

9. D. (4) 110; P. Lehmann (date); A. Steiner (1) and (2); Manitius 186–6; ed. E. Trojel; D. (1), (2), (3).

Averroes : Leff 151.

We can see the extension of sensuous love-imagery, after St Bernard, in mystical accounts of union with God by (a) Richard of St Victor (later 12th c.), (b) Hildegard of Bingen, 1098–1179, (c) the Cistercian Gérard de Liège (mid-13th c.). Richard explores in detail the imagery of love-longing; he wants men to hammer themselves into the likeness of angels, transformed "into the same image from brightness to brightness." For him "the lover burns with love-longing, inflamed with passion," and so on endlessly, passing from the love that wounds to the love that binds. Hildegard, a woman, has a vision of Love as a radiantly lovely girl; she is much influenced by the cult of the Virgin. Gérard attacks the love of woman as *vilitas, corruptio*, and so on, with the monkish sense of the flesh as filth, dung; but he treats the love of God in terms of the tests and trials of a lover. He himself suggests that the love-poets have drawn on Augustine and other Fathers. (Dronke (1) 59–97 for summaries.)

Here is the counter-line to that of the Troubadours. The latter seek to use the metaphysical structures to illuminate earthly experience; the mystics, while despising early experience or at best seeing it as an imperfect prelude to the otherworldly reality, use its imagery to express what they feel in their onanistic raptures of union with pure Otherness. (Against mystical thesis, Bazzi.)

XIII. The Albigensian Crusade

1. See Wakefield and his bibliography; Strayer, Luchaire, Belperron, Bennett, Douais, Dossat, Douvernoy, Griffe, Guiraud; also ch IV here. For poems : J. (1) ii 213–7; P. Meyer (3) and (1); Raynouard iv 194.

Round 1200 the kingdom of France consisted of the Île de France (with Paris), the Orléannais, Bourges and Rheims; the Domain included Blois, Flanders, Champagne, and part of the duchy of Burgundy; in 1204 Philippe added Normandy.

XIV. Response to the Crusade

1. J. (1) i 409 and 153, 196. Appel (9). W. P. Shepard; Press 217. Aimeric de Belenoi: *vida* supported by documents: J. (1) i 129. J. (14).

2. Raynouard iv 191; J. (1) 221f; Audiau 169. Ricketts; Press 257. Late odd genres: J. (1) i 327ff.

3. J. (1) i 378f, ii 279f; Audiau 154. Cathars: J. M. Vidal, Rev. des quest, hist. i 1909 373. Bonone etc.: J. (1) ii 209–11; AM xv 145f. Vidal at time of Richard's captivity called on the princes to accord. For crusades, cf. Rutebeuf's *Débat du Croisé et du Descroisé*, in north.

4. J. (1) i 290; Levy 264, 280. Raynouard iv 271, Guillem Anelier of Toulouse curses "the clergy and the French," apparently from Gascony, addressing count d'Astarac.

Granet etc.: J. (1) i 230–2; *pastorela* 290.

XV. The Inquisition

For refs, see chs. IV and XIII. Catalan area: J. (1) i 186ff.

XVI. Peire Cardenal

1. Gironi: Fontanals 377. J. (1) 428f. Sordello: Boni; Press 237–55; J. (1) 429f. Folquet: Stronski (2) 149–52; J. (1) i 130. Religious *alba*: Eos 377.

2. Lavaud; J. (1) i 404f, ii 184f, 225; Vossler (3); Audiau 111, 181, Fable: Debenedetti – Montanhagol uses a slightly different version.

3. Pfaff; Press 306–25.

He has a set of six *pastorelas*, which make up a sort of short story.

She is lively and gay in the first three, then after marriage develops a gentle gravity, dull. "Alas, lord Giraut, I am no longer she who sang those airs." "Will you accept bed and fire with me tonight?" "You think me, sire, rather a light woman. Why do you ask me?" "Have you, shepherdess no care for me?" "For you and for love I have neither care nor cure." Yet in the first, making a wreath of flowers, she answered the question, "Do you know love?": "It's true, sir, I've already given myself."

Treatises: Marshall, Eos 379, P. Meyer, Rom. vi 353ff.

For later life in Languedoc: E. Le Roy Laduire's books, *Montaillou, village occitan de 1294–1324* and *Paysans de Languedoc*.

Bibliography

Abbreviations:
AA: Al-Andalus. AESC: Annales, economiques, sociétés, civilisations. AR: Archivum Romanicum. AnM: Annuale Mediaevale.
BGSL: Beitrage zur Geschichte der deutschen Sprache und Literatur.
CF: Casiers de Fanjeaus. CHR: Catholic Hist. Review.
EHR: English Hist. Rev. Eos: see Hatto.
MKNAL: Medelingen der Konink. Nederlandse Akadamie, Afd. Lett. MLN: Modern Language Notes. MP: Modern Philology. MS: Medieval Studies.
PMLA: Publications Mod. Lang. Soc.
RCSF: Rivista critica di storia della filosofia. RF: Romanische Forschungen.
RHSLL: Revue hist., scient, et litt. de Languedoc. RHSLT: Do. du dépt. du Tarn. RL: Romanische Lit. studien. RLR: Revue des langues romanes. Rom. Romania. RP: Romance Philology. RR: Romance Review. RRAL: Rendiconti della Reale Accad. dei Lincei.
SATF: Soc. des anciens textes français. Sp.: Speculum.
ZfFSL: Zeitschrift für francoz. Spr. u. Lit. ZfRP: Z. f. romanische Philologie.

(Places of publication for English books, when not given, is London; if French, Paris.)

Afnan, S. M., Avicenna: *His Life and Work* 1958.
Agus, I. A., *Urban Civilisation in Pre-Crusade Europe* (Leiden) 1965.
Ahsmann, H. J. M., *Le culte de la sainte Vierge et la litt. fr. profane du m.â.* 1923.
Alan of Lille (1) *Anticlaudianus* ed. R. Bossuet 1955 (2) *Liber poenitentialis* ed. J. Longère (Louvain) (3) *Textes inédit,* ed. M. T. d'Alverny 1965.
Alonso, D., *Riv. de Filol* esp. xxxiii 1949 297–349.
Alverny, M. Th. d', *Deux traductions latines du Coran au m.â.* (*Archive d'hist. doctrinale et litt, du m.â.* xvi 1948).
Anastos, M. V., in Clagett 131–88.
Andraud, P. (1) *Quae judicia de litteris fecerint provinciales* 1902 (2) *La vie et l'œuvre du troub. Raimon de Miraval* (thesis) 1902.
Andreas Capellanus: *De Amore livros tres,* ed. A. Pagès (Castella de la Plana) 1930.

287

Anglade, J. (1) *Les Troubadours* 1908 (2) *Hist. Sommaire de la litt. merid, au m.â.* 1921 (2) ed. *Leys d'Amors* (4) *Les poésies de Peire Vidal* 1913 (4) RLR, with Chabaneau. *Rigaut de Barbezieux* 1919.

Appel, C. (1) *Bernart von Ventadour* (Halle) 1915 (2) *Die Lieder Bertrans von Born* (Halle) 1932 (3) ZfRP lii 1932 770–91 (4) *Raimbaut von Orange* (Berlin) 1928 (5) *Das Leben u. die Lieder der Trob. Peire Rogier* (Berlin) 1882 (6) RLR xxxiii 404 (7) *Archiv* cvii 1901 338–49 (Rudel) (8) *Provenzal. Chrestomathie* (6th ed. Leipzig) 1930 (9) *Der Trob. Cadenet* (Halle) 1920.

Arberry, A. J. (1) *Moorish Poetry* (Camb.) 1953 (2) *Ring of the Dove* 1953 (3) *The Doctrine of the Sufis* (Camb.) 1935.

Asin Palacios, M. (1) *El Islam cristianizado* (Madrid) 1931 (2) *Abenmassara y su escuela* (Madrid) 1914.

Atiya, A., *Crusade, Commerce and Culture* (NY, London) 1966.

Aubert, M., *L'Architecture cistercienne en France* 1947.

Audiau, J. (1) *Nouvelle anthologie des Troub.* 1928 (2) *La pastourelle dans la poésie occitane du m.â.* 1923 (3) *Les poésies des quatre Troub, d'Ussel* 1922 (4) *Les Troub. en Angleterre.*

Auerbach, E., RP iv 65ff.

Avalle, D'A. S., *Peire Vidal* (Milan, Naples) 1960.

Averroes, *Incoherence of Incoherence*, transl. S. van der Bergh 1954.

Avicenna (1) *Avicenna Commemoration Vol.* (Calcutta) 1956 (2) *A.'s Psychology*, transl. F. Rahman 1952 (3) *A. on Theology*, transl. Arberry 1951.

Axhausen, L., *Die Theorien über den Ursprung der Provenz. Lyrik* (Diss. Marburg) 1937.

Axton, R., in *Med. Drama*, ed. N. Denny 1973.

Azais, *Les Troubadours de Béziers* (2nd ed., Béziers) 1869.

Baehr, R., ed. *Der Provenzal. Minnesang* 1967.

Bartsch, K. (1) with E. Koschwitz, *Chrestomathie Provençale* (6th ed.) 1904 (2) *Romances et Pastourelles: Altfranz. Romanze u. Pastourelles* 1870.

Bath, Van, *The Agrarian Hist. of Western Europe.*

Bauchy, J. H., *Récits des temps carolingiens* 1973.

Bazzi, C. E., *Riv. d'Italia* (June 1911) 971–98.

Beaton, J. F., *Self and Society in Med. France* (G. of Nogent) NY 1970.

Bédier, J (1) *Revue des Deux Mondes* (May 1896) (2) *Les Fabliaux* (5th ed.) 1925 (3) *La Chanson de Roland* 1927 (4) as (1) 1906 398–424.

Beer, R., *Die Handschriften des Klosters Santa Maria Ripoll* (Sitz. d. k. Ak. Wien) clv 1907 and clviii 1908.

Belperron, P., *La Croisade contre les Albigeois* 1942.

Bennett, R. F., *The Early Dominicans* (CUP).

Beroukhim, M., *La pensée iranienne à travers l'histoire* 1938.

Berry, A., *Florilège de Troubadours* 1930.

Bezzola, R. R. (1) *Les origines et la formation de la litt. courtoise en occident* 1944–63 (5 vols.) (2) *Rom.* lxvi 1940.

Bigongiari, D. RR xxxvii 1946 205–24.

Bishop, E., *Liturgica Historica* (Oxf.) 1918.

Bloch, N. (1) *Feudal Society* (2) *Land and Work in Med. Europe* 1967.

Boni, M., *Sordello* (Bologna) 1954.

Bonnassie, P., in *Colloques* 187–219.

Bonner, A., ed. *Songs of the Troubadours* 1974.

Bosch Vila, J., *Los Almoravides* (Tetuan) 1956.

Brandl, A., *Sitz. d. kon. preuss. Ak.* xli 1910.

Bréhier, L., *L'église et l'orient au m.â.* 1907.

Briffault, R., *Les Troub. et le sentiment romanesque* 1945.

Brinkmann, H., *Enstehungsgeschichte des Minnesangs* (Halle) 1926.

Brockelmann, C. (1) *Geschichte der arabischen Lit.* (Leiden) 2nd ed. 1943, 1949 (2) three suppl. vols. 1937–42.

Brooke, C. (1) *The Twelfth Century Renaissance* 1969 (2) *Bull. J. Rylands Lib.* 1967 13–33 (3) *Europe in the Central M.A.* 1964.

Brown, A. C. L., *The Origin of the Grail Legend* (NY) 1966.

Brown, E. G., *Arabian Medicine* (Camb.) 1921.

Burchhardt, T., *Moorish Culture in Spain* (Camb.) 1972.

Butler, Dom Cuthbert, *Western Mysticism* 1927.

Caesarius of Heisterbach (1) *Dialogus Miraculorum*, ed. J. Strayer (Cologne) (2) *The Dialogue on Miracles*, transl. H. von Essen Scott and C. C. Swinton Bland (Camb.) 1929.

Calmette, J., ed. *Moyen Age* (2nd ed.) 1953.

Canello, U. A., *La vita e lo opere del trov. A. Daniel* (Halle) 1883.

Casella, M., *Archivio storico ital.* xcvi 1938 3–63, 153–99.

Chabaneau, C. (1) *Les biographies des troub. en langue provençale* (Toulouse) 1885 (2) RLR xxxv 382 (Eblo) (3) RLR xx 5360, xxvi 157–67 (4) RLR xxxii 50–60.

Chambers, E. K., *Med. Stage* (Oxf.) 1903.

Chaytor, H. J. (1) *The Troub. in England* (Oxf.) 1923 (2) *Hist. of Aragon and Catalonia*.

Chenu, M. D. (1) *L'éveil de la conscience sous la civil. med.* 1969, Conf, Albert-le-Grand 1968 (2) *Nature, Man and Society in the Twelfth C.* (Chicago) 1968 (3) *La théologie douzième s.* 1957.

Claggett, M, with G. Post, R. Reynolds, ed. *Twelfth-century Europe and the Foundations of Modern Society* 1961.

Clarembald: *Life and Works of C. of Arras*, ed. N. M. Häring (Toronto) 1965.

Clerval, L'Abbé, *L'école de Chartres* (Frankfurt) reprint 1965.

Cobban, A. B., *The Med. Universities* 1974.

Coghill, N. K., in Lawlor 141–56.

Colloques internat. du centre nat. de la recherche scient. (Sc. humaines): Toulouse 28–31 March 1968: Les Structures Sociales de l'Aquitaine, du Languedoc et de l'Espagne au premier âge féodal (Paris) 1969.

Conant, K. J., Carolingian and Romanesque Architecture 1959.

Coppolani, J., Toulouse (Toulouse) 1954.

Corbin, H. (1) Avicenna and the Visionary Recital (Tehran) 1952 (2) Hist. de la philosophie arabe i (Paris) 1964.

Coulet, J., Le Troub. G. Montanhagol (Toulouse) 1898.

Coulton, G. G. (1) Social Life in Britain (CUP) 1919 (2) Inquisition and Liberty 1938 (3) Art and the Reformation (CUP) 1953.

Cour, A., Ibn Zaïdoun (Constantine) 1920.

Crombie, A. E., Augustine to Galileo i 1961.

Curtius, E. R. (1) Europäische Lit. u. latein. Mittelalter (2nd ed.) 1954.

Davenson, H. (H. I. Marrou) (1) Les Troubadours 1961 (2) Le Livre des chansons (Neufchâtel) 1946 (3) Traité de la misique selon l'esprit de S. Augustin (Neufchâtel) reprint 1944.

Davis, H. W. C., England under the Normans and Angevins.

Debenedetti, M. S., RRAL xxxix fasc, 7–8 1920.

Dejeanne, J. M. L. (1) AM xvii no 2 (Cercamon) (2) Poésie complète du troub. Marcabrun (Toulouse) 1909.

Delaruelle, E. (1) CF iii 19–41 (2) i 107–22 (3) in N. Hunt 191–216.

Del Monte, A., Peire d'Alvernha, Liriche (Turin) 1955.

Denomy, A. J. (1) MS vi 1944 175–260 (2) MS vi 1945 139–207 (3) The Heresy of Courtly Love (NY) 1947 (4) MS viii 1946 107–49 (5) MS xiii 1951 177ff.

Dodwell, C. R., ed. and transl. Theophilus, De diversis artibus 1961.

Donaldson, E. T., The Myth of Courtly Love 1966.

Dondaine, A. (1) Riv. di st. d. Chiesa in Italia vi 1952 47–78 (2) ed. Un traité neo-manichéen du XIIIe s. (Rome) 1939.

Dossat, Y. (1) RHSLT ix 1943 75–90 (2) RHSLL i 1944 66–87 (3) Rev. du Languedoc no 1 (Albi) Jan. 1944.

Douais. C., ed. La somme des autorités à l'usage des prédicateurs mérid. 1896.

Dronke, P. (1) Med. Latin and the Rise of the European Love-Lyric (Oxf.) 1965 (2) The Med. Lyric 1968 (3) Poetic Individuality in the Middle Age (Oxf.) 1970 (4) RP lxxiii 1961 327ff (5) Med. Aev. xxxii 1963 56ff.

Drouart la Vache, Li Livres d'Amours ed. R. Bossuet 1926.

Duby, G. (1) Rural Economy and Country Life in the Med. West (2) Europe of the Cathedrals (Geneva) 1966.

Duchesne, L., The Beginnings of the Temporal Sovereignty of the Popes 1908.

Duvernoy, J., *Les Albigeois dans la vie sociale et écon. de leur temps* (Ann. Inst. d'Etudes Occitanes: Actes du Coll. de Toulouse i 1962–3) Toulouse 1964.

Ecker, L., *Arabischer, provenzal. u. deutscher Minnesang* (Berlin) 1934.

Economou, G. D., *The Goddess Nature in Med. Lit.* (Harvard) 1972.

Errante, G., *Sulla lirica romanza delle origini* (NY) 1943.

Evans, J. (1) *Romanesque Architecture of the Order of Cluny* (Camb.) 1938 (2) *Cluniac Art of the Romanesque Period* (Camb.) 1949.

Fabre, C. (1) *Miscellany of Studies pres. to L. E. Kastner* (Camb.) 1932 217–47 (2) A, xxi 5–28 (3) RR ii 1970 195–222.

Faral, E. (1) *Les Jongleurs en France du m.â.* 1910 (2) *Les arts poétiques du xiie et du xiiie s.* 1958.

Farnham, F., RP xviii 1964 143–64.

Farriel, *Hist. de le poésie provençale* 1841.

Flores, A., ed. *Med. Age* (NY) 1963.

Fontanals, Mila y, *De los trovadores en España* (2nd ed.).

Font Ruis, J. M., in *Colloques* 63–77.

Fournier, P., and G. Le Bras (1) *Hist. des colls, canoniques en occident* 1931–2 (2) *Nouv. rev. hist. de droit* 1917.

Fourquier, G., *Hist. écon, de l'occident méd.* 1969.

Frank, G. (1) MLN lvii 1942 (rev. of Casella) 528–31 (2) MLR lxix 1944 526–31.

Frank, I. (1) *Trouvères et Minnesänger* 1952 (2) *Répertoire métrique des poésies des troub.* 1953–7.

Frings, T. (1) *Minnesinger u. Troubadours* 1949 (Deut. Ak. Wiss., Berlin fasc. 34) (2) BGSL; xxiii 1951 176 (3) *Die Anfänge der europäische Liebes-Dichtung im 11 u. 12 Jahrhundert* (Bayer. Ak. Wiss., Sitzb. München) 1960.

Gandilhac, M. de, *Cahiers de civil. méd.* 1961 (Abélard).

Garcia Gomez, E. (1) AA xxi 1956 303–38 (2) *Las jarchas romances de la serie árabe en su marco* 1965 (3) as (1) xiv 1949 407–17 (4) xv 1950 158–77 (5) *Clavileño* May–June 1950 17–21.

Gautier, L., *Les épopées français* (2nd ed.) ii (ire p.) 1892 (jongleurs in Italy and Spain).

Gennrich, F. (1) *Der musikal. Nachlass der Troub.* (3 vols. 1958 on) (2) *Troubadours, Trouvères, Minne- u. Meistergesang* 1951 (3) *Bibliog. der ältesten franz. u. latein. Motetten* 1958 (4) *Altfranz. Lieder* 1953–6 (5) *Rondeaux, Virelais u. Balladen*, Bd. ii (Göttingen) 1927.

Ghellinck, J. de (1) *l'ssor de la litt. latine au xiie s.* (Brusels–Paris) 1946 (2) *Le mouvement théologique du xxe s.* (2nd ed.) 1948.

Gibb, *Hist. of Ottoman Poetry.*

Gilson, E. (1) *Héloise et Abélard* 1938 (2) transl. L. K. Shook (3) *La théologie mystique de S. Bernard* 1934 (4) *The Christian Philosophy of St Augustine* 1960 (5) *Christian Philosophy in the M.A.* 1958.

Ginzburg, B., *Le divan d'Ibn Guzman* (Berlin) 1896.

Goff, J. le, *Les intellectuels au m.â.* 1957.

Goldin, F. (1) *Lyrics of the Troub. and Trouvères* 1973 (NY) (2) *German and Italian Lyrics of the M.A.* (NY) 1973.

Goldstein, D., *The Jewish Poets of Spain* 1971.

Gorra, E. (1) *Rendiconti del r. istit. Lombardo di Sc. e Lett.* 1911–12 (2) *Fra Drammi e poemi* (Milan) 1900.

Green, R. H. (1) AM viii 1967 3–16 (2) Sp. xxxi 1956 649–74.

Greene, R. L., *The Early English Carols* (Oxf.) 1935.

Gregory, T. (1) *Anima Mundi: La filosofia di G. di Conches e la scuola di Chartres* (Florence) 1955 (2) *Platonismo med.* (Rome) 1958.

Griffe, F. (1) *Les débuts de l'aventure cathare en Languedoc* 1969 (2) *Le Languedoc cathare* 1971.

Grivot, D. and G. Zarnecki, *Gislebertus.*

Grunebaum, von, AA xxi 1956.

Guiraud, J., *Hist. de l'inquisition au m.â.* i 1935.

Guyer, F. E., MP xxvi 1929 257–72.

Hallinger, K., in N. Hunt 29–55.

Hardie, C., in J. Lawlor 26–44 (Dante).

Hartmann, M. P. W., *Das arab. Strophengedicht* i, *Das Muwassah.*

Harvey, J., *Antiquaries J.* xlviii 1968 87–99.

Harward, V. J., *The Dwarfs of Arthurian Romance and Celtic Tradition* 1959.

Haskins, C. H. (1) *The Renaissance of the xii c.* (Camb. Mass.) 1927 (2) *Studies in the Hist. of Med. Science* (3) *Studies in Med. Culture* (OUP).

Heger, K., *Die bisherveröffentlichen Hargas u. ihre Deutungen* (Tübingen) 1960.

Hell, J. (1) *Oriental. Literaturzeitung* xxxviii 1935 (2) *Islamica* ii 1926 277–301.

Hell, V., and Hellmut Hell, *The Great Pilgrimages of the M.A.* 1961.

Herlihy, D., *Med. Culture and Society* (ed.) 1968.

Higounet, C. (1) *Mél. d'hist, du m.â. déd. à L. Halphen* 1951 313–22 (Toulouse and Barcelona) (2) CF ii 15–22 (3) AESC viii 1953 1–24 (population movements) (4) AM 1942–3 489–98 (Toulouse pop.) (5) in *Colloques* 221–37 (6) *Vaudo-languedociens et pauvres catholiques* (Touolouse) 1967.

Hill, R. T., and Bergin, T. G., *Anthology of the Provençal Troubadours* (Yale) 1974.

Hodgett, C. A. J., *A Social and Econ. Hist. of Med. Europe* 1972.

Hoepffner, E., *Les troub. dans leur vie et dans leur œuvres* 1955.

Hofmann, K., *Joufray's altfranz. Rittergedicht* (Halle) 1880.

Huiszinga, J., MKNAL lxxxiv 1932 89–198 (Alan).

Hunt, N. (1) ed. *Cluniac Monasticism* 1971 (2) *Cluny under St Hugh* 1967.

Hunt, R. W. etc, ed. *Studies in Med. Hist. . . . to F. M. Powicke* (Oxf.) 1946.

Jackson, J., with Chatto, W. A., *Wood Engraving*, 1861.

Jackson, W. T. H. (1) RR xlix 1958 243–58 (Andreas) (2) *The Lit. of the M. A.* (Columbia) 1962.

Jeanroy, A. (1) *La poésie lyrique des Troubadours* 1934 (2) *Les chansons de Guillaume IX* (2nd ed.) 1927 (3) *Origines de la poésie lyrique* (3rd ed.) (4) *Mél. de Lang. et de Litt. offerts à M. A. Jeanroy* 1928 (5) *Hist. de la langue et de la litt. fr.* 1896 (6) *Rom.* lvi 496ff (early Troub. (7) *Rev. des Pyrénées* 3rd trim. 1914 (T. Consistory) (8) *Les poésies de Cercamon* 1922 (9) *Bibliog. sommaire des chansonniers provençaux* 1916 (10) A, ii (*tenson*) (11) *Les chansons de Jaufre Rudel* (2nd ed.) (12) *Rom.* xxxiv 497–544 (Gavaudan) (13) *De nostratibus medii aevi poetis* 1899 (14) with Salverda de Grave, *Poésies d'Uc de Saint-Circ* (Toulouse) 1913.

John of Salisbury, *Metalogicon*, transl. D. D. McGarry (Univ. Calif. Press) 1962.

Jolivet, J., *Achive d'hist. doctrinale et litt, du m.â.* 1960 (Abélard).

Jones, M. P. (1) PMLA xlvi 1931 307–11 (2) *The Pastourelle* (Camb. Mass.) 1931.

Keissmann, R., *Ueber die Bedeutung Eleonorens von Poitou für die Lit. ihrer Zeit* (Bernsburg) 1901.

Keller, M. W., *Das Sirventes Fadet joglar* (Erlungen 1905) = RF xxii.

Kjellman, H., *Le Troub. Raimon-Jordan* (Upsala) 1922.

Klein, C., *Die Dichtungen des Moenchs von Montaudon* (Marburg) 1885.

Klibansky (1) *The Continuity of Platonic Tradition during the M.A.* 1905 (2) in Claggett 3–14 (Chartres).

Kluckholm, F., *Der deutsche Minnesang* (Darmstadt) 1961.

Knight, C., *Old England* n.d.

Knowles, D., *Monastic Order in England* (Camb. 1940, new ed. 1963).

Knudson, C. A., *Rom.* lxiii 1937 284–53 (dicing).

Koch, G., *Frauenfrage u. Ketzertum in Mittelalter* (Berlin) 1962.

Kolsen, A., *Saintliche Lieder des Trob. G. de Bornelh* (Halle) 1910, 1935.

Krappe, A. R., viii 1924 110ff.

Kritzeck, J., *Anthology of Islamic Lit.* 1964.

Kuzzler-Ratye G., *Arch. Rom.* i 1917 161–82.

Ladurie, E. Le Roy (1) *Hist. de Languedoc* 1962 (2) *The Peasants of Languedoc* transl. J. Day (Univ. Illinois Press) 1974 (16th–17th cs.).

Lafont, R., *Cahiers du Sud* lv 1963.

Langfors, A. (1) *Les chansons de G. de Cabestanh* 1924 (2) AM xxvi 1914 5–51, 189–225, 349–56.

Lapa, M. R. (1) *Liçoes de literatura portuguesa: Epoca medieval* (Lisbon) 1934 (6th ed. 1966) (2) *Das Origens da poesia lirica en Portugal na Idade-Media* (Lisbon 1929.

Lavaud, R. (1) *Poésie complète du troub. Peire Cardenal* (Toulouse) 1957 (2) *Les poésies de A. Daniel* (Toulouse) 1910 (3) *Les troub. cantaliens* ii (Aurillac).

Lawlor, J. ed. *Patterns of Love and Courtesy* 1966.

Leach, A. F., *Educational Charters and Docs.* (OUP) 1911.

Leclercq, H., *The Love of Learning and the Desire for God* 1961.

Leclercq. J. (1) *Pierre le Vénérable* (St Wandrille) 1946 (2) in N. Hunt 217–37.

Lee, Vernon, *Euphorion* 1899.

Leff, G., *Med. Thought* 1958.

Legge, M. D., *Anglo-Norman Lit.* (Oxf) 1963.

Le Goff, J., *Les intellectuels du m.â.* 1957.

Lehmann, P., Sp. vii 1932 75–9.

Leigh, D. J. in *Med. Eng. Drama* ed. J. Taylor and A. H. Nelson (Univ. Chicago) 1972 274–8.

Lejeune, R., with J. Stiennon, *La Légende de Roland dans l'art du m.â.* (Brussels) 1966.

Lemay, R., AESC 1963 (Arabic into Latin, 12th c.).

Léonard, E. G., *Cat. des Actes de Raimon V, comte de T.* (Nîmes) 1932.

Levi-Provençal, E. (1) *Arabica* i 1954 208ff (2) *Islam d'Occident* 1948.

Levy, RLR xxi 1882.

Lewent, K., ZfRP xxxvii 1913 313–37, 427–51.

Lewis, B., with S. M. Steen in *Eos*.

Lewis, C. S. (1) *Courtly Love* (OUP) 1958 (2) PMLA xxxvii 1922 141–82 (3) *Neophilol.* v 1920 209ff (4) *The Discarded Image* 1964 (CUP).

Limouzon-Lamothe, R., *La Commune de Toulouse* (T. and Paris) 1932.

Lindsay, J. (1) *Med. Latin Poets* 1934 (2) *Song of a Falling World* 1948 (3) *The Normans and their World* 1974 (4) *Short History of Culture* 1962.

Linskill, J., *The Poems of the Troub. R. de Vaqueiras* (Hague) 1964.

Lloyd, R., *The Golden M.A.* 1939.

Loi, Raimon de, *Trails of the Troubadours* 1927.

Loomis, R. S. (1) MLN xxxix 1924 319ff (2) *Wales and the Arthurian Legend* 1956 (3) *Arthurian Trad, and C. de Troyes* (Columbia).

Lopez, R. S. (1) *The Birth of Europe* 1967 (2) with I. W. Raymond, *Medit. Trade in the Med. World* (NY) 1955.

Lot-Borodine, M. (1) *Mél. de ling. etc. à M. A. Jeanroy* 1928 223–42 (2) *De l'amour profane à l'amour sacré* 1961.

Lowinsky, V., ZfFSL xx 1898 168–74.

Luchaire, A., *Innocent III et la croisade des Albigeois* 1911.

McKeon, R., MP xliii 1946 217–34 (rhetoric 12th c.).

Mahn, C. A. F. (1) *Die Werke der Trob.* 1846–86 (Berlin) (2) *Dedichte der Troub. in provenzal. Sprache* 1856–73.

Maisonneuve, H., *Etudes sur l'origine de l'inquisition* (2nd ed.) 1960.

Majnon-Martier, E., in *Colloques* 115–42.

Mâle, E. (1) *L'art religieux du xiie s. en France* 1898 (6th ed. 1953) (2) ditto, xiiie s. 1922.

Manitius, M., *Geschichte der lat. Lit. des Mitt.* iii (Munich) 1931.

Manteuffel, T., *Naissance d'une hérésie* 1969.

Marshall, J. H., *The Razos de Trobar de R. Vidal* (OUP) 1972.

Marshall, M. H., *Symposium* iv 1950 1–39, 366–89.

Martin-Chabot, E., *La Chanson de la Croisade albigeoise* 1960–1.

Massignon, L. (1) *Encyc. d'Islam* iv (2nd) 1929 "Udhri" 990 (2) *La Passion d'Al-Hallaj* 1914–21 (3) *Essai sur les origines du lexique technique de la mystique musulmane* 1914–22.

Menéndez. A., *Riv. di Filol. Epañ.* xliii 1960 279ff.

Merlo, *Giorn. Stor.* iii 1884 386–400 (Faidit).

Meyer, P. (1) ed. *Chanson de la Croisade contre les Albigeois* (2) *Rom.* vi 353ff (3) *Les derniers troub. de la Provence* 1871.

Meyer, R. (1) (with Bédier, Aubry) *La chanson de Bele Aelis* 1904 (2) *Das Leben des tr. G. Faidit* (Heidelberg) 1876.

Monaci, E., RRAL s. v, 2 1893 927ff.

Moore, O. H., *The Young King Plantagenet*.

Morall, J. B., *The Med. Imprint* 1967.

Morghen, R. (1) *Richerche di storia relig.* i 1954 84–107 (2) as Puech 86f, 91–3 (3) in N. Hunt 11–28.

Mulholland, M. A., ed. *Early Gild Records of Toulouse* (NY) 1941.

Müller, F. W., *Der Rosenroman u. d. latien Averroismus des 13. J.* (Frankfurt) 1947.

Mundo, A. M., in N. Hunt 98–122.

Mundy, J. H. (1) *Liberty and Political Power in Toulouse* (NY) 1954 (2) *Traditio* xxii 1916 203–87 (T. charity, social work).

Nasr, S. H. (1) *Science and Civil. in Islam* (Camb. Mass.) 1968 (2) *Intro. to Islamic Cosmological Doctrines* (ib.) 1964.

Nelli, R. (1) *La vie quotid. des Cathars* 1969 (2) *Les Troubadours*, with Lavaud 1966 (2) *La Musée du Catharisme* (Toulouse) 1967 (4) *Le phénomène cathare* 1968 (5) *Dictionnaire des hérésies mérid.* (Toulouse) 1968 (6) *L'Erotique des troub.* 1961 (7) *Ecritures cathares* 1968 (83 CF iii 177–97.

Nicholson, R. A. (1) *Studies in Islamic Mysticism* (2) *J. of R. Asiatic Soc.* i 1906.

Niel, F., *Albigeois et Cathars* 1955.

Nitze, W. A., *Sp.* xxiii 1948 464–71.

Norton, A. O., *Readings in the Hist. of Education* (Harvard) 1909.

Nunes, J. J. (1) *Cantigas d'amigo* 1929 (2) *Cantigas d'amor* 1932.

Nykl, H. A. R. (1) *Diwan* (Aben Guzman) Madrid 1933 (2) *A Book concerning the Risala, known as the Dove's Neck-ring* (Paris) 1931 (2) *Hispano-Arabic Poetry* (Baltimore) 1946 4() *Troub. Studies* (Camb. Mass.) 1944 (5) *AR* xix 1935 226–36 (6) *Bull. hisp.* xli.

Nykrog, P., *Les Fabliaux* (Copenhagen) 1957.

Oakeshot, W., *Classical Inspiration in Med. Art* 1959.

Obolensky, D., *The Bogomils* (Camb.) 1948.

Ogilvy, J. D. A., *Sp.* xxxviii 1963 603–19.

Olschki, L., *The Grail Castle and its Mysteries* (Berkeley) 1966.

Ordericus, HE ed. A. Prévost.

Ourliac, P., *AESC* iv 1949 268–77 (Toulouse).

Oursel, R., *Les pèlerins du m.â.: les hommes, les chemins, les sanctuaires* 1963.

Packard, S. R., *Twelfth-Century Europe* 1973.

Pagès, A., *Andreae Capellani de Amore libri tres* (Castello de la Plana) 1930.

Panofsky, E. (1) *Meaning in the Visual Arts* (NY) 1955 108–45 (Suger) (2) *Renaissance and Renascence in Western Art* (Stockholm) 1960 (3) *Abbot Suger on the Abbey-Church of Saint-Denis* (Princeton) 1946.

Parducci, A., *Rom.* xxxviii 286 (song of ill-married).

Paré, G., with A. Brunet, P. Trembley, *La Renaissance du xiie s., les écoles* (Ottawa–Paris) 1933.

Paret, R., *Früharab. Liebesgeschichten* (Bern) 1927.

Paris, G. (1) *Rom.* xii 520–5 (2) *Hist. poétique du Charlemagne* (3) *Mél. de litt. fr. du m.â.*

Parry, J. J., *The Art of Courtly Love by Andreas Cap.* (NY) 1941.

Paterson, L. M., *Troubadours and Eloquence* (Oxford) 1975.

Pattison, W. T., *Life and Works of the Troub. R. d'Orange* (Minneapolis) 1952.

Pauphilet, A., *Poètes et romanciers du m.â.* 1951.

Pegge, S., *Fitz-Stephen's Description of London* 1772.

Péres, H. (1) *La Poésie andalouse en arabe classique au* ˣie *s.* (2nd ed.) 1953 (2) Ist ed. 1937.

Petit-Dutaillis, *Les Communes fr.* 1947.

Pevsner, N., *Outline of Europ. Architecture* (8th ed.) 1857.

Pfaff, S. L. H., in Mahn iv 1853 (Riquier).

Philippson, E., *Der Moench von Montaudon* (Halle) 1873.

Picavet, F., *Gerbert* 1897.

Pidal, H. (1) *Cantar de Mio Cid* (Madrid) 1954 (2) *La Chanson de Roland et la trad. épique des Francs* 1960 (3) *España, Eslabón entre la Cristianidad y el Islam* (Madrid) 1956 (4) *Poesía arábe y poesía europea* (Madrid) 1963 (5) *La España del Cid* 1956 (6) *Poesía juglaresco y juglares* (Madrid) 1924 (7) *Bull. hisp.* xl 1938 337ff (8) *Rev. Fil. Esp.* xliii 1960 279–354.

Pirenne, H., *Ann. d'hist. écon. et social* 1929 (instruction of merchants).

Powicke, F. M., EHR xlix 1934 509–11.

Press, A. R., *Anthology of Troubadour Lyric Poetry* (Edinburgh) 1971.

Puech, H. C. (1) *Convegno di scienza morali, stor. e filol.: Oriente et Occidente nel med. oevo* (Ac. naz. Lincei xii, volta) Rome 1957 8of.

Raby, F. J. E. (1) *Hist. of Christian Latin Poetry* (2nd ed. Oxf.) 1953 (2) *Hist. of Secular Latin Poets in M. A.* (Oxf.) 1934 (3) *Sp.* xliii 1968 72–7.

Rajna, P. (1) *Rom.* vi 115 (2) *Mél. M. A. Jeanroy* 1928 349–60.

Raynouard, *Choix des poésies originales des troub.* 1816–21.

Read, J., *The Moors in Spain and Portugal* 1974.

Reise, G., *Music in the M.A.*

Renier, R., *Il tipo estetic della domna nel m.â.* 1885.

Renoir, A., *Eng. Studies* (Amsterdam) xlvii 212f.

Richard, A., *Hist. des comtes de Poitou.*

Rickard, P., *Med. Comic Tales* (Camb.) 1972.

Ricketts, P. T., *Les poésies de G. de Montanhagol* (Toronto) 1964.

Riquier, M. de, *Historia de la lit. catalana, part antigua* 1964.

Ritter, H., *Der Islam* xxi 1933.

Roddy, K., in *Med. Drama* ed. N. Denny (Stratford-on-Avon Studies) 1973 155–72.

Roncaglia, A. (1) *Cultura neolatina* viii 5–46 (2) *ib.* xi 1951 213–49.

Rosenfeld, H., *Die Mittelalterliche Totentanz* (Münster–Köln) 1954.

Röthlisberger, A., *Die Architektur des Graltempels* (Bern) 1917.

Rougement, D. de, *Love in the Western World* (transl. M. Belgion) 1953 (NY).

Russell, J. B., CHR li 1965 31–44.

Rychner, J., *Contrib. à l'étude des fabliaux* (Geneva) 1960.

Sachse, M., *Ueber das Leben u. die Lieder des Troub. Wilhelm IX* (Leipzig) 1882.

Salmen, W., *Der fahrende Musiker in europäischen Mittelalters* 1930.

Saye, G., *Les Juifs en Languedoc antérieurement au xive s.* 1881.

Schell, E. T., as with Leigh 279–91.

Scheludko, D., *Neuphil. Mitt.* xxxv 1934 1ff.

Schrötter, W., *Ovid und die Troubadours* 1908 (rev. in *Rom.* xxxviii).

Shepard, W. P., with F. M. Chambers, *The Poems of Aimeric de Péguilhan* (Evanston) 1950.

Sherwin-Bailey, D., *The Man–Woman Relationship in Christian Thought* 1959.

Sicard, G., *Rec. de la Soc. Jean Bodin* xxi pt. 2, 405–28 (Brussels) 1969.

Siciliano, I., *Les origines des Chansons de Geste* (transl. P. Antonetti) 1951.

Sikes, J. G., *Peter Abailard* (Camb.) 1932.

Simonet, F. J., *Historia de los Mozarabes de España* (Madrid) 1903.

Smythe, B., *Trobador Poets* 1929.

Southern, R. W. (1) *The Making of the M.A.* 1959 (2) *History* xlv 1960 201–16 (3) in Hunt 27–48.

Spanke, H. (1) *G. Raynauds Bibliog. des altfranz. Lieder* i 1955 (2) *Marcabrustudien* (Göttingen, Abh.) 1940.

Spitzer, L. (1) *L'amour lo(i)ntain de J. Rudel* (Univ. N. Carolina *Studies in Romance Lang.* v, Chapel Hill) 1944 (2) *Comparative Lit.* iv 1952 1–22 (3) in Claggett 115–30 (4) RL 363–417 (Rudel).

Steiner, A. (1) *Sp.* iv 1929 92–5 (2) *Sp.* xiii 1938 304–8.

Stemmler, T., *Die engl. Liebesgedichte des Ms. Harley 2253* (Bonn) 1962.

Stern, S. M. (1) AA xiii 1948 299–346 (2) *Eos* 299–301 (3) *Les Chansons mozarabes* (Palermo) 1953.

Storost, W., *Gesch. d. altfranz. u. altprovenz. Romanzenstrophe* (Halle) 1920.

Strayer, J., *The Albigensian Crusade* (NY) 1971.

Stronski, S. (1) *La Légende amoureuse de B. de Born* 1916 (2) *Le troub. Folquet de Marseille* (Cracow) 1910 (3) AM 1913 273.

Sutherland, D. R., *French Studies* x 1956.

Sylvester, D. W., *Educational Docs.* 1970.

Taylor, A. B., *Intro. to Med. Romance* 1930.

Thorndyke, Lynn (1) *University Records and Life in the M.A.* (NY, Columbia) 1944 (2) *Hist. of Magic and Experimental Science* i (NY) 1929.

Tobler, A., *Ein Minnesinger der Provence* 1865 (reissued in *Verm. Beiträg.* v 1912 125–89).

Toja, G., *Arnaut Daniel, Canzoni* (Florence) 1960.

Topfer, B., in *Vom Mittelalter zur Neuzeit* ed. H. Sproemberg and H. Kretzschmer (Berlin) 1956 420–39.

Topsfield, L. T. (1) *Neuphilol. Mitteil.* lxix 1968 280–302 (G. IX) (2) *Troubadours and Love* (CUP) 1975.

Turberville, A. S., *Med. Heresy and the Inquisition* 1920.

Uitti, K. D., *Song, Myth and Celebration in Old French Narrative Poetry* (Princeton) 1973.

Valency, M., *In Praise of Love* 1958.

Vallicrosa, *Cahiers d'hist. mondiale* 1954 (science translators xiiie s.)

Varty, K., *Christine de Pisan* (Leicester) 1965.

Vasoli, C., RCSF xvi 1961 153–87.

Verrier, P., *Les Vers franc.* i 1931 ch. vii.

Vicaire, H. H., *Saint Dominic and his Times* (NY) 1965.

Villard, U. Monneret de., *Lo studio dell'Islam in Europa nel xii e nel xiii s.* (Studi e Testi 110, Vatican City) 1944.

Villemain, *Litt. du m.â.* 1830.

Viscardi, A., *Le origini* (Milan) 1939.

Vossler, K. (1) in *Miscellanei di studi in onore di S. Hortis* (Trieste) 1910 (2) *Sitz. d. Kais. Ak. Wiss., philos.-philol. Klasse* 1918 133ff (3) *Sitz. Ak. Wiss.* München (6th diss.) 1916 (4) *Die Dichtungsformen der Romanen.*

Waddell, H., *Wandering Scholars* 1932.

Waley, D., *The Italian City-Republics* 1969.

Watt, W. M., *Hist. of Islamic Spain* (Edinburgh, 2nd ed.) 1967.

Wechssler, E. (1) *Das Kulturproblem des Minnesangs,* i, *Minnesang und Christentum* (Halle) 1909 (2) ZfFSL xxiv 159ff.

Werner, E., *Die gesellschaftlichen Grundlagen der Klosterreform im 11 J.* (Berlin) 1953.

Weston, J. (1) *Legend of Sir Perceval* 1906 (2) *Rom.* xxxiv 1905 100ff (3) *Rom.* liii 1927 84–92.

Wetherbee, W. (1) *Traditio* xxv 1969 87–125 (2) MS xxxiii 1971 264ff.

Whicker, G. F., *The Goliardic Poets* (NY) 1949.

Wickens, G. M., ed. *Avicenna: Scientist and Philosopher* 1952.

Wilcox, J., *Michigan Acad. of Sc. Art and Letters* xii 1930 313–25.

Wilhelm, J. J., *The Cruelest Month* (New Haven, NY) 1965.

Williams, W., *Saint Bernard of Clairvaux* (Manchester) 1935.

Wilson, E. F., *The Stella Maris of John of Garland* (Med. Acad. of America) 1946.

Wilson, E. M. *Eos* 301–21.

Winterfeld, P. von, *Z. f. deut. Alt.* xlv 133–47.

Wolff, P. (1) *The Awakening of Europe* 1968 (2) with J. Dieuzaide, *Voix et Images de Toulouse* (T.) 1962 (3) *Commerce et marchands de T.* 1954 (4) *Hist. du Languedoc* (T.) 1967 (5) *Hist. de T.* (T.) 1958.

Wood, M. M., *The Spirit of Protest in Old French Lit.* (NY) 1917.

Wright, T. (1) *Domestic Manners and Sentiments* (14th c.) (2) *Womankind in W. Europe,* 1869.

Young, K., *The Drama of the Med. Church* (Oxf.) 1933.

Zamthor, P., *Langue et techniques poétiques à l'époque romane* 1963.

Zanders, M. J., *Die altprovenzal. Prosanovelle* (Halle) 1913.

Zenker, R., *Die Lieder Peires von Auvergne* (Erlangen) 1900.

Zingarelli, M., *Richerche sulla vita di B. de Ventadour.*

Index

PERSONS

Abelard, 35–7, 39, 43, 47, 214, 218, 270
Abraham ben Ezra, 48
Adalbert of Hamburg, 118–19
Adam of Bremen, 118
Adelard of Bath, 34, 45
Adhémar, 141
Aimeric de Péguilhan, 238–9, 274
Aimeric de Sarlat, 90
Al-Ahnaf, 159
Al-Farabi, 47
Al-Ghazali, 161, 225
Al-Idris, 44
Al-Kindi, 47
Al-Tutili, 165
Alan of Lille, 109–11
Alcuin, 23
Alegret, 115
Alexander III (Pope), 95, 124; IV, 253
Alphonse Jourdain, 63
Amaury, 235
Ambrose, 197–8
Andreas the Chaplain, 89–91, 106–8, 112, 217–18, 224–5
Anselm, 35, 39, 43, 47, 218–19
Aquinas, 93
Aristotle, 35, 38, 47, 162, 220, 225
Arnaut Daniel, 167–72, 184, 222, 271
Arnaut de Mareuil, 90, 120, 180–1
Arthur, 146–7, 281
Aucassin, 21, 160
Averroes, 47, 114, 225
Avicenna, 47, 162–4, 225, 272
Azalais, 88, 173, 180, 223

Bacon, Roger, 45
Barral de Baux, 172–4
Béatrice de Die, 184–8
Béatrice de Montferrat, 86
Becket, Thomas, 37
Berdic, 1
Bernard Silvester, 109–10
Bernart Marti, 114–16, 270
Bernart Sicart, 240–1, 271
Bernart de Vensac, 115

Bernart de Ventadour, 23–4, 89, 99–113, 122
128, 158, 164, 221–2, 269, 270
Bertolai, 1
Bertran d'Alamanon, 123, 128, 245, 355
Bertran d'Aurel, 125
Bertran de la Barta, 236
Bertran de Born, 126, 144–53, 167, 271, 274
Bertran de Gourdon, 126
Bertran de Panassac, 215
Bertran de Rovinac, 125, 245
Blacatz, 238, 257
Bleheris, 23–4
Boethius, 108, 220
Boniface de Castellane, 245–6
Boniface of Montferrat, 177
Brémon, G., 83
Brown, T., 43
Bruno of Cologne, 31
Burchard of Worms, 42

Cabra, 120
Cadenet, 201, 237–8
Calega Panzan, 245
Calixtus II, Pope, 95
Cardailhac, 126, 128
Cardenal, 120, 153, 213, 223, 258–65, 269, 271, 273
Castelloza, Lady of, 184–5
Catrola, 55
Catullus, 269
Cercamon, 23, 50–2, 122, 270
Cerveri di Girona, 196, 267
Charlemagne, 1, 190
Charles of Anjou, 245–6, 256
Chaucer, 168, 273
Chrétien de Troyes, 24, 155, 223, 282, 284
Christine de Pisan, 179
Clara d'Anduza, 184–5
Claudian, 108, 111
Cobham, T. de, 124
Conon de Béthune, 177

Dante, 144, 167, 172, 222, 253, 256, 258, 273
Daude de Pradas, 221–2
Dionysios the Areopagite, 86

PLACES